CITY VISIONS

CITY VISIONS
Imagining Place, Enfranchising People

Edited by
Frank Gaffikin and Mike Morrissey

Pluto  Press

LONDON • STERLING, VIRGINIA

First published 1999 by Pluto Press
345 Archway Road, London N6 5AA
and 22883 Quicksilver Drive, Sterling, VA 20166-2012, USA

British Library Cataloguing in Publication Data
A catalogue record for this book is available from the British Library

ISBN 0 7453 1356 6 hbk

Library of Congress Cataloging in Publication Data
City visions : imagining place, enfranchising people / edited by Frank
    Gaffikin and Mike Morrissey.
        p.   cm.
    Includes bibliographical references.
    ISBN 0–7453–1356–6 (hbk.)
        1. City planning—Northern Ireland—Belfast. 2. City planning
—Europe. 3. City planning—United States. 4. Urbanization
—Northern Ireland—Belfast. 5. Belfast (Northern Ireland)—Social
conditions. 6. Belfast (Northern Ireland)—Economic conditions.
    I. Gaffikin, Frank. II. Morrissey, Michael, 1940–   .
    HT169.G72B4933   1999
    307.76—dc21   99–22541
                                                                   CIP

Designed and produced for Pluto Press by
Chase Production Services, Chadlington, OX7 3LN
Typeset by Stanford DTP Services, Northampton
Printed in the EC by TJ International, Padstow

Contents

Foreword   viii
Introduction   x

CONTEXT

1. **Understanding the Contemporary City**   3
   Frank Gaffikin and Mike Morrissey

2. **The Urban Economy and Social Exclusion:
   The Case of Belfast**   34
   Frank Gaffikin and Mike Morrissey

URBAN PATTERN

3. **The Future Planning of City Regions**   61
   Peter Hall

4. **The Just City and the Efficient City**   79
   Wim Wievel and Joseph Persky

5. **Sustainable Cities**   90
   Frank Gaffikin and Mike Morrissey

6. **Urban Regeneration: Lessons from Europe and
   the UK**   104
   Michael Parkinson

7. **Urban Regeneration: The New Policy Agenda**   116
   Frank Gaffikin and Mike Morrissey

8. **The Role of Culture in Remaking Cities**   151
   Charles Landry

9. **The Role of Culture in the Regeneration of a
   Divided City: The Case of Belfast**   164
   Frank Gaffikin and Mike Morrissey

IMPLEMENTING POLICY

10. **The Future Governance of Cities**   183
    Patsy Healey

11. **Belfast: A Partnership Approach to Local
    Governance**   194
    Brian Hanna

12. **Conclusion: The Development of Cities and
    the Future
    of Belfast**   207
    Frank Gaffikin and Mike Morrissey

Notes on Contributors   236
Index   238

List of Figures

1.1   Percentage Employment in Manufacturing and
      Services, 1971–93   11
1.2   Phases of Capitalist Development   22
2.1   Numbers Unemployed in Northern Ireland (Claimant
      Count)   40
2.2   Percentage Change in Unemployment, 1992–97   41
2.3   Gross Annual Household Income: Northern Ireland and
      Belfast City, 1991–92   50
7.1   Total Expenditure in Urban Programmes   138
10.1 Tendencies in Urban Governance   185
10.2 Model 1: Delivering Services   185
10.3 Model 2: Multiple Initiatives   186
10.4 Model 3: Strategic Capacity-Building   188
12.1 The Development Decades   210
12.2 Diverse Aims of Local Economic Development   212
12.3 The Development Spectrum   218
12.4 Income Flows within Communities   220
12.5 Model of New Planning   225

List of Tables

1.1   Employment Changes by Sector in Different Types of
      Area, 1951–81   18
1.2   Unemployment Rates by Area of Residence, 1951–81   19
2.1   Rates of Unemployment (Selected Regions), 1946–54   37
2.2   Employment Status, Northern Ireland and Belfast DC,
      1983–92   45

2.3 Comparative Change in Sectoral Employment
(Manufacturing and Services), 1981–91   45
2.4 Dimensions of Poverty and Exclusion   47
2.5 Indicators of Relative Deprivation (Robson Index):
Belfast and Derry City Council Areas   51
2.6 Deprived and Non-Deprived 'Regions' in Belfast Urban
Area, 1971–91   52
7.1 Share of Inner Cities Expenditure   123
12.1 Neighbourhood and Downtown in the Regeneration
Debate   214

Foreword

In 1994, the Department of the Environment initiated a debate about how best to accelerate the regeneration of Belfast, drawing on the successes already achieved but recognising that much more had yet to be done. As a result, in July 1996 an alliance of elected representatives, business leaders, trade unionists and community activists formed the Belfast City Partnership Board. The aim of the Board is first, to facilitate the widest possible community input to the formulation of a 25-year strategic vision for Belfast and, then, to oversee its realisation. Aware that a visionary approach has been successfully adopted by a number of cities around the world, the Board has been keen to provide a new strategic and policy framework by seeking widespread agreement on what Belfast could be like in 25 years' time. Some have referred to this as 'backcasting', that is, securing agreement on what you want to achieve and then working backwards to identify the steps to realise the vision.

This publication records a series of public lectures on 'City Visioning' sponsored by the Belfast City Partnership Board. Designed to provide an opportunity for those interested in the Belfast Vision process to hear at first hand case studies and policy insights from a range of eminent practitioners in the field of urban regeneration and city visioning, the lecture series provided an invaluable opportunity to validate a visioning approach and to raise horizons about how Belfast could strive towards its fullest potential.

From the beginning, the Board recognised that renewing the city involved an integrated look at the many dimensions of effective urban living. Thus, this book addresses the wide range of issues we have had to consider, including city governance, cultural diversity, urban economics, social exclusion and regionalism. The outcome has been mutually reinforcing for all those involved – not only have we taken the opportunity to learn from the experience of other cities, but we are now convinced that there are useful lessons which can be drawn from the urban regeneration experience in Belfast. As a manifestation of this cross-fertilisation, practitioners in the field of urban regeneration in Belfast and Chicago have developed an exchange programme, funded by the MacArthur Foundation, which has served to inspire and strengthen the resolve of those involved to tackle the common challenges confronting both cities.

I have no doubt that this publication will contribute significantly to the body of knowledge on urban regeneration and the process of city visioning. I wish to acknowledge the efforts of all who participated in the public lecture series, those who delivered papers now reproduced in this book and the University of Ulster's Urban Institute in organising the lecture series and editing this publication.

R B SPENCE
Permanent Secretary of the Department of the
Environment for Northern Ireland and
Co-Chairperson of the Belfast City Partnership Board
26 April 1999

Introduction

We live in an increasingly urban world. Whereas at the turn of the twentieth century, one in ten of the world's people lived in cities, a quarter of the way into the next century, about seven in ten of the planet will be urban dwellers. Far from being a relic of an industrial age, the city is the habitat of the future. But, the nature of cities will change. In the advanced economies, this challenge is pressing. It involves remaking the purpose of places that were once the site of smoke stack industries and large public bureaucracies in an age when both are in decline. Future urban prosperity will depend more on producing and using information cleverly.

But how are we to help shape this future when so much of local development seems to be at the mercy of huge private corporations and large economic blocs in a new global economy? One argument in this respect is that resignation to such external determination disenfranchises people. Conversely, an active citizenship intent on taking responsibility for future development generates an empowering process in itself. This attitude to 'taking power' derives from a view that the best way to predict the future is to help create it. As expressed by Ellyard: 'The future is not a probable place we are being taken to, but a preferred place we are creating. The tracks to it are not found and followed, but made by laying and constructing a trail.'[1]

In this way, vision planning is designed to foster an inspiring and imaginative approach to developing cities. It seeks to get round the limitations of conventional urban planning, which has tended to:

- separate the physical from the social, the economic and the environmental, rather than treating all of these elements in an integrated fashion;
- be tied down by contemporary economic restraints, public spending projections or immediate practicalities of institutional arrangements;
- in effect, exclude many sections of society, left with little sense of ownership of planned change in their city; and
- be based on projected trends of social life which can often be flawed or overtaken by events.

As the world becomes a less predictable place, the effectiveness of trend planning, based on trajectories of present patterns, is severely compromised. Such planning tends to be over-influenced by what appears to be inevitable social destinies to a point that it becomes self-fulfilling. What is needed is a widely agreed view of where the city wants to be two decades or so hence, with in-built flexibilities to review that vision and its related goals. Taking a long span like 20 years permits a more ambitious picture of a desired future, since any radical transformation will demand that kind of time period.

Vision planning, in seeking to get beyond land use and zoning (the traditional concerns of planning), attempts to dissolve old demarcations, integrating the various dimensions needed to ensure a holistic development. It looks far enough ahead to avoid the immediate concerns about 'feasibilities' such as cost. Such considerations inhibit imagination about preferred futures by emphasising the current limits of resources, agencies, or the disposition of key actors. By contrast, vision planning, supported by an informed view, is offering more of a blank canvas to sketch from, and scratch the shape of tomorrow's society. Thus, the vision is intended to be free from a blinkered view, which perceives current problems and divisions to be largely unchangeable. It allows participants to leap ahead of such immediate obstacles. Accordingly, vision planning is not designed for crisis management or even coping with change. It is about making positive change happen.

Moreover, since the visioning process is not just about *where* we want to go, but also about *why* we want to go there, it inevitably throws up the need for explicit discussion about the values and principles underpinning the goal. The process of inclusive engagement across all the diverse urban interests is itself helpful. A compelling vision that comes from such encounters and networking is well placed to rally and motivate people throughout the city. It can produce openness to change and innovation. It demands wide ownership because its ultimate success depends on it being something people appreciate, share and pledge backing to. As expressed by Klein et al.: 'Proponents of visioning believe that plans that resonate with citizens' deepest aspirations and values have the best chance of being implemented.'[2]

Critics of vision planning might charge that it amounts to no more than wishful thinking at best and authoritarian utopianism at worst. But, this is to misunderstand the nature of an effective vision plan. It is not the product simply of untamed imagination and flights of fancy. Rather, the vision is influenced by an acute understanding of the complex forces driving social change. Thus, the process deploys techniques such as scenario planning, which allow people to step mentally into possible, probable and preferred futures to script a number of narratives for their city decades hence.

Such a forward-looking approach to development highlights key aspects of a changing social and economic environment, such as:

- the new *importance of languages* in a multi-lingual Europe;
- or the need to respond to the *changing nature of work*, e.g. teleworking, electronic commerce, and the redeployment of surplus office/retail space that might follow such trends;
- or the way certain *health technologies* such as scanner software for home PCs could revolutionise diagnostic medicine, and our use of acute care.

Other methods, such as visualisation, can be used. This is designed to show participants concrete examples of proposed change (models or photographs) since some people have difficulty with an abstract perception of changed urban form. A variation of this is the Visual Preference Survey, which in broad terms is a device to test people's assessment and prioritisation of a range of options for the future of their city and/or community.

This type of vision planning took off first in the USA. By the late 1980s, a series of cities and communities were involved. For instance, Rock Hill, South Carolina produced an award winning effort called 'Empowering the Vision' in 1989; Gresham in Oregon started their visioning process in 1986, with their final plan emerging in 1991; the city of Torrance in California designed theirs in 1995 following a year-long planning process tied to comprehensive consultation; following the production of a vision for Greater Vancouver in 1993, the 1995 City Plan in Vancouver offered a long-term vision for the city's future, embodying a framework for prioritising city programmes and actions. However, not all of the plans that claim to be visionary are entitled to the name. For instance, Cleveland's Civic Vision 2000 concerns mostly its Downtown and Waterfronts. Critics of the planning processes adopted in Cleveland charge that it is not inclusive of the poorest constituencies and does not embody essential values like equity.[3]

Interestingly, the visionary approach has been slower to take off in the UK. Yet, as Shipley and Newkirk note: 'There is some irony in this because, unlike Canada and the United States, where visioning does not seem to have been mandated, Britain has new Regional Planning Guidelines (RPGs) that require that visions be prepared.'[4]

Visioning Beyond Division: The Case of Belfast

This book has come from the visioning process in Belfast, a city that has experienced not only the universal processes of economic restructuring and traditional decline, but also the particular stresses of its deep political conflict. Necessarily, its drive for regeneration has to be twinned with an effort to redress the polarisation of its sectarian and cultural division. With this in mind, Belfast formed a City Partnership Board, comprising representation from the City Council, business, trade unions, community and public sectors. Over a period of two years, this Board engaged in widespread consultation across the city, attempting to engage the imagination of its diverse constituencies in a series of workshops and forums.

In crafting its Vision Plan, the Belfast City Partnership had to consider a complex range of issues affecting prosperity, equity and quality. Thus, it recognised that it would be helpful in catching the popular imagination to have one 'hook' or overarching theme to hang the total Vision upon. Insofar as the messages from its consultations provided some guidance, the general idea of a connected city emerged. Such a connected or *Mutual City* was one that encouraged links and collaboration among all sections and areas, and opened the city up to the wider world, e.g. linking:

- the city with its wider metropolitan hinterland;
- the social, economic, cultural and environmental aspects of development to that of the physical and land use;
- the statutory, private and voluntary sectors into collaborative multi-agency partnerships;
- City Hall with all government departments and with active citizenship into a 'joined up' governance of the city;
- different stages of education in pathways of lifelong learning;
- the progress of work-rich areas of the city with that of the work-poor parts;
- the development of Downtown and Waterfront to that of neighbourhood 'urban villages';
- those with a weak attachment to the labour market to the world of work;
- the goals of social cohesion and environmental enhancement with those of economic competitiveness and overall sustainability;
- the young to the elderly in projects which bridge generations and develop mutual respect;
- Protestant to Catholic where there is a wish to have cross-community interaction;
- the future to the past in creative ways that help provide a recognisable tread from its best traditions.

The *Mutual City* concept does not deny real contests of interest. It does, however, suggest that such conflicts should not preclude the practice of common action and collective support, which ties the fortunes of all sectors and parts of the city together as much as possible. As the vision emerged, the following components were prioritised.

A Buoyant City Economy demanded consideration of *structural* changes – getting a strategic framework for integrated development, sectoral selection, role of the social economy, and such like – and of the *cultural* – the need for changes in attitude and behaviour towards risk, enterprise and quality. There was a need to get *beyond fragmented development* whereby a myriad range of urban initiatives tended to operate in isolation. Greater cohesion and synergy required development to come within an overall strategic framework. The search was for 'win-win' scenarios rather than zero-sum games such as out-of-town retailing depleting Downtown, which could amount to expensive displacement rather than net gain.

Moreover, the nature of the development itself demanded consideration, since *development was more than growth*. Thus, economic progress needed to be tied to targeting social need, fair employment and equal opportunity, with the integration of underdeveloped areas, and groups such as the long-term unemployed. A more diversified economic base would require *specialisation in clustered growth sectors*. There were recognised benefits in concentrating on certain sectors, which could be clustered to achieve optimal critical mass and service and supply linkages. Within this, Belfast could identify appropriate *niches* that complemented the rest of the region, with corporate champions to drive competitiveness and investment. Whatever the sector, the importance of more export-led, high valued-added industries and tradable services was recognised. But, there was a need for a *mixed portfolio*. The focus on sectoral specialisation did not imply one source of prosperity. Thus, the expansion of services should not preclude the contribution of manufacturing. Nor should the drive for inward investment distract from the effort to nurture home grown business into a vibrant Small and Medium Enterprise sector. Similarly, the role of the private sector needed to be balanced with the economic scope of community enterprise and the public sector.

In this respect, there was an important *role for the social economy*. In the most depressed areas in particular, there would be advantage in strategically developing a social economy that tied projects for local social, cultural and environmental improvement with local job creation. In general, the city had to *build on its strengths*.

A range of positive factors had been associated with location in Belfast: proximity to customers and suppliers; good labour relations; quality of communication; availability of premises, availability and ease of recruitment of management and technical staff; and quality of working environment. Building on such attributes, the city had to tackle the traditional negatives in business operation: such as low skills, and poor productivity and profitability together with problems in accessing finance.

The benefits of linkage were affirmed. Here, there was a need for a more proactive effort to integrate inward investors into the business community to foster greater local linkages. Another example was the benefit of a cross-fertilisation of ideas and experience between public and private sectors, e.g. staff exchanges.

Less dependence on low factor costs. We used to compete for investment and trade on the basis of low costs (e.g. in labour and rental costs). But, in future we could be increasingly squeezed between low cost areas like Eastern/Southern Europe and Asia for low valued-added markets and higher productivity locations in Europe for the high value-added. Certain aspects of production costs would remain significant, for example the high local cost of energy, particularly affecting profitability in low margin industries. But, in the main, factors such as ingenuity and quality would be ever more critical, requiring:

1. A new culture. This involved a move away from a conservative and insular culture to one that fostered risk-taking, global perspective, continuous improvement and quality control. Centres of excellence with exportable learning product and mentoring to spread best practice could advance such approaches.
2. Opening up the city labour market. There was some recognition that the economic zone in cities included the wider urban hinterland. This would require a concept of a Greater Belfast labour market. Such a city-region approach chimes with European thinking on urban and regional development.
3. An arterial routes strategy. There was recognition of the need to reclaim and renew the economic role of the main radial roads, through such initiatives as niche retailing, cultural quarters, etc.
4. Fostering knowledge assets. The basis of competitive edge was shifting to the knowledge and skills base. This implied a premium role for research and development, and the spread of know-how to the widest population. To optimise the capacity of the city's human capital would require, among other things, an increasing alignment of education to enterprise. More than that, it involved the establishment of a whole new learning culture for a 'learning city'.

The overriding message is that in a city which has become increasingly polarised in sectarian terms, voluntary integration can be facilitated. However, any intervention in this field has to respect the complexities, insecurities and sensitivities that arise. At least four developments in the city may point to progress in addressing division: new local initiatives for peace and reconciliation; the area partnerships, which are cross-community instruments for regeneration; the higher profile of ethnic groups, which contribute to a greater multi-cultural complexion in the city; and new schools – integrated and Irish language – which acknowledge the virtue of diversity.

The Source of this Book

As part of the effort to engage the citizens of Belfast and to identify the salient driving social forces shaping the future pattern of cities, a series of public addresses were held, with renowned speakers from a number of disciplines in urban development. This book brings together those key addresses. In the opening two chapters, we seek to set the theoretical context of urban change and the challenge of building a competitive city that can accommodate social inclusion. In Chapter 3, Peter Hall sets out a detailed understanding of how the modern city form has to be appreciated in its metropolitan context. This has involved the spreading out of the urban, and indeed suburban, into a wider economic hinterland of a city region. Such a wider economic geography of investment and employment is matched by settlement patterns. However, Wim Wievel and Joseph Persky caution against a pattern of low-density development that sprawls into greenfield environments and thins out central cities, in the process losing the economies, efficiencies and especially the equities of a more compact urban form. Citing the US experience, Wievel and Persky contend that continued suburbanisation and edge city development have encouraged a flight of talent and funds from the traditional core of cities, sacrificing the productive use of existing physical and social infrastructures, and creating problems of great social exclusion. In Chapter 5, we comment on these arguments, and seek to contextualise them in the concept of sustainability.

Michael Parkinson summarises the key changes in recent urban policy in the UK and Europe in Chapter 6. This is followed by our review of the lessons to be drawn from these kind of urban interventions, pointing to the likely new urban policy agenda, within which cities' regeneration efforts will be set. Charles Landry reminds us in the next chapter that the premium quality in remaking industrial cities is that of creativity, and in Chapter 9, we seek to build on this analysis in assessing the potential contribution of the cultural industries to cities like Belfast, which endures the consequence of cultural conflict.

Whatever the physical, economic and social pattern of cities in the future, and whatever the policy path they pursue to creatively regenerate, city management will be crucial. Patsy Healey outlines the features of good governance in Chapter 10, emphasising the need to expand the role of participatory democracy and active citizenship. Brian Hanna's follow-up contribution examines this message with regard to the growing role of partnerships as a means to achieve a more inclusive form of urban decision-making. In the Conclusion, we set out the critical considerations about urban development that need to be faced if a credible city vision is to be scripted with the signature of all sections of the population behind it.

Notes

1. Ellyard, P. quoted in Share the Vision, http://www.ci.diamond-bar.ca.us/share.htm
2. Klein, W. et al. (1993), 'Vision of Things to Come', *Planning* 59, 5, p. 10, quoted in Shipley, R. and Newkirk, R. (May 1998), 'Visioning: Did Anybody See Where It Came From?', *Journal of Planning Literature*, Vol. 12, No. 4, p. 411.
3. Krumholz, N. (Nov. 1991), 'Equity and Local Economic Development', *Economic Development Quarterly*, Vol. 5, No. 4.
4. Shipley, R. and Newkirk, R. (May 1998), 'Visioning: Did Anybody See Where It Came From?', p. 411.

CONTEXT

1 Understanding the Contemporary City

Frank Gaffikin and Mike Morrissey

In most of the industrial world, the period since 1945 saw the development of a rational planning system, framed to decentralise jobs, investment and people from concentrated metropolitan areas, while providing incremental improvements to the built environment in the old cities. By the 1980s, the urban issue had changed. More fundamental questions were raised about the very viability of the city, in the context of a radical shift in the political economies of industrialised societies like the UK and USA. This chapter explores the tentative remaking of urban and social theory to make sense of these 'New Times'.

It addresses two key questions: first, whether the standard urban theories are adequately comprehensive and operational in the economic geography behind the contemporary recasting of capitalism; second, whether the recent emphasis on locality studies is a timely rediscovery of the contingency of space, or whether it represents a sidelining not only of totalistic theories of the urban, but of theory itself. The purpose is to contextualise recent urban developments in major social, economic and political change – variously characterised under rubrics such as post-Fordism, post-industrialism, disorganised capitalism, or even more boldly in terms of 'New Times', post-modernism and 'the end of history'. Such understanding is essential if visions of future cities are to be rooted in an analysis of the key drivers for urban change.

Increasingly, urban researchers are wary of restricting their analytical reference to the purely urban, but rather frame urban developments in wider societal change. Some, like Saunders, dispute altogether the relevance of spatial constructs like 'the urban', contending that since modern industrial societies are urban in character, it is more fruitful to examine the impact of macro-policies of collective consumption than to focus on the relatively modest outputs of urban policy per se.[1] This perspective would also accord with a general Marxist claim that the issue is not so much an urban crisis but rather a more fundamental crisis of welfare capitalism, transparent since the 1970s. Implicit in these

3

views is an appreciation that the acute micro-change at the urban level
by this stage could only be explained fully by an account of macro-
change at the national and increasingly global level.

The End of Keynes

By the mid-1970s, the maintenance of full employment and continuous
economic growth was in jeopardy. The central problem for government
was the poor performance of the British economy and the inability to
balance inflation, growth, full employment, currency stability and
external trade. High (relative) levels of unemployment in 1971 and
1972 were reduced by a substantial increase in aggregate demand
accomplished by tax cuts, increased public investment and a large
expansion of the money supply. This 'Barber boom' was accompanied
by a surge in imports and increasing inflation. The principal Keynesian
remedies seemed to be generating as many problems as they solved.[2]

The acknowledgement of the inability of Keynesian macro-economic
policies to respond to these problems was contained in a passage of
the Prime Minister's speech at the 1976 TUC conference described
by Keith Joseph as 'reminiscent of Milton Friedman':[3]

> We used to think that you could just spend your way out of a
> recession and increase employment by cutting taxes and boosting
> government spending. I tell you, in all candour, that that option no
> longer exists, and that insofar as it ever did exist, it worked by
> injecting bigger doses of inflation into the economy followed by higher
> levels of unemployment as the next step. That is the history of the
> past twenty years.

Keynesian demand management seemed to have reached a point
where its major effect was an expansion of the money supply, thus
fuelling inflation and import penetration. In theory, government can
'fine tune' aggregate demand to equal aggregate supply via fiscal
policy. Thus, demand deficits can be compensated by additional
spending and overheating by increasing expenditure. In practice, there
are many reasons why public expenditure will tend to 'overshoot'
appropriate targets. For example, political parties will have made
promises which require expenditure increases. The general upward
trend in the consumption of services will increase the demand on
public services. Demographic and other changes will increase the
resources needed simply to maintain public service levels. Finally, a
commitment to full employment policies will produce a bias towards
high aggregate demand.

With a surplus in aggregate demand (caused by an expansion of the money supply generated principally through the public sector borrowing requirement), two trends emerge: first, supply and demand will move towards equilibrium via price increases – inflation; second, if competitors' prices are increasing more slowly, imports grow in volume (and exports decline) hence precipitating a balance of payments deficit. Both will contribute to unemployment since a growing proportion of aggregate demand will target competitor products, while a balance of payments deficit forces a cut back in government expenditure and/or a currency crisis treated by higher interest rates which, in turn, inhibit private investment.

Apparently, Keynesian solutions had become the 'problem' in a number of different senses:

- first, the practice of 'fine tuning' the level of demand in the economy turned out to be a less than perfect science;
- second, the association between the growth of demand and import penetration had resulted in a period of 'stop-go' policies which undermined the prospect of longer-term planning and minimised the prospects for non-inflationary growth;
- third, no effective comparable international mechanism of demand management had been established – the implementation of Keynesianism at national level was compromised by global economic processes;
- finally, even if the Keynesian promise of perpetual, full employment growth had materialised, there remained the problem of underdevelopment in the Third World and, indeed, the ecological damage generated by the spread of industrialism.

At the same time, supply-side theorists were contending that the public sector, through an excessive fiscal burden on business, was creating a situation where productivity increases were used to reduce costs rather than increase output. This contributed to the growth of unemployment.[4] Gaffikin and Morrissey have explained the popular interpretation thus:[5]

> Under welfarism, wealth redistribution had been allocated greater priority than wealth creation. This had led to a profligate public sector, borrowing beyond its means in a vain attempt to catch up with ever more generous definitions of social need and poverty. The ratchet effect of a universalist welfare system had increasingly crowded out the private sector, feather-bedded the work-shy, demeaned the work ethic, and imposed a penal tax burden on the risk-taking entrepreneur.

Welfarism Under Threat

Central to the political and economic disturbances of the 1970s were the contesting legitimacies of welfarism and capitalism. Certainly, these strains were experienced more sharply in the solidaristic welfare state of the UK, compared to the US liberal version.[6] The objectives espoused by welfarism included those of a social cohesion born of common citizenship; social need redressed by collective provision; equality of opportunity, if needs be via positive discrimination; and full employment sustained by state intervention. These credos were at odds with capitalist imperatives: competitive individualism; the primacy of want, as expressed in market demand, over that of need as generously defined by empire-building welfare bureaucracies; and inequality, properly reflected in the preferential status accorded the risk-taking and industrious entrepreneur. The intriguing aspect of this value conflict was that it engaged both left and right, who differed more in prognosis than diagnosis.

The left believed that welfarism and capitalism were in uneasy coexistence because the former was forever at the discretion of the latter. Wealth creation, inspired pre-eminently by private profit and capital accumulation, was destined to confine the public sphere to a poorly funded casualty station for the individual and spatial victims of a flawed economics. Always the poor relation, the public sector constantly risked being simultaneously marginal to economic policy-making, while being blamed for, and penalised by, its failures. The most cherished welfarist objectives could only be securely attained through socialism.

Whereas the left bemoaned the dilution of welfare by capitalism, the right maintained the converse: 'public' values had trespassed too far into the preserve of the 'private'. Dislocating the relationship between effort, achievement and reward had enfeebled capitalism. The post-war social democratic consensus was supposed to balance an opportunity ladder for the ambitious with a safety net for the dependent. In fact, the net had become a featherbed for the undeserving poor, purchased by a punitive tax burden on the enterprising. This, in turn, had engendered an economic crisis, whereby both work ethic and profit motive had been eroded by an intrusive and profligate state, hooked on taxation and regulation.

But for the right, the malaise existed at multiple levels: cultural, ideological, fiscal and planning. The growth rate of social reproduction costs had pressured government to extend its revenue base not only by means of tax increases but also through borrowing and/or printing money. This, in turn, reduced the supply, and raised the cost, of money for the private sector. Consequently, private investment potential, and with it employment creation, were curtailed. As expressed by Bacon and Eltis,[7] this process involved a fiscal transfer from the marketable to the non-marketable sector, at once 'crowding out' the private economy, while expecting it to sustain productivity growth. The ultimate fall-out was greater unemployment and poverty, most manifest in older industrial spaces, whose problems generated yet more welfare demands. But, more welfare simply reinforced circuitous patterns of extra government spending leading to less investment and employment. In the process, many urban communities had become welfare-dependent.

Apart from the fiscal bind of how to finance welfare, there was also the dilemma of how to plan and administer its delivery.[8] In the USA and the UK, two 'monopoly' parties competed in a political market, demand-led by an electorate, whose rising expectations were stimulated by inflated promises of social consumption. The result was 'government overload'.[9] The law of diminishing returns determined that the more government assumed responsibility, the less competently it accomplished any particular task, a process destined to bring planning itself into disrepute.

According to some, the particular severity of this crisis in the UK, as compared say to the USA, was attributable to the impasse of class stalemate.[10] Specifically, the working class, spatially concentrated in the old urban areas, had been defensively organised to resist pressures from the capitalist class, but was too politically conservative to impose a socialist alternative. Meanwhile, a deteriorating economic performance could not sustain welfarist demands, thereby straining corporatist structures. The very lack of competitiveness made workers resistant to the rationale of economic restructuring, since production change seemed inevitably to bode ill for job prospects. Yet, this attitude confirmed the image of a workforce shielded from realities of massive 'hidden unemployment', a deception in which government had colluded.

A New Production System

The emergence of Fordism as the pre-eminent production form in the post-war growth sectors was a critical contribution to the spatial redistribution of employment to depressed areas. Involving, as it did, mass flowline rather than nodal assembly, producing standardised goods at a scale economy demanded by the new consumer society, it offered numerous, reasonably secure and remunerated labour opportunities. But in its use of mechanisation to rationalise labour, and its focus on low cost formulaic rather than quality design, several rigidities emerged in its vertically integrated corporate decision-making. As change at the local and global levels quickened, its reactions were often stalled, evident in the time lags in transferring innovation into production. By the 1970s, the system's durability was in doubt.

Some characterised the manufacturing job drain at this time in blanket terms of 'de-industrialisation'.[11] But some, like Massey and Meegan,[12] understood it as a significantly differentiated process, requiring disaggregation at two levels. First, job loss was an outcome of changes in output and/or productivity. Second, industry's drive to improve international competitiveness could assume three distinct forms – rationalisation, intensification and technical innovation – each 'justifying' labour shedding. Rationalisation involved a cut in total capacity. Intensification was designed to extract productivity gains without significant new investment or production reorganisation, features inherent in automation and robotisation.

By the late 1970s, it was widely acknowledged that the structural and spatial effects of the new micro-technology on employment would be significant and persistent.[13] While some expressed apprehension, others lamented industry's hesitant embrace of the new opportunities.[14] The issue of whether these changes amounted to a collapse of Fordism is subject to much contest. Harvey has identified three theoretical responses.[15] One detects a seismic shift in which 'markets for standardised mass-produced goods have given way – in part at least – before a growing profusion of shifting niche markets'.[16] These new fragmented consumption patterns have coincided with changing production technologies,[17] prompting, in the view of Piore and Sabel and Lipietz,[18] a distinctive regime of flexible specialisation. It represents a change so profound that some like Aglietta and Scott have designated it as neo-Fordism, a radical attempt by Fordism at self-adjustment, and some like Murray speak of post-Fordism, as a qualitatively new era beyond Fordism.[19]

Post-Fordism, as a new production model, is seen to involve a switch from being operations-led to being market-led. In its new customer-driven guise, the premium is on innovation, quality and design. A finer integration of research, development and production demands decentralisation into less hierarchical control teams, which combine responsibilities for engineering, production, customer services and marketing. Quality with cost control, to be achieved by zero-defect objectives, not only encourages networking, franchising and joint ventures with other producers, but also a more long-term relationship with selected sub-contractors, rather than reliance on competitive advantages from multiple sourcing.[20] Post-Fordist production is more alert to segmented markets, whether divided horizontally around such factors as age or gender, or vertically around income and status. It applies various technological antennae to correlate commodities with lifestyle niches, and in that respect production targeting is about scope as much as scale.

The second theoretical strand is sceptical. Amin and Robins refer to the 'mythical geography of flexible accumulation'.[21] Sayer questions the incapacity of mass production to respond to diverse markets.[22] Gordon[23] sees the arguments about the increased spatial mobility of capital being a feature of its enhanced flexibility, as fatalistically and prematurely demoting the capacity of nation-states to regulate capital. In a similar vein, Pollert characterises claims for a flexible regime of accumulation as complicit with an ideological onslaught against working-class resistance to industrial change, an 'offensive which celebrates pliability and casualisation, and makes them seem inevitable'.[24]

The third approach, and the one in which Harvey positions himself, contends that post-Fordism has a social and spatial reality, but that 'flexible technologies and organisational forms have not become hegemonic everywhere'.[25] This is a view which accords most closely with the confused reality. The experience of Fordism itself for many depressed conurbations and regions has been partial and transitory, even allowing for the decentralisation of production to undeveloped areas under regional policy in the 1950s and 1960s. Instead, therefore, of conceptualising in terms of 'neo' or 'post' Fordism, it is our assessment that a more differentiated system is in operation, which, as Hudson remarks, reproduces in modified form, pre-Fordist and Fordist production methods.[26] This more circumspect approach to restructuring and its local 'reproductions' is found in Warde,[27] while more fundamental doubts as to whether the most important changes in the 1980s have come from consumption rather than production have been floated by Thrift.[28]

While writers like Murray and Lipietz[29] concentrate on changing patterns of consumption and production, a distinctive emphasis of Harvey's work, in this regard, concerns the way innovative techniques and deregulation in financial systems, have contributed to the new volatilities and 'flexibilities'. The pace, scale and global reach of financial flows have unsteadied national strategies for capital accumulation, while appearing to offer governments, corporations and consumers strategies to unblock Fordism, none more evident in the 1980s than what Harvey calls the production of debt, speculative and fictitious 'junk bond' capital:[30]

> Casino capitalism had come to town, and many large cities suddenly found they had command of a new and powerful business. On the back of this boom in business and financial services, a whole new Yuppie culture formed, with its accoutrements of gentrification, close attention to symbolic capital, fashion, design, and quality of urban life.

By the early 1980s, as the pace and scale of economic restructuring became apparent, pessimism about reversing mass unemployment grew. The British Labour Movement proposed an Alternative Economic Strategy, contesting the fatalistic revisionism that full employment was no longer feasible.[31] Contending that any credible programme would have to accommodate reappraisal of the work ethic and new leisure opportunities, Jenkins and Sherman argued that a transitory adjustment phase in the micro-computer age would require government intervention to cushion job displacement. They projected that surplus generated by new technologies could finance generous social compensation for the negative fall-out for some people and places:

> Technological unemployment will be based on high growth, high profits and returns, a highly competitive manufacturing and service base and high incomes, and these enable constructive policies to be adequately funded.[32]

However, by the early 1990s in the UK, the new flexible workforce was more evident than anything resembling a return to full employment. In spring 1993, some 9.7 million (38 per cent of all UK workers) were either in part-time, temporary or self-employment, or on government training schemes or were unpaid family workers – an increase of 1.25 million since 1986. The share of male employment now part of this 'flexible workforce' has grown from 18 per cent in 1981 to 27 per cent in 1993, while for women it has stabilised at around 50 per cent.[33]

Post-Industrialism: 'From Welders to Waiters'?

Economic transformation in this period has been more radically framed in terms of 'post-industrialism'. The term has a pedigree going back to the First World War, when some figures applied it to infer a preference for a return to decentralised artisan workshops.[34] Back in the late 1950s, Riesman equated the concept with the affluent society, in which the diminishing role of work would usher in a leisure society.[35] By the late 1960s, Touraine associated it with a more pessimistic prognosis about technocratic dominance in a 'programmed' society.[36] By the 1970s, Bell projected the axial basis of the new order as not technology per se, but rather theoretical scientific knowledge. In an information society, the social framework rested upon a knowledge theory of value, by which surplus value derives primarily from information rather than productive labour.[37] In this post-industrial age, the service economy would acquire prominence over the goods-

Figure 1.1 Percentage Employment in Manufacturing and Services,
1973–91

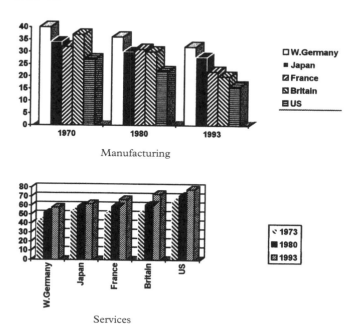

Manufacturing

Services

* *For W. Germany, Japan and France, the last figures are for 1991*

Source: OECD, National Statistics and Industrial Policy in OECD Countries,
Annual Review, 1993

producing one, giving pre-eminence in the occupational structure to
the professional and technical class.

These ideas can be seen as part of the 'stages model' of development,
whereby society moves linearly from pre-industrialism dominated by
agriculture, through to industrialism dominated by manufacturing, to
post-industrialism dominated by services. Basic facts are marshalled
to support this periodisation, for instance that in the industrial world
the service sector accounts for over half the output and labour force.
Manufacturing companies employ one in six workers in the USA, one
in five in the UK, and one in three in Japan and Germany. The shift
is represented in Figure 1.1.

The greatest manufacturing decline is in Britain, where job totals
in this sector have been almost halved since 1970, compared to an 8
per cent drop in the USA over the same period. Since 1970, the

service sector's share of all jobs in Britain rose from just over a half to nearly three-quarters. In the USA, services now account for 78 per cent of all employment. There are only three OECD countries – Greece, Portugal and Turkey – in which fewer than half the workforce is in services.[38] The composition of US service employment growth in the 1980s is shown in Figure 1.1, alongside the increasing share held by services in total exports and GDP.

Plausible reasons are advanced for this move to post-industrialism. The supply-side component of the explanation is that rising manufacturing productivity has created a labour surplus 'pushed' into a more labour-intensive service sector. In the seven largest OECD economies, in the period 1979–90, real output per manufacturing employee grew annually on average by 3.1 per cent, compared to an annual average rate of 0.9 per cent for services.[39] The 'pull' factor stems from the recomposition of demand, whereby as income rises in society, a growing share of expenditure shifts from basic material to non-material needs, such as cultural and leisure services.

Clearly, this narrative of automatic sequence is simplistic. For one thing, a burgeoning service sector can often attend a rise in manufacturing, which requires services such as design, marketing, advertisement and distribution. Second, there is no neat pattern of labour displaced from manufacturing being absorbed by services. Indeed, as one indication, UK labour market trends refute any notion that the loss of full-time male jobs is compensated by the growth of part-time female ones. Between 1978 and 1993, full-time male employment declined by 2.98 million, while part-time female jobs increased by 0.96 million.[40] Moreover, Gershuny has argued persuasively that a buoyant self-service economy is replacing some services with manufactured goods such as television and washing machines, though these in turn rely on services for repair and maintenance.[41] Finally, statistics purporting to show shifts in employment and output are themselves contaminated, since they group under services contracted-out activities once done in-house by manufacturing, such as auditing, catering and cleaning. Some businesses assigned to the service sector, such as computer software, could just as readily be designated as manufacturing.

Nevertheless, these considerations do not preclude radical social reformation linked to a new pivotal role for services, one which is seen to harbour new contradictions. For some, like Bell, these include tensions between the bourgeois work ethic and the individualistic, hedonistic lifestyles generated by a credit-card service economy.[42] For critics of capitalism, like Gorz, the change threatens a social regression, whereby stratifications are accentuated. Overworked economic elites purchase leisure time by sub-contracting personal and domestic tasks to a deskilled servile class for modest remuneration.[43] There is a prevalent concern in the literature that the coming economic order contains a structural tendency for acute labour market segmentation – professional elites and multi-skilled employees at one end, and at the other, an increasingly casualised, flexi-time labour force, forever perched precariously close to unemployment.[44]

Alongside this common ground, different emphases abound. For instance, Castells prefers to assign the term 'informationalism' to the new era. For him, the key social and spatial dynamic derives from 'the interaction and the articulation between the informational mode of development and the restructuring of capitalism'.[45] In the competitive scramble to secure state-of-the-art technology markets, the state will be pressured to fund expensive requisite infrastructure, thereby demoting its redistributional functions. These government fundings are likely to be legitimated in the form of public–private partnerships, as part of a general interpenetration of state and capital. But, it is a transformed capital from its oligopolistic concentration in industrialism:[46]

in the informational era large corporations set up specific alliances for given products, processes and markets: these alliances vary according to time and space, and result in a variable geometry of corporate strategies that follow the logic of the multiple networks where they are engaged rather than the monolithic hierarchy of empire conglomerates.

Disorganised Capitalism

Lash and Urry[47] frame these transitions within a more general paradigm, which posits a shift from 'organised' to 'disorganised' capitalism. In summary, they denote the latter as representing the current period in which: industrial, financial and commercial capital are becoming increasingly globalised; the coalition of state and big capital is overtaken because of the growing autonomy of large private monopolies; and the core economies are suffering the dislocations of deindustrialisation as they sectorally realign towards services, paralleled by competitive industrial development in the periphery.

In turn, these restructurings are exhibiting discernible social, political and cultural ramifications. Social relations of production are being reconstituted. On the one hand, managerial hierarchies are assuming more complicated forms as the trend towards the separation of ownership and control becomes accentuated. On the other, organised labour is losing its national collectivity as plant size contracts, 'smoke stacks' collapse and the blue-collar working class is deskilled as part of a general recomposition of employment. In a later work,[48] Lash and Urry propose that since post-industrialism is denoted by knowledge-intensive production requiring innovatory process, it is naturally aligned with post-Fordism, in which flexibility is inherently not only knowledge intensive, but also reflexive. Reflexive accumulation involves the greater unification of conceptualisation and execution, evident in the increased role for R&D and design,[49] and greater expectation of initiative and hermeneutic sensibility at shopfloor level.

But in the new production form, social and spatial hierarchies are changed, not erased. The U-form of hierarchy, based on unitary organisation, divided on functional lines, and the M-form of hierarchy, based on operational divisions within a more collegiate and less rigid compartmentalisation may both give way to the model of Value Added Partnership. This involves firms in a sector, from the raw material to final consumption stage, networking so that each focuses on a single task in the chain, in a way conducive to cost reduction, shared information, de-layering and downsizing. In this manner, some conglomerates may disintegrate, since operating in partnerships permits 'the coordination and scale associated with large companies and the flexibility, creativity and low overhead usually found in small companies'.[50] The spatial implications of such corporate reorganisation are addressed later in this chapter.

Politically, these changes are manifested in a diminution of class-based electoral appeals. Corporatist decision-making, designed to promote consensual negotiation among relatively monolithic blocs of labour and capital, is deemed to be redundant. The dominance of science and rationality fragments in the face of more diverse cultural idioms, channelled through a globalised media, which promote greater pluralism and less durability in values and fashion.

Cooke cautions against these universalist claims. First, the organisation of both industrial and finance capital, the social relations around them, and the role of the state have all differed over time and space. Second, while mass production became the main 'technological paradigm', it was not always and everywhere the main form of production. Third, while capitalism has experienced a series of crises since the 1970s, its resilience hardly suggests disorganisation. Rather, 'the picture ... is of increasing world economic integration and the reorganisation of spatial production relations, at a rapid pace, without undue signs of disorganisation'.[51]

The Urban and Post-modernity

Reference to concepts such as disorganised capitalism, post-Fordism and post-industrialism suggests, for some, competing explanations. For instance, post-Fordism seems to address changed forms of manufacturing production as a new industrialism, while post-industrialism shifts the gaze to a radical redirection from manufacturing to services. Yet, these terms all infer some periodisation of polity and economy. They acknowledge to varying degrees new pluralisms and flexibilities, and the current pivotal force of information. Most of their variants identify structural tendencies to more acute socio-spatial polarisation, and they view these changes in the context of greater globalisation, and networking among 'wired' organisations on information highways. Among the issues they do contest is the extent to which such upheavals have been transformative or whether they constitute intensified continuities with the past.[52] Those who locate the pronounced changes of our time in a post-modern paradigm unequivocally opt for the latter. The debate about the existence and form of post-modernism is extensive and beyond the scope of this review. What follows is a summative version, relevant to the contours of urban theory.

Post-modernism derides the pretension underpinning the modernist project that the enigma of social reality is subject to order and pattern, discernible by science. Enlightenment concepts of rationality and objectivity belie the problematic of excavating universal truths. Diverse linguistic and cultural prisms beget different worlds and not merely mediate different insights into the same world. Thus, post-modernism travels beyond the standard phenomenological concerns with penetrating meaning or the sociological concern with the action frame of reference.[53] The new self-referentiality[54] disowns settled orthodoxy, exactitude and predictability, even if such concession subverts 'an independent reality',[55] and exposes as illusion, human control of the environment. Forsaking the historicist meta-narratives,[56] it queries not merely the inevitability of 'an emancipatory politics',[57] but its very validation.

This forfeited certitude is intrinsic to the post-modernist discourse itself, since it is a concept resistant to specific usage. Thus, the 'New Times' can be characterised simultaneously as a barely comprehensible fragmented hyper-reality[58] of signs and images, by which style is elevated over content, and as auguring a dynamic pluralism rooted in cultural diversity. In the case of the former, the pervasive pastiche, montage and whimsy in many recently built environments, reflect not only the eclectic in contemporary design and planning, but also the penchant for creating the new in recycled nostalgic motifs.[59] Adopting the latter emphasis, the rupture with the past coincides with the 'end of the American century'. The new mapping of political economy, in which the creative drive associated with modernity has relocated from the West to the Far East, nullifies the conventional equation of globalisation with Americanisation:[60]

if an increase in global flows has contributed to the 'de-territorialisation' of populations, commodities, money, images and ideas, the consequence has not so much been in the direction of cultural homogenisation as the reconstitution or regeneration of differences in and through displacement.

Cooke grasps this straw as a chance to resolve tensions between an increasingly centralised and bureaucratised capitalist state and an atomised population, ever more individuated under market relations. The new flexible specialisation underscoring Japanese inventiveness places a premium on cohesive, globally networked industrial localities as 'the most dynamic, fast-growing centres of production in the post-modern space economy',[61] and thus offers a model for replenishing citizenship as the basis for a recuperative modernity project. However, not all scholars corroborate this affinity between the spatial clustering of frontier 'propulsive' industries and the formation of vibrant industrial 'ensembles', favourable to the improved adhesiveness of civil society.[62]

Another reading of post-modernism stresses its misgivings about ideologies which privilege one totalising schema over another, and concludes that its pluralist posture is a ruse for depoliticisation:[63] since arbitration between theoretical abstractions is inconclusive, concerted action for social progress is misconceived utopianism. In such a fashion, hand-wringing becomes hand-washing. The collapse of command planning is taken to invalidate planning per se – a view consonant with Chaos Theory, which refutes the Newtonian model of a physical universe governed by discoverable laws. Behind the apparent regulation of complex systems, lies an unpredictability ready to upset the best laid plans.[64]

Yet, for Harvey, one of the key features of the post-modern condition is an intensified compression of time and space. Not only have production and distribution speeded up and spatially extended under flexible accumulation, so also have exchange and consumption. Electronic banking and trading accelerates transfers of currencies and stocks in the global markets. Similarly, consumerist lifestyles, involving a relative shift to the purchase of services over goods, experience great volatility in frenetic search for the novel. Among the consequences he notes, are the increasing commodification not only of culture and leisure, but also of images as simulacra; the 'instantaneity' and 'dis-posability' of both commodities and values; a 'sensory overload'; and a lack of permanence and solidity (reflected right down to the temporary labour contract), which generates its own ironies such as the vogue heritage projects keen to impart a sense of 'mooring' and roots.[65] Rapid turnover in fads, and agnostic tastes, lend the age an ephemer-ality, referred to by Berman[66] in his echo of 'all that is solid melts into air'. It seems to mock any endeavour at long-term planning, particu-larly by public authority immune to market sensitivities.

Implications for the Social Production of Space

The spatial reconfigurations associated with these shifts are acute. Micro-electronics simultaneously allows for the decomposition of the production process and its spatial disaggregation, while integrating management control across distance via on-line information systems and telecommunications. The new territorial dispersal of industry displaces traditional regional specialisation. Alongside this, the urban–rural shift of jobs and population persists, as manufacturing in city cores virtually disappears. Population density in cities declines along with their tax base, leading to neglect of fixed investment in the urban fabric.

Back in the 1960s, the erosion of the manufacturing base in the 'smoke stack' urban zones was characterised in terms of 'an inner city crisis'.[67] By the 1980s, this malaise had, in the view of some,[68] deteriorated into an 'urban crisis', as an accentuated deindustrialisation process extended city economic decline beyond the inner core. There was a changing geography of production associated with this, including the relocation of investment to suburban/rural sites, a certain measure of internationalisation of production, and later for a period in the 1980s a more polarised UK regional divide between the 'core' command South, a semi-peripheral Midlands and a Northern periphery.

This reshaping of the space-economy was theorised in various ways. From neo-classical perspectives,[69] unfavourable cost factors operated in traditional urban areas whereby, for instance, the tradition of organised labour, the scarce supply of appropriate land and the costs of congestion promoted the decentralisation of investment. In this respect, it might be inferred that new firm formation in such mature spaces demanded not just reordering of economic and environmental structure, but also of the social relations of production.[70] For others, it was more the acute repercussion in urban areas of macrochanges in the industrial labour market.[71]

A different view emphasised the interplay of the urban and national. The city was seen to suffer from three features of deindustrialisation. First, there was a national recomposition of employment involving a manufacturing jobs drain and an expansion of service employment. Second, this structural shift was accompanied by poor national economic growth, leading to overall sustained high unemployment. The third aspect, unlike the previous two, has had a specific spatial dimension. The city has been losing manufacturing jobs at a relatively faster rate:[72] 'In every region small towns and rural areas have fared better than larger settlements by a sizeable margin .... . Highly urban regions have declined; more rural regions have grown.' Fothergill et al. have attributed this distinct underperformance to industrial land constraints in cities, which thereby are disadvantaged on two accounts.

Table 1.1 Employment Changes by Sector in Different Types of Area, 1951–81

Sector and Periods	Inner Cities		Outer Cities		Free-standing Cities		Small Towns and Rural Areas		Britain	
	000s	%	000s	%	000s	%	000s	%	000s	%
Manufacturing										
1951–61	−143	−8.0	+84	+5.0	−21	−2.0	+453	+14.0	+374	+5.0
1961–71	−428	−26.1	−217	−10.3	−93	−6.2	+489	+12.5	−255	−3.9
1971–81	−447	−36.8	−480	−32.6	−311	−28.6	−717	−17.2	−1929	−24.5
Private services										
1951–61	+192	+11.0	+110	+11.0	+128	+17.0	+514	+16.0	+944	+14.0
1961–71	−297	−15.3	+92	+8.1	−7	−0.8	+535	+14.5	+318	+4.2
1971–81	−105	−6.4	+170	+17.3	+91	+10.9	+805	+24.8	+958	+14.4
Public services										
1951–61	+13	+1.0	+54	+7.0	+38	+6.0	+200	+8.0	+302	+6.0
1961–71	+25	+2.0	+170	+21.6	+110	+17.7	+502	+17.3	+807	+14.5
1971–81	−78	−7.4	+102	+8.8	+53	+6.5	+456	+14.1	+488	+7.7
Total employment										
1951–61	+43	+1.0	+231	+6.0	+140	+6.0	+1060	+10.0	+1490	+7.0
1961–71	−643	−14.8	+19	+0.6	+54	+2.4	+1022	+8.5	+320	+1.3
1971–81	−538	−14.6	−236	−7.1	−150	−5.4	+404	+3.5	−590	−2.7

Source: Begg, I., Moore, E. and Rhodes, J. (1986), 'Economic and Social Change in Urban Britain and the Inner Cities', in V.A. Hausner (ed.), Critical Issues in Urban Economic Development, Vol. I, Clarendon Press, Oxford, p. 22.

They endure job loss associated with increasingly capital intensive production forms and they fail to attract compensating job gains drawn to greenfield sites in small towns and rural areas.

Table 1.1 illustrates the long-standing trend of the 'deindustrialised city'. In both the 1960s and 1970s, the inner city lost 15 per cent of its employment base. This erosion comprised a manufacturing job drain of over a quarter in the 1960s and over a third in the 1970s. By the latter decade, the inner city was losing jobs in every sector. By then, it was only the small towns and rural areas which were experiencing net job growth. But, even they suffered from industrial job loss as the whole country's manufacturing jobs base contracted by a quarter. The most depressing feature for the urban cores is that while they have endured the greatest manufacturing decline, they have experienced the least compensation from job growth in private and public services. On the other hand, the small towns and rural areas saw their manufacturing jobs base shrink the least, but enjoyed the greatest growth in service employment. In terms of unemployment, this disparity between a buoyant rural/semi-rural site and the inner city is apparent from the table. But, most interesting perhaps, is the way the jobless problem is extending out to the outer city.

Table 1.2 Unemployment Rates by Area of Residence (GB = 100), 1951–81

Residents of:	1951	1961	1966	1971	1981
Inner Cities	133	136	132	144	151
Outer Cities	81	82	82	88	101
Free-standing Cities	95	107	96	112	115
Towns & Rural Areas	95	93	96	90	90

Source: Begg, I., Moore, B. and Rhodes, J. (1986), p. 20.

In all of this, the processes of deindustrialisation and decentralisation are each distinctive. The latter has been most evident in the case of large buoyant cities, subject to the price elasticity of demand for space, whereas the former has most afflicted older industrial cities like Belfast. Another relevant factor in determining urban decline is that of peripherality 'not only in geographic terms but also socially and in terms of trade patterns'.[73] Cheshire argues that the fate of declining cities relates to their particular experience of the permutation of these three causal factors and their adjustment capacity, including their institutional, social and cultural flexibilities.

But, in general, he contends that the city form, built around industry, is primed to adapt to 'post-industrial' opportunities. Cities can revert to their pre-industrial functions as centres of administration, commerce and culture, and as chosen residential locations, and they also can be an employment source around a range of urban services and amenities. In short, the shift to a service-based economy is the basis for a re-urbanisation. The fastest growing parts of the service sector – insurance, finance, hotel and catering, and retailing – rely either on personal delivery or on deal-making, both of which are facilitated by being located in concentrated settlements of population:[74]

> In terms of economic disadvantages, those particular characteristics of cities – congestion, high unit space costs, and high costs of transport for bulky goods – are much less significant for services. Thus services tend still to be attracted to urban locations and, since it is reasonable to expect most output growth, and even more most employment growth over the next 10 to 20 years to be in services, then that provides strong grounds for believing that an urban employment revival is likely.

Alongside the growth in services, the old division between public and private services is disappearing. As recognised by Bagguley et al.,[75] modes of public service provision have become more differentiated, with new roles for the market, neighbourhood informal economies and the voluntary sector. This has potentially beneficial job implications for local communities if means can be devised to link more closely local employment to local services. Residential choice decisions also are now re-favouring cities. The population movement out of urban areas over many decades now means that the cost of urban relative to ex-urban space is decreasing. Moreover, the income and demographic characteristics of those most impelled to re-urbanise – multiple job holding households – stand to disproportionately increase spending on urban services and amenities, improvements in which then lend further stimulation to urban residential location.

For Castells, the informational city will be one which can accommodate the spatial logic of information technology industries, swayed, as they are, by the availability of quality scientific and technical labour, in a location offering an innovative milieu for networking and organisational synergy. But a lot will depend on the product. In the case of semi-conductors, for instance, a phased process involving knowledge-intensive research and design, advanced engineering, unskilled assembly and quality testing, invites variable location, each compatible with a particular skill base. Where appropriate, this decentralisation of production is facilitated by the industry's intrinsic nature:[76]

> Miniaturisation of devices means low weight and low transportation costs. Computer automation of manufacturing makes possible high-quality standardisation of parts that can be assembled anywhere.

Computer-aided flexible manufacturing enables production to be adjusted to market requirements without the different production functions being spatially proximate.

However, other products, such as leading edge genetic engineering, do not imply the same spatial differentiation, but rather more exclusive attributes. Such selective locations become valuable in terms of real estate, and thereby continue to privilege high value-added activity. For Harvey, the irony is that space–time compression and less-anchored capital actually accentuate the issue of locational advantage, while involving hierarchical realignment in the global urban system:[77]

> The local availability of material resources of special qualities, or even at marginally lower costs, starts to be ever more important, as do local variations in market taste that are today more easily exploited under conditions of small-batch production and flexible design. Local differences in entrepreneurial ability, venture capital, scientific and technical knowhow, social attitudes, also enter in … .

While these perspectives focus on the urban implications of sectoral and demographic shifts, other research has focused on the new spatial divisions of labour related to the corporate strategies of 'prime mover' firms, restructuring in an increasingly globalised economy.[78] The internationalisation of capitalist relations involved not just the relocation of production in search of low cost labour or new markets, but also a related expansion of producer services, in particular finance.[79]

Capital was more mobile across space, and operating at greater speed. A world economy centred on the USA gave way to a multi-polar one based around a more integrated industrial core, including Europe and Japan. However, the signature of transnational corporations and banks on this integration has led some to dispute the existence of a sovereign national economy, never mind anything recognisable as a discrete city economy.[80] Castells talks about the new age as 'the last frontier where organizational networks and information flows dissolve locales and supersede societies'.[81]

For those for whom the post-Fordist city is the future, a new economics arises. For example, there is the increasing keenness on the part of big corporations to be in physical proximity to a core set of long-term suppliers capable of 'just in time' production. In its most optimistic trajectory, this new period of uncertainty is seen by some like Stohr[82] to stimulate innovation in a Schumpterian process of creative destruction. But a new urban politics is also likely, one that is more entrepreneurial and enabling, constituted around a wider coalition of interests, capable of differentiating the city region in the more acutely competitive arena that is the new global economy. For city governance,

Figure 1.2 Phases of Capitalist Development

Phase of Cap. Dev.	Long Wave Period	Tech. and Sectoral Dominance
	Late 1780s–1840s (peaking 1820s)	Mechanisation/steam power Iron, cotton
LIBERAL	1850s–1890s (peaking 1870s)	Railways, steam motor, coal, steel
	1890s–1930s (peaking 1914)	Electric power, combustion engines, chemicals, synthetic materials
ORGANISED	1940s–1970s (peaking 1966)	Electrical and light eng. Petro-chemicals Motor and aircraft industries
	1980s (5th Kondratief)	Micro-electronics Information tech.
DISORGANISED		

Spatial Focus	Political Form	Spatial and Industrial Form
Lancashire Shropshire Black Country	Emergence of nation-states	Limited overlapping of locality Key role of big commercial cities
S. Wales, N.E. England Central Scotland		Spread of New urban Institute Centres in rural areas
West Midlands Gt. London	Nation-state Large bureaucratic corp. in advanced societies	Fordist development around labour-intensive regional specialisation
	Imperialism through to post-war boom Increasingly interventionist Ultimately Keynesian state in pluralist democracies	Extractive + heavy indust. Polarisation of core/periphery in global economy
		Homogenisation of consumption patterns Conc./cent. Of Capital
Cambridge M4 Corridor	Reduction of space and time for subjects and objects Fragmented role of state	Decline of distinct regional/national economies and of industrial cities Growth of industry in smaller towns Globalisation of credit and commodities Post-Fordist emphasis on innovation and agglomeration

the role swap from provider to enabler is linked to the new mixed economy of welfare, in which elements of social consumption are becoming more privatised and remaining public provision more marketised. As its social redistributive role is demoted, local government is assuming greater involvement in economic regeneration, though ironically in the context of a diminution in central state development planning.

In their wider interpretative framework, Lash and Urry,[83] periodising capitalism through liberal, organised and disorganised phases, attribute distinct spatial patterns to each. The form of uneven development specific to the 'flexibilities' and 'fragmentations' of the contemporary period of disorganised capitalism, has seen the demise of regional sectoral and functional specialisation, to be substituted by greater spatial dispersion and diversity. This, in turn, has seen the increasing capacity of electronically-based information systems to reduce diseconomies of time and space, which once operated favourably for the traditional industrial cities.[84] Futurists like Tofler locate the current period in a broader sweep: it is the difficult transition period between the second and third wave. Tofler's 'first wave' is the agrarian phase, which drew to a close in the eighteenth century; the second wave of mass industrialisation started to fade by the mid-1960s; and the third wave, based on computerisation and technocratic culture, is in its awkward infancy.

Figure 1.2 attempts some synthesis of these main conceptual frameworks used to explain socio-economic forms over space and time. Scott has drawn attention to the untidy and confusing spatial patterns emerging as a result of these contemporaneous regimes of accumulation – ageing Fordist alongside the developing one of flexibility. Though the complicated reshaping of 'declining' and 'ascending' areas is difficult to delineate in a period of rapid transformation, in his view, it indubitably represents a qualitative change:[85]

> Whatever the future evolutionary path of this system may be, it is evident that the landscape of capitalist production is today drastically different from what it was even a couple of decades ago.

As Soja remarks,[86] spatial forms in the contemporary industrial city exhibit contrary patterns, no longer mosaic, but kaleidoscopic. Taking the prototype of the US city, he charts changing urban form from the mercantile city that still existed in the 1820s to the competitive industrial form by the 1870s. He then takes this through to the corporate monopoly control in the 1920s, which had begun tertiarising downtown and suburbanising industrial satellites, to the state managed Fordist city in the 1970s, which attempted to revalorise and gentrify urban centres, while accommodating expansive metropolitanisation.

He contends that in the present period, neither conventional urban theory nor Marxist political economy can any longer claim convincing purchase on the enigmatic cohabitation of metropolitan sprawl (which now accommodates amorphous landscapes such as silicon villages) and state orchestrated downtown revitalisation. Gottdiener[87] complies with much of this account. Emphasising the increasing public-private coalitions behind the property sector in US cities, he deprecates the way these forces have attenuated working-class social relations in the process of concentrating new real estate away from the high costs and/or fixed built environments of older manufacturing areas. But, properly in my view, Katznelson dissents from Gottdiener's implicit farewell to the city, arguing instead the spread and range of city-types: 'reinvigorated traditional cities, suburban sprawl, and new agglomerations in formerly peripheral areas are developing simultaneously'.[88]

The outcome of similar processes in the UK has been summarised by Cooke:[89]

> In brief, the spatial trend in the 1980s is towards centralization in or near the urban settings where flexible suppliers and workforces are more common and where older managerial styles, often equated with conflict-ridden relations with unionised workers, are absent. Such localities tend to be Southern and suburban or semi-rural, except for the highest level service activities which remain metropolitan.

The Particularity of Place

In Massey's terms, the global generalities of urban spatial reconfigurations are mediated by the particular history of overlaying rounds of investment and disinvestment, and the specific political-economy of the city region under review.[90] In that sense, space matters. It is not just that space is socially constructed. The social is also spatially constructed. Capitalist global integration has not ushered 'the end of geography', any more than the demise of communism has witnessed the 'end of history'. The uniqueness of place, according to Cooke,[91] means that the resolution of the above mentioned dichotomies can only be resolved in any given urban research practice by appreciating the interaction between universal processes, such as capital accumulation and economic restructuring, and local processes. As expressed by Warf, the contingencies of urban formations mean that: 'within limits, local history and geography could always "be otherwise". With these themes in mind, geography is poised to view cities in existential terms as much as it comprehends them as the products of social logics.'[92]

After decades when it has been assumed that community has been 'eclipsed', or that social relations have been commodified within the frame of global markets, or that new mobilities have liberated people from locality, the significance of place is being rediscovered. It entails a more positive engagement between sociological and geographical imaginations.[93] Taking this view, together with some of the logic of post-Fordism, a more optimistic prognosis for urban regeneration emerges. Ironically, it could be argued that the very globalisation of economic life has simultaneously eroded the authority of the nation-state, while providing some opportunity for regions and cities to operate more directly in the global economy. As noted by Strassoldo,[94] far from rendering the local irrelevant, increasing globalisation reconstitutes the significance of space and place.

Clearly, not all cities are going to get in on the game, and a competitive scramble for such selection is linked to the capacity of urban centres to mobilise their full capacities for this end. It might be thought that the current intensification of social and spatial segregation in the city is an unfavourable basis for a common agenda from the various urban fractions. A more hopeful view is that efforts to compose a united portrayal of a city provide new negotiating opportunities for the urban disadvantaged:[95]

> attempts should be made to exploit the structural openness for external groups characteristic of the new local and regional bargaining systems to push for non-exclusive participation and for more representation for marginalised interests.

For researchers like Cooke, space is an active agent, and not merely a stage. Localities are not passive recipients of exogenous change, but can intervene to transform, if not control, their circumstances. They are not merely places or neighbourhoods, but rather the total social relations and activity among individuals and groups operating in a particular space.[96] As expressed by Fainstein, this interaction of people and property is the key urban dynamic:[97]

> This built environment forms contours which structure social relations, causing commonalities of gender, sexual orientation, race, ethnicity, and class to assume spatial identities. Social groups, in turn, imprint themselves physically on the urban structure through the formation of communities, competition for territory, and segregation.

Researching the Urban in Northern Ireland

This issue is of distinct significance in urban research in Northern Ireland. There are two types of research in the region, one that tends predominantly to view the place as 'normal', the other which emphasises the 'peculiarities'. The former highlights Northern Ireland's integration with social and economic processes common to other peripheral industrial regions. The other perspective emphasises the area's specific history, in particular the extent to which it is shaped by the contesting nationalisms, and the way sectarianism overdetermines the political economy. Most particular research projects adopt one or the other, and employ it separately.[98] What is preferable is an approach which combines the two, integrating issues which are prevalent everywhere and those which are particular to place.[99]

This book addresses the various dimensions of new urban visions. But, it does so recognising that cities are distinctive in history and politics. Accordingly, urban theory to help us understand the future of cities needs to eclectically choose from the main positions outlined above, distinguishing commonalities in patterns and processes, and the uniqueness of place. The current revisionism in urban theory, together with the inadequate explanatory power of any one paradigm, determine that a variety of theoretical positions will be advanced.

In summary, this chapter has traced the latest developments in urban theory, and related them to the proposition that the qualitative change evident in the contemporary urban landscape mirrors the decisive shift in the political economies of mature capitalism. It has argued that such universal processes are mediated via the particularities of cities. The next section examines the policy responses to this changing urban arena.

Notes

1. Saunders, P. (1981), *Social Theory and the Urban Question*, Hutchinson, USA.
2. Knight, K.G. (1987), *Unemployment: an economic analysis*, Croom Helm, London, pp. 327–8.
3. Joseph, K. (1987), 'Conditions for Full Employment', in Coates, D. and Hillard, J. (eds), *The Economic Revival of Modern Britain*, Edward Elgar, Aldershot.
4. Bacon, R. and Eltis, W. (1978), *Britain's Economic Problem: Too Few Producers*, Macmillan, London.
5. Gaffikin, F. and Morrissey, M. (1990), *Northern Ireland: the Thatcher Years*, Zed Books, London, p. 9.

6. Categorisation of welfare states in this fashion is subject to considerable contention. See Esping-Anderson, G. (1990), *The Three Worlds of Welfare Capitalism*, Polity Press, Cambridge.

7. Bacon, R. and Eltis, W. (1976), *Britain's Economic Problems: Too Few Producers*, Heinmann, London.

8. Offe, C.(1984), *The Contradictions of the Welfare State*, Hutchinson, London.

9. King, A. (1987), *The New Right*, Macmillan, London.

10. Aaronovitch, S., Smith, R., Gardiner, J. and Moore, R. (1981), *The Political Economy of British Capitalism: A Marxist Analysis*, McGraw-Hill, London.

11. Blackaby, F. (ed.) (1979), *De-industrialisation*, National Institute of Economic and Social Research and Heinemann, London.

12. Massey, D. and Meegan, R. (1982), *The Anatomy of Job Loss: the How, Why and Where of Employment Decline*, Methuen, London.

13. 'Counter Information Services Report No. 23' (1978), The New Technology, and the Advisory Council for Applied Research and Development, The Application of Semi-Conductor Technology, HMSO, London.

14. ACARD (1979), *Joining and Assembly: The Impact of Robots and Automation*, HMSO, London, and Policy Studies Institute (1981), 'Micro-Electronics in Industry: the extent of use', PSI, London.

15. Harvey, D. (1990), *The Condition of Postmodernity: An Enquiry into the Origins of Cultural Change*, Blackwell, Oxford.

16. Cooke, P. (1988), Guest Editorial, *Environment and Planning D: Society and Space*, Vol. 6, p. 242.

17. Saunders, P. (1984), 'Beyond Housing Classes: The Sociological Significance of Private Property Rights in Means of Coonsumption', *International Journal of Urban and Regional Research*, Vol. 8, No. 2, pp. 202–27.

18. Piore, N.J., and Sabel, C.F. (1984), *The Second Industrial Divide: Prospects for Properity*, Basic Books, New York; and Lipietz, A. (1987), *Mirages and Miracles: The Crises of Global Fordism*, Verso, London.

19. Aglietta, M. (1979), *A Theory of Capitalist Regulation: The US Experience*, New Left Books, London; and Scott, A.J. (1988), 'Flexible Production Systems and Regulated Development: The Rise of New Industrial Spaces in North America and Western Europe', *International Journal of Urban and Regional Research*, 12, pp. 171–86; and Murray, R. (1989), 'Fordism and Post-Fordism', in Hall, S. and Jacques, M. (eds), *New Times: The Changing Face of Politics in the 1990s*, Lawrence and Wishart, in association with Marxism Today, London.

20. Boyer, R. (1989), *New Directions in Management Practices and Work Organisation: General Principles and National Trajectories*, OECD, Paris.
21. Amin, A. and Robins, K. (1990), 'The Re-emergence of Regional Economies? The Mythical Geography of Flexible Accumulation', *Environment and Planning D: Society and Space*, Vol. 8, pp. 7–34.
22. Sayer, A. (1989), 'Post-Fordism in Question', the *International Journal of Urban and Regional Research*, Vol. 13, No. 4, pp. 667–95.
23. Gordon, D. (1988), 'The Global Economy: New Edifice or Crumbling Foundations?', *New Left Review*, 168, pp. 24–65.
24. Pollert, A. (1988), 'Dismantling Flexibility', *Capital and Class*, 34, pp. 42–75.
25. Harvey, D. (1990), *The Condition of Post-Modernity*, p. 191.
26. Hudson, R. (1988), 'Labour Market Changes and New Forms of Work in "Old" Industrial Regions', in Massey, D. and Allen, J. (eds), *Uneven Redevelopment: Cities and Regions in Transition*, Hodder and Stoughton, in association with the Open University, London.
27. Warde, A. (March 1988), 'Industrial Restructuring, Local Politics and the Reproduction of Labour Power: Some Theoretical Considerations', *Society and Space*, 6.
28. Thrift, N. (June 1989), 'New Times and Spaces? The Perils of Transition Models', *Society and Space*, 7.
29. Lipietz, A. (1987), *Mirages and Miracles: The Crises of Global Fordism*, Verso, London.
30. Harvey, D. (1990), *The Condition of Post-Modernity*, p. 332.
31. CSE London Working Group (1980), *The Alternative Economic Strategy: A Labour Movement Response to the Economic Crisis*, CSE Books, London, p. 49.
32. Jenkins, C. and Sherman, B. (1979), *The Collapse of Work*, Methuen, London, p. 176.
33. Watson, G. (July 1994), 'The Flexible Workforce and Patterns of Working Hours in the UK', *Employment Gazette*.
34. Rose, M. (1991), *The Post-Modern and the Post-Industrial*, Cambridge University Press, Cambridge and New York.
35. Riesman, D. (1958), 'Leisure and Work in Post-Industrial Society', in Larrabee, E. and Meyersohn, R. (eds), *Mass Leisure*, Glencoe, Illinois.
36. Touraine, A. (1971), *The Post-Industrial Society*, Random House, New York.
37. Bell, D. (1980), 'The Social Framework of the Information Society', in Forester, T. (ed.), *The Micro-Electronics Revolution*, Basil Blackwell, Oxford.
38. Industrial Policy in OECD Countries (1993), *Annual Review*, OECD, Paris.

39. 'The Manufacturing Myth' (19 March 1994), *The Economist*, p. 98.

40. Parliamentary Question, 3 March 1994, *Employment Gazette*, April 1994.

41. Gershuny, J. (1978), *After Industrial Society? Emerging Self-Service Economy*, Macmillan, London.

42. Bell, D. (1976), *The Cultural Contradictions of Capitalism*, Basic Books, New York.

43. Gorz, A. (1982), *Farewell to the Working Class: An Essay on Post-Industrial Socialism*, Pluto Press, London, and by the same author (1989), *Critique of Economic Reason*, Verso, London.

44. Allen, J. (1992), 'Post-Industrialism and Post-Fordism', in Hall, S. et al. (eds), *Modernity and its Futures*, Polity Press in association with the Open University, Oxford.

45. Castells, M. (1989), *The Informational City: Information Technology, Economic Restructuring and the Urban–Regional Process*, Blackwell, Oxford, p. 28.

46. Ibid., p. 32.

47. Lash, S. and Urry, J. (1987), *The End of Organised Capitalism*, Polity Press, Cambridge.

48. Lash, S. and Urry, J. (1994), *Economies of Signs and Space*, Sage, London.

49. Garnham, N. (1990), *Capitalism and Communication*, Sage, London.

50. Johnston, R. and Lawrence, P. (1991), 'Beyond Vertical Integration – The Rise of the Value Adding Partnership', in Thompson, G, Frances, J., Levacic, R. and Mitchell, J. (eds), *Markets, Hierarchies and Networks: The Coordination of Social Life*, Sage, London, p. 200.

51. Cooke, P. (1988), 'Spatial Development Processes: Organised or Disorganised?', in Massey, D. and Allen, J. (eds), *Uneven Redevelopment*, p. 237.

52. Allen, J. (1992), 'Post-Industrialism and Post-Fordism'.

53. Lambert, J., Paris, C. and Blackaby, B. (1978), *Housing Policy and the State*, Macmillan, London.

54. Poster,M. (1990), *The Mode of Information: Post-Structuralism and Social Context*, Polity Press, Cambridge.

55. Callinicos, A. (1990), 'Reactionary Post-Modernism?', in Boyne, R. and Rattansi, A. (eds), *Post-Modernism and Society*, Macmillan, London.

56. Lyotard, J.F. (1986), *The Post-Modern Condition: A Report on Knowledge*, Manchester University Press, Manchester.

57. Sayer, D. (1991), *Capitalism and Modernity: An Excursus on Marx and Weber*, Routledge, London.

58. Baudrillard, J. (1988), *America*, Verso, London.

59. Sudjic, D. (1992), *The 100 Mile City*, Andre Deutsch, London.
60. Smart, B. (1993), *Post-Modernity*, Routledge, London, p. 149.
61. Cooke, P. (1990), *Back to the Future: Post-Modernity and Locality*, Unwin Hyman, London, p. 164.
62. Storper, M. and Walker, R. (1989), *The Capitalist Imperative: Territory, Technology and Industrial growth*, Basil Blackwell, Oxford.
63. Jameson, F. (1991), *Post-Modernism or the Cultural Logic of Late Capitalism*, Verso, London.
64. Parker, D. and Stacey, R. (1994), *Chaos Management and Economics*, Institute of Economic Affairs, London.
65. Harvey, D. (1989), *The Condition of Post-Modernity*.
66. Berman, M. (1985), *All That is Solid Melts Into Air: The Experience of Modernity*, Verso, London.
67. CDP (1977), *Gilding the Ghetto*, CDP Interproject Editorial Team; and Lawless, P. (1986), *The Evolution of Spatial Policy*, Pion, London.
68. Byrne, D. (1989), *Beyond the Inner City*, Open University Press, Milton Keynes; and Hasluck, C. (1987), *Urban Unemployment: Local Labour Markets and Employment Initiatives*, Longman, Harlow.
69. For a review of these arguments see Scott, A. (1982), 'Locational Patterns and Dynamics of Industrial Activity in the Urban Metropolis', *Urban Studies*, Vol. 19, pp. 111–42.
70. Abernathy, W., Clark, K. and Kantrow, A. (1983), *Industrial Renaissance: Producing a Competitive Future for America*, Basic Books, New York.
71. Massey, D. and Meegan, R. (1978), 'Industrial Restructuring Versus the Cities', *Urban Studies*, Vol. 15, pp. 273–88.
72. Fothergill, S., Gudgin, G., Kitson, M. and Monk, S. (1988), 'The Deindustrialisation of the City', in Massey, D. and Allen, J. (eds), *Uneven Redevelopment: Cities and Regions in Transition*, Open University, Hodder and Stoughton, London, p. 70.
73. Cheshire, P.C. (1989), 'Urban Change and Economic Transition: The European Dimension', in Klaassen, L., van den Berg, L. and van der Meer, J. (eds), *The City: Engine Behind Economic Recovery*, Avebury, Aldershot, p.16.
74. Ibid., p. 19.
75. Bagguley, P. et al. (1990), *Restructuring: Place, Class and Gender*, Sage, London.
76. Castells, M. (1989), *The Informational City*, p. 80.
77. Harvey, D. (1989), *The Condition of Post-Modernity*, p. 295.
78. Massey, D. (1984), *Spatial Divisions of Labour: Social Structure and the Geography of Production*, Macmillan, London; Gaffikin, F. and Nickson, A. (1984), *Jobs Crisis and the Multinationals*, Third World Publications, Birmingham; and Dicken, P. (1992),

Global Shift: The Internationalisation of Economic Activity, Paul Chapman, London.

79. Coakley, J. (1984), 'The Internationalisation of Bank Capital', *Capital and Class*, No. 23, pp. 107–20.
80. Radice, H. (1984), 'The National Economy – A Keynesian Myth?', *Capital and Class*, No. 22, pp. 111–40.
81. Castells, M. (1989), *The Informational City*, p. 32.
82. Stohr, W.B. (ed.) (1990), *Global Challenge and Local Response: Initiatives for Economic Regeneration in Contemporary Europe*, Mansell & United Nations University, Guildford.
83. Lash, S. and Urry, J. (1987), *The End of Organised Capitalism*.
84. Martin, R. (1988), 'Industrial Capitalism in Transition: The Contemporary Re-organisation of the British Space Economy', in Massey, D. and Allen, J. (eds) (1988) *Uneven Re-Development: Cities and Regions in Transition*, Hodder and Stoughton in association with the Open University, London.
85. Scott, A. (1988), 'Flexible Production Systems and Regional Development: The Rise of New Industrial Spaces in North America and Western Europe', *International Journal of Urban and Regional Research*, 12, p. 183.
86. Soja, F. (1989), *Post-Modern Geographies: The Reassertion of Space in Critical Social Theory*, Verso, New York and London.
87. Gottdiener, M. (1985), *The Social Production of Urban Space*, University of Texas Press, Austin.
88. Katznelson, I. (1993), *Marxism and the City*, Clarendon Press, Oxford, p. 300.
89. Cooke, P. (ed.), (1989), *Localities: The Changing Face of Urban Britain*, Unwin Hyman, London, p. 9.
90. Massey, D. (1984), *Spatial Divisions of Labour: Social Structure and the Geography of Production*; and Massey, D. and Allen, J. (eds.), (1988), *Uneven Re-Development: Cities and Regions in Transition*.
91. Cooke, P. (1989), *Localities*.
92. Warf, B. (1990), 'The Reconstruction of Social Ecology and Neighbourhood Change in Brooklyn', *Environment and Planning D: Society and Space*, Vol. 8, p. 92.
93. Agnew, J.A. and Duncan, J. (eds), (1989), *The Power of Place: Bringing Together Geographical and Sociological Imaginations*, Unwin Hyman, Cambridge.
94. Strassoldo, R. (1992), 'Globalism and Localism: Theoretical Reflections and Some Evidence', in Milnar, Z. (ed.), *Globalisation and Territorial Identities*, Avebury, Aldershot.
95. Mayer, M. (1992), 'The Shifting Local Political System in European Cities', in Dunford, M. and Kafkalas, G. (eds), *Cities*

and *Regions in the New Europe, The Global–Local Interplay and Spatial Development Strategies*, Belhaven Press, London, p. 267.
96. Cooke, P. (1989), *Localities*.
97. Fainstein, S. (1994), *The City Builders, Property, Politics and Planning in London and New York*, Blackwell, Oxford, p. 1.
98. O'Dowd, L. (1989), 'Ignoring the Communal Divide: The Implications for Social Research', in Jenkins, R. (ed.), *Northern Ireland: Studies in Social and Economic Life*, Avebury, Aldershot.
99. Darby, J. (1989), 'The Prospects for Social Policy Research in Northern Ireland', in Jenkins, R. (ed.), *Northern Ireland: Studies in Social and Economic Life*.

2 The Urban Economy and Social Exclusion: The Case of Belfast

Frank Gaffikin and Mike Morrissey

Most cities in the developed world are undergoing rapid change. In some cases, the primary causes are economic. The place of the city within national economies has dramatically shifted while the internal distribution of economic activity within the city – both in terms of jobs and production – has become more volatile. In other cases, the changes have been essentially political – the reinvention of Berlin as the capital of a united Germany or the virtual destruction of Sarajevo during the conflict in Bosnia. Both kinds of development have significant social impact on city populations. The spatial effects of change have benefited many but damaged many others.

Those responsible for city management are grappling with these problems. While it is clear that change cannot be reversed, vital policy questions focus on how its impact can be moderated and how cities can see change as an opportunity rather than a threat. Since the end of the Second World War, many cities in the developed world have faced a continuous series of economic challenges. The lengthy post-war boom, coupled with the introduction of welfare states, saw a general increase in prosperity. Harris describes the process in Britain as follows:[1]

> The structural changes completed in the 1940s were followed by almost three decades of prosperity and growth in the UK. Rising levels of output, high employment, rising living standards and expanded trade within a relatively stable framework marked the 'long post-war boom' that stretched from the mid-1940s through the 1950s, 1960s and part of the 1970s.

There was a general conception, however, that a major consequence of such growth would be significant physical and economic stress on existing cities. Accordingly, the primary purpose of planning at that time was to decant industry and jobs away from existing cities to contain their overdevelopment. Yet by the 1970s, and particularly by the 1980s, it was clear that cities were suffering both population and job loss:[2]

> It is generally accepted that, for the last fifteen or so years, urban policy has been concerned with urban decline. For much of the period between 1945 and 1977 there was little awareness of such a decline; indeed, attention was focused on the planned decentralisation of jobs, industry and population away from urban areas.

Moreover, key sections of the populations that remained in cities were characterised by high levels of unemployment and poverty. With diminishing local tax bases and falling support from central government, city governments were decreasingly able to successfully intervene. Indeed, there is evidence of falling standards in local, mainstream services. All of this was occurring within a context of generally rising unemployment and, in many cases, the economic decline of the regions in which cities were located.

More recently however, it has been argued that changes in the nature of production and the globalisation of economic processes have created the potential for new economic niches for regions and cities:[3]

> There is, however, a growing argument that globalisation is actually reinforcing the role that geographic clusters of production play in the competitive international arena ... There appears to be a paradox ... in that although the technological revolution has provided the infrastructure for the increasing globalisation of economic structures, both cities and regions are becoming increasingly crucial agents of economic development.

Such opportunities for cities to seize a competitive niche in the international economy depend on having the right industrial structures, appropriate governance systems and a culture capable of meeting the exacting demands of the transition. Without these, cities will continue to be dependent on public subsidy, remain economically marginalised and, crucially, will contain concentrations of the most socially disadvantaged.

In short, new opportunities do exist for the urban economy. Spatial constraints on production have become less significant as important components of the production process have dematerialised. The emphasis on services, particularly traded services in the new cultural industries, can give a priority to city locations provided the skill base is high and the information infrastructure is advanced. City government has to be sufficiently flexible to seize emerging opportunity and be creatively interventionist in pursuit of integrated development initiatives.

Most of all, the skill drain on urban populations has to be reversed through substantial investment in education and training:[4]

> An aim of human investment is to promote economic self-sufficiency in a technologically complex world. Such a policy does not foreclose a social responsibility to provide for those who are temporarily or even permanently dependent, but human investment itself is guided by the desirability of making economic self-sufficiency as broad based as possible.

The purpose of this chapter is to examine the situation of Belfast within this context of urban change. The concern will not only be with economic development but also with its social consequences, particularly poverty and social exclusion. Belfast has a legacy from an old manufacturing past. Its education system continues to produce a majority of children less well qualified than regional averages and such averages are themselves comparatively low. It is a highly unequal city, divided by class, politics and religion. Currently, it lacks the social cohesion that many see as the basic ingredient of urban transformation. Finally, within a region characterised by a violent political conflict, it has seen the greatest number of political deaths and each political crisis sees more violent eruption in Belfast than elsewhere. Nevertheless, it will have to overcome these obstacles. It cannot remain heavily dependent on public subsidy in an era of growing fiscal caution. It cannot afford to be a city where, in places, the private sector is an endangered species. Most importantly, there is no long-term future in having such extraordinary concentrations of deprivation as exist there.

The Belfast Urban Economy: Regional Context

The North East of Ireland had successfully industrialised in the mid nineteenth century in a pattern similar to British regions. This pattern, known as regional sectoral specialisation,[5] consisted of a concentration in key industrial sectors in which particular regions had comparative advantage. The very narrowness of its industrial base made Northern Ireland vulnerable to the structural changes of the inter-war and post-war periods. Although the development of regional sectoral specialisation had served the region well, it also meant that the region was affected by economic change in four respects:

- first, it was sensitive to structural shifts in demand – typified by the shift in demand towards cotton and away from linen;
- second, it was affected by structural shifts in supply – particularly the rise in international competition in shipbuilding;

- third, one of its key sources of employment, the linen industry, competed on the basis of low costs (largely through paying low wages to women) and thus was sensitive to cost factors – as happened with rising prices of flax in the 1920s;
- finally, its industries were export oriented and therefore depended on Britain maintaining its share of global trade – this steadily declined after 1914.

Corresponding to the rest of the UK, unemployment rates in Northern Ireland fell after the Second World War. However, the region's unemployment remained substantially more serious than even in depressed British regions.

Table 2.1 Rates of Unemployment (Selected Regions), 1946–54

	1946 (June)	1948 (July)	1950 (June)	1952 (June)	1954 (June)
Northern	5.0	3.0	2.6	2.3	2.0
Scotland	4.5	3.0	2.7	3.2	2.4
Wales	8.5	5.5	3.4	2.6	2.1
N. Ireland	8.8	6.5	5.5	10.6	6.3
Britain	2.5	2.0	1.4	2.1	1.1

Source: Isles, K. and Cuthbert, M. (1957), *The Northern Ireland Economy*, HMSO, Northern Ireland, p. 18.

The problem was that the regional economy was still heavily dependent on traditional manufacturing and had not experienced the rapid industrial restructuring seen in Britain during the 1930s. It was thus in no position to take advantage of the bouyant demand conditions prevailing after the immediate post-war difficulties. Harris describes the comparative position of the region thus:[6]

the average unemployment rate between 1949–59 was 7.4% compared to 3.0% for Scotland (which had the next highest regional rate) and 1.7% for the UK; net outward migration of the labour force was 7.2% between 1951–61, while in Scotland it was 5.7% (and 0.5% for the UK);

earnings in industry were 83% of the UK for non-manual workers in 1951 and 80% for manual workers (the comparable figures for Scotland were 93% and 95%);

the average growth in manufacturing net capital stock (plant and machinery) over the 1948–58 period was 0.3% per annum (which compares with 5.5% pa growth in the UK).

By the 1950s, it was clear that Northern Ireland relied on industries which were in long-term, in some cases terminal, decline. The rate of indigenous industry formation was too low to tackle the scale of unemployment. Accordingly, the view was taken that only a policy of attracting inward investment would introduce new products and new technologies while broadening the narrow industrial base.

In response to these perceived defects, a regional development strategy was adopted in the 1960s to improve physical infrastructure, to enhance the incentives package for industrial development, and to sell to potential external investors the particular resources which the local economy could offer – good water supplies and a surplus of labour with a record of low stoppages and accustomed to low pay. The objective was to attract transnational capital, which could help diversify the industrial base away from a dependence on shipbuilding, natural textiles and engineering. As such, this strategy was typical of the regional policy approach adopted by depressed regions in Britain since 1945. Northern Ireland caught up with this form of indicative planning in the late 1950s.

In Northern Ireland this development plan met with some success. Up to 1971 around 34,000 jobs were created in the manufacturing sector. As noted by Canning et al.:[7]

> The dominant feature of the period (1961–1971) is the large differential growth in Northern Ireland's manufacturing employment after allowing for its industrial structure. We attribute this primarily to the greatly strengthened regional policies.

In these years, Northern Ireland was one of the most successful regions in the UK for employment creation. However, this reindustrialisation process halted and then went into reverse in the 1970s. The impact of two 'Oil Shocks' on the artificial fibre industry, most of which used a crude oil base, was considerable. Moreover, international mobile capital, upon which the drive to rejuvenate depended, became both more scarce and subject to greater competition, given the whole process of the internationalisation of production and the related reorganisation of the global division of labour. In this changing world economy, Northern Ireland's comparative advantages were being eroded – a situation made worse by its steadily deepening political crisis.[8]

Gudgin has summarised the general condition of the Northern Ireland economy thus:[9]

Its industrial base is small with little local competition in most sectors. Local suppliers or industrial services are limited in number and in the scope of products or services on offer. Like most of the northern regions of the UK, Northern Ireland's clusters (in linen and standard clothing) were established long ago and in most cases face intense competition from competitors with much lower labour costs. Local consumer and industrial markets in Northern Ireland are at the low income end of the UK spectrum and are not in general either sophisticated or fast changing. Although the upper third of the secondary education system is the best in the UK, the low level of local demand for highly educated manpower means that many well-educated young people leave the region. This results in a labour force which is not particularly well educated even by the UK's low standard.

This pessimistic assessment must be qualified by a recognition that the regional economy grew rapidly over the 1990s. Between 1990 and 1995, Gross Domestic Product per head increased from 78.2 per cent to 83 per cent of the UK average.[10] Manufacturing output rose by just over 20 per cent between 1990 and the final quarter of 1997 compared to around 4 per cent in the UK.[11] Moreover, manufacturing productivity increased by 2.5 per cent each year between 1993 and 1996 compared to 2 per cent in Britain.[12] Indeed by 1997, manufacturing productivity was 21.9 per cent higher than in 1990. Finally, the number of employees in employment increased by 6.6 per cent between 1990 and 1995 compared to a fall of 3.1 per cent in the UK as a whole.[13] Provisional figures indicate that male employees increased by 12,450 between 1991 and 1997 and female employees by 30,770.[14] However, while it is predicted that there will be 14,100 net new jobs in Northern Ireland by 2001, all of the jobs increase will be in just two sectors – distribution, hotels and catering and financial and business services.[15] Thus, although Northern Ireland grew faster than Britain in the first half of the 1990s, it is anticipated that growth will level off and new jobs will not be in those sectors traditionally recruiting among the unemployed.

The level of unemployment has always been the key indicator of the condition of the regional economy. Yet in 1996, the short-term unemployment rate was only 1 per cent higher than in Britain (5.9 per cent compared to 4.9 per cent) while overall unemployment was at the European average. Moreover, the female unemployment rate was one of the lowest in Europe.

Figure 2.1 indicates the falling numbers unemployed since 1994. For both genders, the most dramatic decline occurred since 1996. However, some argue that the biggest impact on headline unemployment figures has been changes in the unemployment count and

Figure 2.1 Numbers (000s) Unemployed in Northern Ireland (Claimant Count)

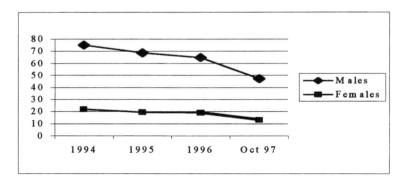

increasingly stringent benefit conditions, as manifested in the Jobseeker's Allowance, rather than the demand for jobs in the economy. Indeed, unemployment in Northern Ireland fell by 19 per cent between October 1996 (the date of the introduction of the Jobseeker's Allowance) and April of the following year. This may reflect some redistribution of those previously defined as unemployed into other forms of benefit rather than a genuine welfare to work effect. Interestingly, the percentage of those leaving the unemployment register and finding jobs fell in the year following the introduction of the Jobseeker's Allowance – from 52.2 per cent to 48.6 per cent. Similarly, the proportions going into training and education fell from 11.7 per cent to 6.5 per cent. Meanwhile, those moving to other forms of benefit increased from 10.5 per cent to 13.8 per cent.[16]

Unemployment fell substantially in Belfast during the 1990s. Figure 2.2 indicates the percentage fall in the numbers unemployed in the four Belfast parliamentary constituencies between August 1992 and August 1997. Interestingly, unemployment decline in the North and West of the city was greater than in the other two constituencies. Indeed, unemployment there had fallen from 66 per cent of the city total in 1992 to 58 per cent in 1997.

However, the figures on long-term unemployment have not demonstrated a similar improvement since 1994. In the spring of that year, 65 per cent of all male unemployed had been workless for a year or more. The equivalent figure for women was 36 per cent. By spring 1997, 66 per cent of unemployed men and 32 per cent of unemployed women were long term (although based on a lower total figure for unemployment).[17] Thus, there remains a persistent problem of long-term unemployment in the region.

Figure 2.2 Percentage Change in Unemployment 1992–97

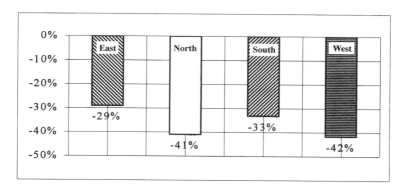

In short, recent economic indicators for Northern Ireland have been positive although there remain worrying structural features about the local economy.

- Key industries continue to compete on the basis of low costs and their long-term sustainability may be threatened both by the even lower lost competitiveness of new entrants to the European Union and minimum wage legislation within the UK.
- A large segment of employment is concentrated in low technology industry (over 60 per cent of manufacturing employment is in low technology industries and a quarter in the vulnerable textile industries while R&D accounts for 0.57 per cent of GDP compared to 1.3 per cent in the UK) and low-grade services, which inhibits the possibility of convergence with UK GDP per head levels. Moreover, high value-added activity, like financial and business services account for only 17.2 per cent of GDP compared to 26.6 per cent in the UK as a whole.[18]
- Core sections of the unemployed remain stubbornly in the long-term category with some evidence that many of those moving off the register are taking up alternative forms of benefit.

Indeed, the 1998 Coopers & Lybrand assessment of the regional economy notes in its introduction:[19]

Despite Northern Ireland's strong economic performance during 1997, dark clouds were beginning to gather on the economic horizon as we reached the end of the year. Consequently, our view of the prospects for the Northern Ireland economy over the next two years is less optimistic than we expressed at the beginning of 1997.

However, since 1997, the region has been subject to a new Labour administration and many commentators suggest that the range of policies being developed and implemented are likely to affect regional development positively. For example, the Northern Ireland Economic Council commented on the first Labour Budget:[20]

> Whilst many of the policy objectives build on the experience of the previous Conservative Administration, the emphasis on equality, fairness, and trust and the restoration of employment alongside growth as the central economic objective signifies a new point of departure.

Indeed, the Council's assessment was that the Budget's distributional impact in Northern Ireland was generally progressive in cash terms. Such developments have been reinforced by the 1998 Spring Budget. Employment opportunity was enhanced by the £75 per week subsidy for employers to take on the long-term unemployed. The Working Families Tax Credit reduced the severity of the unemployment trap and the Child Care Tax Credit offers significant support to child-care arrangements. Moreover, changes in National Insurance will diminish the effects of the poverty trap. In general, the impact of such reforms should be greater in Northern Ireland. Small firms account for a higher proportion of private sector employment (45 per cent compared to 35 per cent in the UK).

In relative terms, both the unemployment and poverty traps affect a greater proportion of the population. There is a greater concentration of low wages, and part-time work accounts for a significant amount of all employment. Moreover, the overall approach is as important as the detail. While the UK has been committed for some time to a shift from passive to active labour market policies, Labour has both increased the resources and modified the tax and benefit structures so as to reduce disincentives to work. In the final analysis, despite reservations about New Deal, this offers a more positive framework for tackling disadvantage in Northern Ireland. Much of this programme will be the responsibility of the new Assembly – a return to a regional administration lacking for almost 25 years.

The challenge is to transform Northern Ireland into a region with high value-added, quality products that can be marketed internationally. The Northern Ireland Growth Challenge has identified seven key goals in effecting such a transformation:

- building world-class firms and industrial clusters;
- creating networks of common interest;
- creating a 'best investment' environment;
- developing human assets for the twenty-first century;

- building the region's infrastructure to support twenty-first century competition;
- marketing Northern Ireland to the world;
- creating a community that values and benefits from enterprise.

The Economic Council's study on what makes European regions successful also identified such factors as a high level of consensus and networking among key industrial actors, an appropriate institutional/governance framework and a high degree of social cohesion.[21] From both, a vital message is that investment in people and the reduction of social exclusion are vital preconditions for successful regional and city development.

Belfast

A century ago, Belfast was the industrial heartland of Ireland. Its rapid advance had given it a global status as a production site. In shipbuilding, for instance, the technical and design skills won international plaudits, and its business boomed.[22] A commentary of the time proclaimed:[23]

> we mark the eminent status of Belfast in the modern world, her high commercial and industrial distinction, her wealth and influence, her constant growth, and the meritorious character of her municipal institutions. ... we are bound to admit that very few cities of the present age owe more to the splendid public spirit of their residents ... .

An economic base centred around shipbuilding, engineering and linen, also accommodated a ropeworks, which by 1900 was the largest in the world, and a printing industry which in the same year employed 1,400 men.[24] This vibrant growth had seen the old Georgian town remade into a buoyant Victorian and Edwardian city, and population rise from under 20,000 at the start of the nineteenth century to nearly five times that in mid-century to 349,180 by 1901 – unsurpassed growth of any urban centre in the British Isles.[25] It had also witnessed the cramming of large families into mazes of terraced housing, where squalor, poverty and disease were common.[26] Sectarian conflict persistently divided its working-class communities,[27] only briefly and very partially abated in the 1930s depression years.[28] Though in 1960, the city's shipbuilding employed close to 20,000,[29] deindustrialisation saw a loss of 14,000 manufacturing jobs in the Urban Area between 1961 and 1968.[30] By the end of the decade, the shipyard employed around half of what it did at the start, attempts at stalling the job drain in traditional sectors like linen were failing,[31] and the outcome was severe unemployment in Belfast, particularly acute in districts pre-dominantly Catholic.[32] By the 1970s, with its significant public sector dependence for jobs and income,[33] Belfast's future as an industrial city seemed doomed.

Between 1971 and 1991, Belfast lost a third of its population – from 416,700 to 279,230. During this period, its share of the Belfast Urban Area population fell from 70 per cent to 59 per cent. The big decline happened in the 1970s. Between 1971 and 1981, there was a 25 per cent drop in population, followed by an 11 per cent drop in the following decade.[34] The big decline happened in the inner city. In the 1970s it saw a population loss of 42 per cent, and in the 1980s a loss of 23 per cent. Between 1971 and 1991, inner-city residence decreased by over half (55 per cent). Much of this pattern is familiar in industrial cities like Liverpool and Glasgow. What is distinctive about Belfast is the way this change has been also tracked by deepening segregation during a period of massive public housing redevelopment and prolonged violent conflict.

Both Catholics and Protestants have left the city. But, while the period 1971–91 saw a 16 per cent decline in the Catholic city population, it saw a much more significant decline of 41 per cent in the Protestant population. Thus, whereas Catholics were 34 per cent of city population in the early 1970s, two decades on they were 42 per cent. Increasing residential segregation has been based on both religion and class. Whereas west of the River Lagan is 55 per cent Catholic, east it is only 12 per cent. There is a close link between social housing and such segregation:[35]

> In early 1969, in the Urban Area, 59 per cent of public sector households resided in streets that were completely or almost completely segregated; by 1977, this proportion had risen to 89 per cent. For housing in the private sector there was also an increase, but a much more modest one – in this case, from 65 to 73 per cent.

Typically, industrial cities have experienced chronic decline in their manufacturing base over the last 30 years. Belfast is no different. Within this weak, underperforming regional economy, Belfast in the 1980s fared less well than the region as a whole. Its share of the region's population fell by just over 3 per cent, while its share of regional employment fell by nearly 4 per cent. The job gains Belfast city centre achieved in the 1980s disproportionately benefited commuters over city residents.[36]

Moreover, the percentage of the Belfast working population in unskilled occupations has remained consistently higher than the regional average, as have the proportions in semi-skilled manual occupations. In contrast, the percentage in professional and managerial occupations in Belfast remained below the regional norm. Just over a third of those employed in Belfast were in semi-skilled or unskilled manual occupations. By the late 1980s, Belfast's employment composition was also somewhat different from that of Northern Ireland as a whole, with 15 per cent of employment in manufacturing and 81.4 per cent in services, compared to 20 per cent and 71.2 per cent respectively in the region.[37] A more detailed picture of employment status is presented in Table 2.2.

Table 2.2 Employment Status, Northern Ireland and Belfast DC, 1983–92 (percentages)

| | 1983–85 | | 1989–92 | |
	N. Ireland	Belfast	N. Ireland	Belfast
Males				
Working full time	73	66	78	73
Working part time	3	3	3	4
Unemployed	23	29	15	20
Gov. schemes	1	1	4	3
Females				
Working full time	53	53	56	52
Working part time	33	32	32	35
Unemployed	13	13	8	8
Gov. schemes	1	1	4	4

Source: 'Belfast Residents Survey' (1992), Department of the Environment, Table A3.17 a and b.

A comparison of Belfast with British cities reflects its relatively acute experience of deindustrialisation, but relatively modest growth in service employment (see Table 2.3). Most of the cities have had twice or three times the increase in service jobs.

Table 2.3 Comparative Change in Sectoral Employment (Manufacturing and Services), 1981–91

| | Manufacturing | | | Services | | |
	1981	1991	% change	1981	1991	% change
Belfast	37,925	22,242	−41.3	124,253	132,740	+6.8
Nottingham	50,378	38,481	−23.6	100,170	115,181	+15.0
Leeds/Hunslet	85,487	64,244	−24.8	187,421	227,648	+21.5
Cardiff	21,364	19,539	−8.5	103,195	118,518	+14.8
Dundee	21,535	16,008	−25.7	52,557	51,377	−2.2

Sources: Belfast figs calculated from Department of Economic Development (NI); other cities from NOMIS, via DoE (NI) (1994), 'Urban Policy in Belfast'.

The four parliamentary constituencies of Belfast contained 26 per cent of all Northern Ireland's unemployment in May 1998 of which 15 per cent were located in North and West Belfast. Within the city itself, 1991 Census figures revealed the male unemployment rate at 25 per cent and female unemployment at 14 per cent, while the general unemployment rate for the travel to work area was around 12 per cent.

Unemployment is also distributed unevenly between religions. The 1991 Census unemployment rate for Catholic males in the Belfast Urban Area was 29.4 per cent compared to 15.2 per cent for Protestant males. Relevant rates for women were 15.6 per cent and 9.3 per cent respectively. In 1991, six Belfast wards had unemployment rates greater than 40 per cent, almost ten times higher than those in the 'work-rich' wards. The worst unemployment rates were concentrated in the Catholic wards of the West and North.[38] By the early 1990s, nearly eight in ten of the inner-city unemployed were in North and West Belfast.[39] The 1991 Census recorded that as a share of all those 'out of employment' in Belfast, North and West accounted for just over two-thirds.

Moreover, patterns of unemployment are compounded by spatially segmented labour markets. Over 25 years of violent political and inter-communal conflict have imposed severe limitations on where people in Belfast are prepared to work. West Belfast (predominantly Catholic) stands out as having extraordinarily low percentages of those prepared to work in East Belfast (predominantly Protestant). Higher proportions are prepared to work in Britain or elsewhere in the European Union. This 'chill factor' deterring some unemployed from availing of the full wider labour market is a product of both deepening residential segregation and the heightened insecurity of political violence.

The future of Belfast hinges on the development of the regional economy as a whole, although, simultaneously, the Urban Area's economic significance within the region is such that it can significantly affect its trajectory. Belfast also has a new city administration and a renewed commitment to development. Its programmes in this respect have still to develop but the approach is more than just rhetoric. Moreover, the city has seen the development of a series of area partnerships bringing together the public, private and community sectors to work for integrated development. Co-ordination among the efforts of the new Assembly, city government and area partnerships offers the possibility of raising the development of the city to a new, higher trajectory. However, the embedding of a peace process is a primary precondition – a renewal of conflict would consign the city to permanent peripherality.

Social Exclusion and the City

Teague comments that the term 'social exclusion' has jumped into the heart of the poverty debate without paying an admission price in the shape of an adequate definition.[40] Room argues that the confusion in this respect arose because the concepts of poverty and social exclusion have been derived from very different theoretical traditions. The former emerged from an 'Anglo-Saxon Liberalism' which, viewing society as atomised individuals engaged in market competition, focused on the sufficiency of resources which such individuals have at their command.[41] Even Townsend's formulation that asserted a causal relationship between command over resources and a capacity for social participation was shaped by the same intellectual tradition.[42] In any case, as Ringen argues, there is a contradiction between defining poverty directly (in terms of lifestyle) and measuring it indirectly (via income measures).[43] In contrast, Room sees social exclusion as coming from a notion of society as a hierarchy or set of collectivities bound together by mutual rights and obligations that are, themselves, 'rooted in some broader moral order'. Social exclusion is being marginalised from such collectivities and becoming detached from the moral order.

The essential difference is that poverty is an outcome whereas social exclusion is a process. The latter is thus relevant to understanding the social dynamics associated with a period of rapid economic change that generates risk and uncertainty in people's lives. Berghman usefully distinguishes the concepts via the matrix shown in Table 2.4.[44]

Table 2.4 Dimensions of Poverty and Exclusion

	Static Outcome	Dynamic Process
Income (resources)	Poverty	Impoverishment
Multi-dimensional	Deprivation	Social exclusion

Within this framework, poverty refers to an insufficiency of resources. Widening the scope of the concept via recognising that there are many dimensions to poverty generates the idea of deprivation. If the situation is seen dynamically, then impoverishment results in poverty and social exclusion in deprivation.

Lawless and Smith suggest that the term 'social exclusion' has at least four dimensions:[45]

- The first refers to the impact of wider processes of global economic change that 'conspire to accentuate the scale and intensity of urban unemployment'. From this perspective, economic restructuring contributes significantly to social division.
- The second focuses on the declining real value in benefit incomes and the growing incapacity of welfare to affect redistribution – hence the emergence of a new poor and growing divisions between 'work-rich' and 'work-poor' households. In Northern

Ireland, work-rich households have three clear advantages over those that are work-poor. Most obviously, a high proportion of household members are in employment, frequently full-time, relatively well paid employment. Second, a high proportion are in public sector employment and enjoy nationally determined wage levels (admittedly, the growth of decentralised wage bargaining is reducing this), while cost of living estimates, for example by Regional Reward Surveys, suggest that Northern Ireland is one of the cheapest places to live. Finally, linked to the last, house prices are significantly lower than in other UK regions, suggesting that outstanding mortgages are also lower. Since housing costs are generally the largest single item in household expenditure, this last factor is said to augment disposable household income. Indeed, the income of a two earner couple with children was, on average more than twice that of a no earner couple with children in 1998.[46] It has also been suggested that this 'surplus' of household income is spent on leisure services and imported consumption goods, neither of which contributes much to the region's development.

- Third, there are institutional factors that segment housing markets leading to the creation of a spatially divided society characterised by both rich enclaves and areas with high concentrations of marginalised groups.
- Finally, some commentators emphasise the moral and behavioural deficits emerging out of long-term welfare dependency theories of the underclass.

Cities are increasingly the terrain of social exclusion. Urban deprivation refers to a particular subset of the poor. It has two distinguishing, and related, characteristics: the first is the spatial concentration of deprivation where certain areas are dominated by poor households; as a consequence, there is second dimension – an extremely uneven distribution of deprivation across the city, described by Byrne as 'socio-spatial segregation'.[47] The poor thus not only live in poverty but among other people who are also poor and separated from those who are not. This may have distinctive consequences with the generation of structures of informal welfare – sometimes termed 'community spirit' – or indeed in some instances in Northern Ireland an alternative culture and anti-statist solidarity in the form of Republicanism. However, even within such cultures, the struggle to subsist imposes harsh physical and psychological burdens. Other areas less identified by attachment to place and community spirit are more characterised by demoralisation and despair.

As a result, the concept of space becomes central. The poor are not simply those with inadequate standards of income or consumption, but the inhabitants of certain spaces which are insulated from more prosperous areas of the city – inner cities bounded by new road systems or peripheral estates served with inadequate transportation. Those who live there are frequently stigmatised simply because of their address. They may have considerably greater difficulty finding employment and are even perceived as a threat to those outside such areas. They are a potent symbol of what it means to fail within the market economy. As the market economy becomes more volatile, particularly for those at the edge of, or detached from, the labour market, the process of social exclusion results in concentrated patterns of deprivation. It may be that the concept of social containment, rather than social exclusion, better represents the condition. Social exclusion infers a lack of access to certain elements of lifestyle and implies being outside key social processes – essentially a form of isolation.

Social containment is both isolation and insulation referring to the means by which society in general is 'protected' from too close contact with the poor. In this sense, the concept of peripheralisation is much more than a geographical construct. US polarisation does provide a forbidding warning of what might be in Britain unless the gap in opportunity and social contact is addressed.[48]

> In the context of a modern economy, the underclass is largely bereft of the language and routines of technology and science, making its members inept in dealing with the daily rigours of politics, commerce, and culture in this country. In a very real sense, the underclass becomes estranged from and hostile to – yet is largely dependent on – a middle class it envies but cannot join. In turn the envy and anger of the estranged underclass drives the middle class out of the city, thereby deepening the intellectual isolation of the poor. At that point cities become reservations for the poor which the middle class, through its control of ... Government must manage in order to preserve its own safety and well being.

Many deprived spaces were constructed via an urban planning mechanism and characterised by specific assumptions about how such development would eliminate 'old style' inner-city poverty. The central thrust of this planning was the provision of new housing without consideration of the need for employment. The stark reality of inner-city tower blocks and bleak peripheral estates has confounded such assumptions. These failures have been exploited by neo-liberals to castigate any form of city planning and to stigmatise the inhabitants of these 'enclosures'. This interpretation is flawed – if poor people are allocated houses within the resources to maintain them, poor housing results – although planning needs to be both more sensitive and more accountable than the socio-spatial engineering of the 1960s. Equally,

the local state, having created such spaces, has an enhanced responsibility for the resolution of the problems created.

The available evidence suggests that Belfast contains many such
deprived spaces. Gross annual household income data show that the
share of higher income households is smaller in Belfast city relative to
the region. Within the region generally, there is substantial inequality
in household incomes. The average net income for households in the
lowest decile in 1998 was £93.02 weekly compared to £543.64 for
households in the highest decile.[49] Both groups live in different spaces
with the former disproportionately in Belfast (see Figure 2.3).

*Figure 2.3 Gross Annual Household Income: Northern Ireland and Belfast
City, 1991–92*

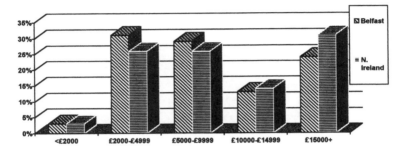

Source: 'Belfast Residents Survey' (May 1992), Table A3.20, Department of the
Environment (NI), Belfast.

Income differentials between Belfast and the region are a function
of many factors. For instance, certain demographic differences have
a bearing, such as the higher proportion of single, widowed and
separated people in Belfast than in the region, and the notably higher
share of families headed by a lone parent in Belfast (26 per cent)
compared to that in Northern Ireland (19 per cent).[50] However, a major
factor is the differential incidence and composition of unemployment.
Not only is there a higher rate in Belfast, as indicated earlier. There
is also a higher share of the unemployed in the long-term category. In
1989/90–1991/92, 69 per cent of Belfast's jobless had been unemployed
for one or more years, compared to 60 per cent in the case of Northern
Ireland's unemployed (1991/92).[51] Many indicators reflect the income
disparity between Belfast and the region. For instance, 44 per cent of
children in secondary schools and 41 per cent in primary schools in
the city are recipients of free school meals, compared to 34 per cent
and 30 per cent respectively for the region.[52]

Within Belfast, the areas in greatest need (within the responsibility of the Making Belfast Work [MBW] programme) show a more pernicious trend, particularly in regard to the very long-term unemployed category. Data for September 1993 show that whereas one-third of MBW's unemployed had been without work for three or more years, the corresponding figure for the Belfast Urban Area was less than half that (14.3 per cent).[53] These demographic and labour market characteristics are reflected in the pattern of benefit receipts across Belfast, whereby inner-city areas show a heavy reliance on Income Support/Jobseeker's Allowance. Inner West Belfast, for instance, has nearly half (46 per cent) on this benefit, compared to just under a third (32 per cent) for the city as a whole.[54]

A social mapping of deprivation in Belfast District Council on the Robson index of degree, intensity and extent,[55] produces the pattern shown in Table 2.5 between the two largest cities in the region. There is interesting symmetry: both have half their wards and populations included as 'deprived'. The significant difference is that Belfast's deprived represent over three times the 'regional share' than do those of Derry.

Table 2.5 Indicators of Relative Deprivation (Robson Index): Belfast and Derry City Council Areas

	Derry	Belfast
Number (and percentage of wards included)	15 (50%)	26 (51%)
Proportion of the District Council population included	49.0 %	48.9%
Proportion of population covered (as share of N. Ireland pop.)	3.0%	9.8%

Source: DoE (NI) Briefing Paper sourced from PPRU Occasional Paper 28.

A slightly different 'social mapping' for the Urban Area, which emphasises unemployment, has been produced by the Fair Employment Commission (see Table 2.6).[56] The pattern emerging is one of substantial population decline in the deprived area – particularly of Protestants, just over a quarter of whom left the Urban Area between 1971 and 1991; and a considerable decline in economic activity in the deprived area.

Belfast contains some of Northern Ireland's most deprived wards. Of the 50 most deprived wards in Northern Ireland (as measured by the *degree of deprivation* in the Robson Index[57)]), six are in North Belfast (43 per cent of all North Belfast wards) and eight are in West Belfast

Table 2.6 Deprived and Non-Deprived 'Regions' in Belfast Urban Area, 1971–91

	Inside Deprived Region			Outside Deprived Region			Urban Area Total		
	1971	1991	%change	1971	1991	% change	1971	1991	% change
Persons	271,279	172,590	−36.4	321,906	303,377	−5.8	593,185	475,967	−19.8
Households	81,164	64,582	−20.4	96,874	113,361	17.0	178,038	177,943	−0.1
Catholics	98,102	93,416	−4.8	43,207	54,879	27.0	141,309	148,295	4.9
Protestants	141,083	66,573	−52.8	251,211	221,802	−11.7	392,294	288,375	−26.5
Not stated	32,094	12,601	−60.7	27,488	26,696	−2.9	59,582	39,297	−34.0
Households without car	59,467	44,748	−24.8	38,286	37,238	−2.7	97,753	81,986	−16.1
Unemployed	13,582	20,649	52.0	5,959	14,099	136.6	19,541	34,748	77.8
Econ. active	112,046	69,354	−38.1	136,505	144,751	6.0	248,551	214,105	−13.9

Source: FEC (October 1994) *Spatial Distribution of Disadvantage,* based on Table 3.

(62 per cent of all West Belfast wards). This compares to one in South Belfast (10 per cent) and three in East Belfast (27 per cent). A different study using Townsend's indices of deprivation (unemployment as a percentage of the economically active; the percentage of private households without cars; the percentage of households not owner occupiers; the percentage of households with more than one person per room), suggested that 57 per cent of wards in North and West Belfast were deprived with only 2 per cent judged affluent. This compares unfavourably with South and East Belfast (20 per cent deprived and 54 per cent affluent).[58]

The most significant factor in accounting for such concentrations of deprivation is unemployment, particularly long-term unemployment that is concentrated both spatially and within households. This degree of inequality has profound implications for regeneration programmes. Building a new social and political order will be severely inhibited by such divisions, particularly since those areas of greatest affluence have been least touched by two and a half decades of political conflict.

Conclusions

On the surface, Belfast seems badly placed either to take a leading role in developing Northern Ireland or to hold its own among the successful cities of Europe. It has adjusted badly to rapid industrial change with long-term manufacturing loss and inadequate replacement with high value-added, traded services. It continues to require substantial public subsidy to maintain both services and employment. Moreover, despite high levels of public expenditure per head of population, the city has high concentrations of deprivation particularly in the North and West. Finally, the city continues to be divided by religion, politics and violence.

At the same time, the unfolding peace process, even though punctuated by crisis and new eruptions of violence, has liberated energy and enthusiasm for development. The regional economy has grown fastest when the prospects for peace are highest. Moreover, the city is experimenting with new forms of governance, detailed in later chapters. If it can sustain peace and if it can learn from the experience of other cities, it could unlock a future very different from its past.

Notes

1. Harris, L. (1988), 'The UK Economy at a Crossroads', in Allen, J. and Massey, D. (eds), *The Economy in Question*, Sage, London, pp. 13–14.

2. Atkinson, R. and Moon, G. (1994), *Urban Policy in Britain,* Macmillan, London, p. 17.

3. Huggins, R. (1997), 'Competitiveness and the Global Region: The Role of Networking', in Simmie, J. (ed.), *Innovation, Networks and Learning Regions,* Jessica Kingsley and Regional Studies Association, London, pp. 101–2.

4. Imbroscio, D., Orr, M., Ross, T. and Clarence, S. (1995), 'Baltimore and the Human Investment Challenge', in Wagner, F., Joder, T. and Mumphrey, A. (eds), *Urban Revitalisation: Policies and Programs,* Sage, London, p. 39.

5. See Byrne, D. (1978), 'The Deindustrialisation of Northern Ireland', paper to the *Social Administration Annual Conference.*

6. Harris, R.I.D. (1991), 'The UK Economy at a Crossroads', p. 16.

7. Canning, D., Moore, B. and Rhodes, J. (1987), 'Economic Growth in Northern Ireland: Problems and Prospects' in Teague, P. (ed.), *Beyond the Rhetoric: Politics, the Economy and Social Policy in Northern Ireland,* Lawrence and Wishart, London, p. 221.

8. Freeman, J. Gaffikin, F. and Morrissey, M. (1987), *Making the Economy Work,* Transport and General Workers Union, Belfast.

9. Gudgin, G. (May 1996), 'Prosperity and Growth in UK Regions', *Local Economy,* Pitman Publishing, London, p. 19.

10. Coopers & Lybrand (January 1998), 'Northern Ireland Economy: Review and Prospects', Belfast, Table A1.

11. Figures provided the Northern Ireland Economic Council.

12. Coopers & Lybrand (January 1997), 'The Northern Ireland Economy: Review and Prospects', Belfast, p. 5.

13. Figures provided by Northern Ireland Statistics and Research Agency.

14. Coopers & Lybrand (1998), 'The Northern Ireland Economy: Review and Prospects', Belfast, Table D12.

15. Gudgin, G. (October 1997), *The Economic Outlook and Medium Term Forecasts 1997–2001,* NIERC, Belfast, p. 15.

16. Figures provided by the Northern Ireland Economic Council.

17. Department of Economic Development (Jan. 1997), 'Northern Ireland Labour Force Survey: Historical Supplement, Spring 1984 to Autumn 1997', Table 6.

18. Northern Ireland Statistics and Research Agency (1997), 'Focus on Northern Ireland', Belfast, pp. 25–6.

19. Coopers & Lybrand (1998), 'The Northern Ireland Economy: Review and Prospects', p. 6.

20. Northern Ireland Economic Council (Nov. 1997), 'The 1997 UK Budget: Implications for Northern Ireland', Report 125, Belfast, p. 9.

21. Dunford, M. and Hudson, R. (1996), *Successful European Regions: Northern Ireland Learning from Others*, Northern Ireland Economic Council, Research Monograph No. 3, Belfast.
22. Moss, M. and Hume, J.(1986), *Shipbuilders to the World: 125 years of Harland and Wolff, Belfast 1861–1986*, Blackstaff Press, Belfast.
23. Crawford, W.H. (intro.) (1986), *Industries of the North One Hundred Years Ago: Industrial and Commercial Life in the North of Ireland, 1888–91, Incorporating Industries of Ireland, Part 1, Belfast and the Towns of the North, Published in 1891*, Friar's Bush Press, Belfast, p. 35.
24. Collins, B. (1988 edn), 'The Edwardian City', in Beckett, J. et al., *Belfast: The Making of the City*, Appletree Press, Belfast.
25. Walker, B. and Dixon, H. (1983), *No Mean City: Belfast 1880–1914*, Friar's Bush Press, Belfast.
26. Mc Fall, D. (undated), *The Development of Belfast: Book 2*, BDO, DoE, Belfast; Beckett, J. and Glasscock, R. (1967), *Belfast: The Origin and Growth of an Industrial City*, BBC Publications, Belfast.
27. Boyd, A. (1969), *Holy War in Belfast*, Anvil Books, Tralee.
28. Devlin, P. (1981), *Yes We Have No Bananas: Outdoor Relief in Belfast 1920–39*, Blackstaff Press, Belfast; Munck, R. and Rolston, B. (1987), *Belfast in the 30s: an Oral History*, Blackstaff Press, Belfast.
29. Boal, F.W. (1987), 'Belfast: The Physical and Social Dimensions of a Regional City', in Buchanan R.H. and Walker, B.M. (eds), *Province, City and People: Belfast and its Region*, Greystone Books, Antrim.
30. Building Design Partnership (1969), *Belfast Urban Area Plan*, 1, Belfast.
31. Probert, B. (1978), *Beyond Orange and Green: The Political Economy of the Northern Ireland Crisis*, The Academy Press, Dublin.
32. Boal, F.W., Doherty, P. and Pringle, D.G. (1974), *The Spatial Distribution of Some Problems in the Belfast Urban Area*, Northern Ireland Community Relations Commission, Belfast.
33. Rowthorn, R.E. and Wayne, W. (1988), *The Political Economy of Conflict*, Polity Press, Cambridge.
34. The analysis in this section is based on the 1991 Census, but largely on: Boal, F. (1995), 'Shaping a City: Belfast in the Late Twentieth Century', The Institute of Irish Studies, Queen's University, Belfast; and Compton, P. (March 1995), 'Demographic Review: Northern Ireland 1995', Northern Ireland Economic Council, Research Monograph 1, Belfast.
35. Boal, F. (1995), 'Shaping a City: Belfast in the Late Twentieth Century'. Boal uses the definition of a segregated street as one in which 90 per cent of its households are either all Protestant or all Catholic.

36. Based on data supplied by DoE (NI) Statistics Branch and analysis for DoE (NI) by Andreas Cebulla, NIERC.
37. Touche Ross (1993), 'Economic Report on Belfast for Belfast City Council', Belfast, p. 23.
38. Touche Ross, 'Economic Report on Belfast for Belfast City Council', p. 28. The wards were Ardoyne (46.23 per cent); Falls (49.33 per cent); New Lodge (48.27 per cent); St Anne's (42.59 per cent); Upper Springfield (43.76 per cent); and Whiterock (49.04 per cent). Source: 1991 Census.
39. NOMIS data, the reference is to parliamentary constituencies.
40. Teague, P. and Wilson, R. (1996), 'Social Exclusion/Social Inclusion', *Democratic Dialogue*, Belfast.
41. Room, G. (1995), 'Poverty and Social Exclusion: The New European Agenda for Policy and Research', in Room. G. (ed.), *Beyond the Threshold*, The Policy Press, Bristol, pp. 6–7.
42. Townsend, P. (1979), *Poverty in the United Kingdom*, Penguin, Middlesex.
43. Ringen. S. (1988), 'Direct and Indirect Measures of Poverty', *Journal of Social Policy*, Vol. 17, Part 3, pp. 351–65.
44. Berghman, J. (1995), 'Social Exclusion in Europe: Policy Context and Analytical Framework', in Room. G. (ed.), *Beyond the Threshold*, p. 21.
45. Lawless, P. and Smith, Y. (1998), 'Poverty, Inequality and Exclusion in the Contemporary City', in Lawless, P., Martin, R. and Hardy, S. (eds), *Unemployment and Social Exclusion*, Jessica Kingsley Publishers and Regional Studies Association, London, pp. 203–4.
46. Northern Ireland Economic Council (1998), 'The 1998 UK and EU Budgets: Implications for Northern Ireland', Belfast.
47. Byrne, D. (1989), *Beyond the Inner City*, Open University Press, Milton Keynes.
48. Andrews, M. (1994), 'On the Dynamics of Growth and Poverty in Cities', *Cityscape: A Journal of Policy Development and Research*, Vol. 1, No. 1, p. 63.
49. Northern Ireland Economic Council (1998), 'The 1998 UK and EU Budgets: Implications for Northern Ireland'.
50. Department of the Environment (DoE) (NI) (May 1994), 'Belfast Residents Survey'.
51. Ibid.
52. Department of Education (NI), Table on DoE (NI) (1995), 'Belfast Database'; note that figures refer to 1992/93, and 'secondary schools' exclude grammar schools.
53. Breen, R. and Miller, B. (1993), *A Socio-Economic Profile of the Making Belfast Work Area*, Queen's University, Belfast.

54. Department of the Environment (DoE) (NI) (May 1994), Table A4.4.
55. Robson's index is based not just on degree of deprivation in a ward, but also the spatial extent of deprivation, measured at ward level as the share of the ward's residents living in the poorest 10 per cent of Northern Ireland's Enumeration Districts (EDs) (which are areas of about 400 houses), and the intensity of deprivation, calculated at ward level as the average score of the three worst EDs (MBW (1994), *Strategy Proposals*).
56. Fair Employment Commission (October 1994), 'A Re-examination of the Making Belfast Work Strategy Proposals', FEC, Belfast. This analysis uses percentage unemployed and of households with no car (as a surrogate for low income) from the 1971 Census, and the percentage unemployed; percentage unemployed among 16–30-year-olds; percentage with no car; and percentage of workforce without a job in ten years for the 1991 Census.
57. Robson, B. et al. (1995), *Relative Deprivation in Northern Ireland*, PPRU, Belfast.
58. North and West Belfast Health and Social Services Trust (1996), 'Key Indicators of Deprivation in North and West Belfast', p. 21.

URBAN PATTERN

3 The Future Planning of City Regions

Peter Hall

What exactly do we mean by this term, 'City Region'? It has been around quite a long time in the jargon of planners: to be exact, about 30 years. It first began to swim into our consciousness in the writings of a very distinguished journalist: Derek Senior, the local government and planning correspondent of the *Guardian* during the 1960s. It is a measure of his distinction that not only was he appointed to the Royal Commission on Local Government in England in 1966, the so-called Redcliffe-Maud Commission, but that he dominated its proceedings, culminating in the point at which he broke with his colleagues and produced a Memorandum of Dissent.

Derek Senior became almost personally identified with the idea of the city region, which was always expected to be the basis of the Royal Commission's recommendations – and indeed was, save for the irony that Senior and his colleagues finally disagreed as to what the term meant in practice.

In its main report, the Commission pointed out that not only Senior, but the old English Ministry of Housing and Local Government (MHLG), had identified themselves with the city region principle. That was because at the core of the MHLG at that time was a group of extra-ordinarily able, very academically-minded geographer-planners: Jimmy James the Chief Planner, Christie Willatts, Geoffrey Powell, and many others. Because they were geographers, they had studied work coming out of the United States at that time, based on the concept of what was then known as the Standard Metropolitan Statistical Area (SMSA). This was a city region not in any physical sense, defined in terms of bricks and mortar, but in the sense of functional relationships: the everyday, or sometimes every-week, flows of people and information across geographical space. The central idea was first to define a central area, much wider as a rule than the so-called Central Business District – another piece of geographer's jargon that has almost become part of everyday consciousness – and effectively extended over the entire central city. Then it was to consider how wide an area around this central city was in effect partially urbanised, in terms of population densities that were distinctly higher than rural levels, and was also – this is the really important point – tributary to it, in terms of commuter movements, shopping trips for higher-order goods, and the circulation of newspapers or radio or TV stations. The official definition the Americans use for their SMSAs, now renamed MSAS, is critically based on at least 15 per cent of the resident workforce commuting into the central city – a low cut-off, it might be thought until it is recognised that everywhere a very large proportion of people work quite locally.

So that was, and indeed is, the central principle behind the concept of the city region. The Royal Commission's report in 1969 put it succinctly in a footnote: a city region 'consists of a conurbation of one or more cities or big towns surrounded by a number of lesser towns and villages set in rural areas, the whole tied together by an intricate and closely matched system of relationships and communications, and providing a wide range of employment and services'.[1] That principle produces a region that stretches in a semicircle some 30 miles, or 50 kilometres, from the centre of Belfast.

The English Royal Commission, in 1969, concluded that the idea 'has value because it takes account of the fact that people are now much more mobile than they were'. But when it got to implementing the idea, it found witnesses putting forward a variety of schemes, ranging in number from 25 to 45 for England; and that suggested that the city region was not an idea that could be implemented uniformly across the whole of England, 'and in some parts of the country it did not seem to us to fit reality'.

Around the big conurbations, and the larger free-standing cities of the English shire counties, it did; but in more thinly populated areas like the South West, it seemed to mean 'creating artificially constructed areas whose people have no sense of looking to a city centre or of sharing interests peculiar to themselves'; while in the South East of England.[2] London's influence overshadowed that of a score of other centres. So the Commission went back to the drawing board, and after a great deal of cogitation concluded that over most of England, a single tier of city-region authorities – 58 in number – was practicable. (It concluded that this would not work for the West Midlands, Greater Manchester or Merseyside, where a two-tier system was called for.)

Senior disagreed: he criticised his colleagues for accepting the premise that 'the unitariness of an all-purpose local authority has inherent advantages of such transcendent value in themselves that almost any sacrifice of other values is worth making to attain it; and conversely, that any apportionment of functions between two levels of local government, however articulated, entails disadvantages so intolerable that almost any sacrifice is worth making to avoid it'. He could not, he wrote, 'accept this implicit premise'.[3]

He had a point, of course. The work which the Commission commissioned from a team of us, working at the London School of Economics, showed that even in densely populated South East England, it was all too easy to find areas that did not have strong connections with larger cities and towns; and, as the Commission itself recognised, as one moved out to more sparsely populated areas like the South West or East Anglia, this problem increased exponentially. Here, one found huge tracts that had virtually no organic connection with the relatively few medium-sized cities. In effect, in such areas the Royal Commission majority report sacrificed the city region principle in favour of another overriding objective, which was to create areas of such minimum population size that they were both simple (i.e. comprehensible to the public) and efficient.

For Senior, this represented a Procrustean bed: hence his preferred solution based on extending the two-tier solution to the entire country. The problem is that the resulting map 'is somehow complex, messy, unmemorable. The majority proposals are a fudged compromise, but they have a startling clarity; anyone could understand them.'[4] That is why the failure to implement them, under the Heath government in 1972, was such a tragedy.

However, there was one real problem with all this, and that was the fact that neither the majority proposals, nor the Senior memorandum, really dealt with the problem: did the city region idea represent a reality in people's everyday lives? Senior said they did: that 'they play a dominant and ever-increasing part in the lives of well over 90 per cent of the population'; but he produced no research to justify that sweeping remark. For the vast majority of people lived their lives within very circumscribed areas, within which they lived, worked, shopped or sent their children to school. Above that very parochial level, there was in fact no unit that made much sense in terms of people's everyday lives.

I commented: 'The city region remains like the unicorn in Thurber's garden: a mythical beast.'[5] And yet, there was a need for wider units, in fact much wider units, for planning purposes. For, even then, the dispersal of people and jobs, in ever widening rings around the conurbations, meant that London impinged on Hampshire, Birmingham on Shropshire, Liverpool even on North Wales. For handling these relationships, neither prescription would work. That was why both had to allow for high-level provincial or regional councils above the entire structure: 8 in the majority's case, 35 in the Senior case.

I concluded from this that maybe the only way was to base local government for most personal services on smaller, more local units, on the Senior prescription, with much larger regional units, indirectly elected, to cover planning issues where the interrelationships extended over far wider areas.

Interestingly, that is exactly what the parallel Royal Commission for Scotland (the so-called Wheatley Commission) concluded.[6] For strategic planning and for associated functions like transport, they said, wide areas were needed, based on socio-geographic criteria, while personal services required smaller areas. Therefore, there should be no single tier of all-purpose authorities on the English model; instead, there should be a regional level for strategic planning and associated services, and also – this was doubtless more contentious – housing and personal social services; all other services should go down to districts, at shire level.

In practice, given the extraordinarily sparse population over much of Scotland, this meant for instance that the Glasgow-based authority (the Strathclyde region) extended from Crianlarich, deep in the Highlands, in the north nearly to Stranraer in the south, while the Edinburgh-based region (the Lothian region) extended to the English border at Berwick. Again, as with the English debate, there could be no real pretence that most people at the far edges of these vast regions had any but the most distant, residual affinity with their core cities.

Interestingly, the Wheatley prescription for the lower-level district authorities was in general to include all of the contiguous physically built-up suburbs, such as Milngavie and Bearsden and Rutherglen around Glasgow: a perfectly logical prescription.

All this is of course a matter of history. The Redcliffe-Maud recommendations were never implemented; after a fierce campaign by the shire districts, they were replaced by the prescription of the County Councils, a two-tier system of counties and enlarged (merged) districts across the entire country, metro and non-metro areas alike, but with stronger district powers in the six conurbation areas, doubled in number from the original Royal Commission recommendations. Then, in recent years, an extraordinarily protracted and acrimonious further review has produced a patchwork of authorities rather closely resembling the system that prevailed before the Royal Commission, a patchwork that will make effective strategic planning extraordinarily difficult. In Scotland there has been a very similar dismantling of the structure, involving the disappearance of the regions; if anything, an even more regressive step, since the Scottish model was widely cited among experts worldwide as a model of its kind.

From the 1960s to the 1990s: How Much is Different?

So, why rake over old history? Because, as usual, it reminds us of some uncomfortable and basic facts. We are so unhistorically minded nowadays, that we are often in danger of reinventing wheels without ever realising that an earlier generation has been through the process before. The basic question is, what exactly has changed over the three decades since the publication of these historic inquiries? Has the passage of history, the socio-economic evolution of our country, rendered their prescriptions irrelevant and if so, how?

To clarify these considerations it is useful to argue both sides: first to find arguments that indeed the world has changed, and second to turn around and postulate that the recommendations are as startlingly fresh and relevant as ever. The world appears to have changed in at least three important respects, but they are strangely contradictory. The first is that – at least in the 1980s – the agenda of planning changed: it was much less concerned with guiding or controlling the complex processes of outward decentralisation of people and jobs, far more concerned with trying to slow that process by inner-urban regeneration. This was first evident in Scotland in 1974, with the abandonment of the Stonehouse new town and the diversion of funds into the Glasgow Eastern Area Renewal Project (GEAR); it was definitively extended into England in 1977/78, with the publication of the three consultants' reports on the problems of inner Liverpool and Birmingham and London, and the succeeding Inner Urban Areas Act of 1978, which effectively did the same job of reversing policies. And the interesting point about the Thatcher era was that – for all the talk of radical reversals of previous policies – here they concerned means of implementation: the Urban Development Corporations and the Enterprise Zones were the preferred instruments, supplementing and even supplanting the partnerships, but the inner-city regeneration emphasis remained.

The important point was that the cities turned in on themselves, seeking to solve their own inter-linked problems of economic restructuring, physical regeneration and social construction; overspill was no longer on the agenda, and of course the entire social housing programme was being slashed. In essence, two reversals happened: the emphasis was on the cities, and the historic link between housing and planning was severed. This was not at all unique to the United Kingdom. One can see the same shift of emphasis in France, in the contrast between the 1965 *Schéma Directeur* with its stress on constructing huge new cities, and its 1994 successor, largely concerned with creating poles of economic growth in the decaying inner suburbs around the *Périphérique*, or in the Netherlands, in the contrast between the first and second reports of the late 1950s and the early 1960s, with their emphasis on outward deconcentration to new towns, and the fourth report (Extra) of 1989, with its emphases on compaction and regeneration. It was a pan-European trend.

Nonetheless, there is an odd irony, which is that there was very little evidence that the new policies were achieving their stated objectives. They did achieve some selective regeneration in places like the London or Salford or Cardiff docklands (and their mainland European equivalents); what they conspicuously failed to do was to stem the outward drift of people and employment, even though ever-hopeful academic observers were always noting the beginnings of dramatic reversals, at best they marked a stemming of the population decline – and that largely because the closure of industry and of dockland activities was making available one-off windfall gains in the form of vast tracts of land for housing development.

The city of Belfast recorded a loss of nearly 120,000 people, nearly 29 per cent, over the 23 years 1971–94, while the remainder of the region grew by close on 148,000. Now, the latest household projections suggest that with 4.4 million additional households predicted in England between 1991 and 2016, housing and planning issues are very firmly on the political agenda. The reaction of Mr Gummer, as English Secretary of State at the time, was to propose putting 60 per cent of the resultant housing on to brownfield land, and to welcome another report proposing that we raise the target to 75 per cent; many, including myself, doubt that it can be done or that it should be done.

The Town and Country Planning Association has been arguing that the right answer would be to plan for substantial greenfield development along major public transport corridors radiating out from the major conurbation cities, forming a twenty-first-century variant of Ebenezer Howard's famous polycentric Social City.[7]

Deconcentration: A Fact of Urban Life

So outward dispersion is a fact of life, like it or not. And urban regeneration, though it remains an aspiration with which few if any planners would quarrel, is likely to do little more than compensate in part for continuing job losses in more traditional sectors – as the London experience over the past decade so eloquently shows. How many people appreciate that despite all the hype that accompanied Big Bang in the City of London, during the 1980s not only did London employment fall overall, but in nearly every sector save financial services? Urban economic regeneration is essentially a matter of running very fast to stand still. The forces behind outward movement of employment are all too evident: the desire and even the need to put activities at key points on the motorway network, the development of major freight logistics complexes here and at ex-urban container port locations, the outward move of retail and business park complexes to the same kinds of locations. Belatedly, planning policies in England are being reversed to try to bring these activities back into the cities; I doubt whether they will have more than a marginal effect, and if they do it will be through physically dismembering the urban physical structure.

The other consideration, however, comes from the opposite end of the spectrum. Some American academic writing is suggesting that the dispersal of urban areas is now reaching a new stage, such that cities are literally turning themselves inside out: while traditional centres like Detroit revert to wasteland, new downtowns or Edge Cities are springing up on greenfield land in the spaces between the cities, in places like Aurora between Denver and Fort Worth, Mesa outside Phoenix, or San Ramon-Dublin-Pleasanton in the San Francisco Bay Area.[8] And these are serious places: Tyson's Corner outside Washington, DC which 30 years ago was a filling station and grocery store at the top of a hill on US Route 50, is now the largest commercial downtown in the entire state of Virginia, exceeding in floorspace even the state capital of Richmond.

Something like this is beginning to happen here, not only through the construction of new regional shopping centres like the Metro Centre outside Gateshead, Meadowhall in Sheffield, Merry Hill in Dudley and Lakeside in Thurrock, most of which are incidentally very much urban and even inner-urban phenomena, but also in subtler processes like the translation of BAA airports into edge-of-town shopping centres with attached flying facilities. These places are truly becoming the new town centres because they combine traditional central qualities (including, in the British cases, excellent public transport) with car access; they are what the Dutch Fourth Report calls B-locations, places that have the best of both worlds.

To return to the main line of the argument: in the UK as in North America, hyper-deconcentration is producing a very complex polycentric pattern of living and working, with many small and medium-sized employment centres forming nodes in the system, some of them older, a few newer, and with geographically circumscribed patterns of movement around and between them, such that journey lengths remain in some kind of equilibrium. This is the argument of Peter Gordon and Harry Richardson at the University of Southern California, who argue that Los Angeles is now the norm and not the exception, and that in such places employment is so widely diffused that most people do not have to travel far to work.[9] In my view, analysis of UK data will show much of the same trend, albeit with the limited development of some hyper-long-distance commuting along exceptionally fast lines such as the high-speed rail lines out of London. However, the point is not the existence of the phenomenon, but what it says about the city region.

The Nonplace Urban Realm: Here at Last?

Just about at the point that the city region debate was beginning in the UK, an American academic planner called Melvin M. Webber wrote two rather remarkable papers, intriguingly entitled 'The Urban Place and the Nonplace Urban Realm', and 'Order in Diversity: Community without Propinquity'.[10] In them he developed two linked arguments: that an increasing number of people essentially related at a global scale rather than locally (though of course they would also have local relationships); and that this was powerfully being assisted by the development of modern telecommunications. The only thing he got wrong in these papers was the timing: he was 30 years too early.

It is now possible to see very clearly that in a very wide range of jobs, from financial securities dealing to academia, people do indeed relate globally and that they do so through a variety of information technologies, the more important of which have essentially developed over the past two decades. The important point, however, is what this says about where they work. And here a doubt enters. Webber, 30 years ago, clearly thought that geographical space was becoming more and more homogeneous, a kind of level plain. He wrote:

Increasingly in the future, when high-level specialists are able to locate their establishments in outlying settlements or even in the mountains, as at least one electronics group already has in the Sierra, what is hinterland and what is centre becomes, at best, but a difference in magnitudes of information flow and of volumes of activity.[11]

And so, as they interrelated in all kinds of ways and over greater distances, the pull of places would weaken:

The enlarged freedom to communicate outside one's place-community that the emerging technological and institutional changes promise, coupled with an ever-increasing mobility and ever-greater degrees of specialisation, will certainly mean that urbanites will deal with each other over greater and greater distances. The spatial patterns of their interactions with others will undoubtedly be increasingly disparate, less and less tied to the place in which they reside or work, less and less marked by the unifocal patterns that marked cities in an earlier day.[12]

Manuel Castells, in *The Rise of the Network Society*, similarly argues that a space of flows replaces a space of places.[13] Yet, notwithstanding this, all these interactive people also identify with a particular place on the earth's surface: they live in one place (sometimes two, rarely more); they tend to have one primary workplace, though they may spend less and less time in it, more or more time perhaps working at home, perhaps in hotels and foreign meeting places. And, despite all the losses of jobs from the centres of New York and London in recent years, they remain outstandingly attractive places for those kinds of work, generally the most specialised high-level work, that involve face-to-face interaction: international finance, headquarters of large corporations, national and international organisations, the media.

Graham and Marvin's recent comprehensive study of telecommunications and the city suggests that in France, over more than a century, the curves of telecommunications and personal traffic have marched in parallel together, strongly suggesting that telecommunications act less as a substitute for face-to-face meeting than as a preliminary to it[14] and this is fortified by similar evidence for transatlantic telephone and aeroplane traffic, for instance. Indeed, one could agree with Saskia Sassen: that if anything, as production activities diffuse across the world to newly industrialising countries, these command and control activities concentrate into fewer and fewer such centres worldwide.[15]

Trying now to put this picture together, what emerges is a very complex pattern, partly hierarchical but with a great deal of overlapping of functions and competition between places. Well over 30 years ago, at the same time that Melvin Webber wrote his classic papers, one of his Berkeley colleagues wrote another. Christopher Alexander argued that a city was not a tree but a semi-lattice; it was not so much dendritic, with a trunk and branches, but like a network in which all kinds of interactions could and should be possible.[16] His ideas related to Webber's, and both were very influential, for instance in the original planning of the new town of Milton Keynes. One can argue, again, that like much Californian thinking this was well in advance of its time. The old dendritic, hierarchical pattern is still there, but it is in course of being overlain by different kinds of non-hierarchical structure of many-to-many relationships.

A Global Urban Hierarchy

So, the hierarchy is still there; indeed it is now a global hierarchy, in which the most important centres of information exchange relate to each other and also compete with each other. Sassen's three indisputable global cities – London, New York, Tokyo, each occupying a distinct place in world time zones within a 24-hour financial trading economy – are the classic case. What is interesting, however, is the subtle effect of geography on the next level of the system, above all here in Europe. For the distinctive feature of this continent, even in the age of the Single European Market and the possible arrival of EMU, is the fact of many nation-states and many different linguistic-cultural systems which remain to some degree, even in the age of universal soap operas and the Internet, closed off from each other.

Robert Maxwell discovered to his cost that the market for a daily European newspaper was very limited; people still read in English about the UK, in French about France; and it is even true that by and large German papers do not penetrate Austria, French papers do not penetrate Wallonie, or vice versa. The same goes without saying for television news and current affairs; this is still a *Europe des patries* on the de Gaulle model, rather than an incipient European superstate. Add to this that people still relate to their national governments, that major institutions like banks are still nationally-based, and one is faced with an extraordinary set of barriers to competition. It is because of this that the smaller European capital cities – the Scandinavian capitals, Amsterdam, Brussels, Lisbon, Dublin are so relatively powerful, punching far above their weight in terms of population or volume of product.

If one adds to this the fact that a number of European nation-states contain powerful elements of regional devolution, it suggests why such cities as Belfast and Edinburgh, Antwerp and Liège, Hamburg and Munich, Barcelona and Milan also are such powerful players on their national scenes. These cities have a cultural and sometimes a linguistic degree of independence: they have their own newspapers, sometimes major ones, their own television stations and sometimes publishing houses, and their own universities.

It is interesting to compare Europe in this regard with the United States. There too, partly as a function of the country's enormous physical size, there are major regional centres, each of which could be said in a very loose sense to control a section of the country: Boston, Atlanta, Minneapolis-St Paul, Dallas-Fort Worth, Denver, San Francisco, Los Angeles and Seattle come immediately to mind. They are the seats of major national newspapers, they have major bank headquarters (aided by the archaic nature of the banking laws until recently), and they have independent cultural lives. But their position is eroded by the fact that this is truly a homogeneous market with few cultural or other barriers to the diffusion of national institutions, and also by the fact that, paradoxically, the huge continental scale makes possible the development of independent sub-centres with their own spheres of influence; so that the major regional centres of the United States simply do not occupy the same privileged place as their European equivalents.

In Japan, the other obvious comparison, there is a remarkably homogeneous and centralised nation-state, in which the power of the national capital and its institutions are all-pervasive. So, again, the role of regional cities – which in Europe are far more than that – is far less significant, even in comparison with the United States. Europe, in this sense, is a unique part of the world, though in time it could be suspected that the emerging urban economies of South East Asia might come to rival it.

What it means is that there is far greater potential turbulence in the European urban system than in those of other parts of the world. In a report called *Four World Cities: A Comparative Study of London, Paris, New York and Tokyo*, commissioned by the Government Office for London,[17] we concluded that London was likely to remain in its predominant position as one of the great global cities, and that indeed it was probably the most indisputably global city of all. That was partly because of its unique position at the junction point of three world cultures: the old British Commonwealth, the North Atlantic trading and cultural economy, and now an increasingly English-speaking Europe, cemented by the dominance of English as a world medium of communication for travel, tourism, diplomacy, business and professional life, and by the unrivalled position of its airports within international air traffic. But the competition, we concluded, was most likely to come from smaller European capital and regional cities that could specialise in particular niches for the global market – Milan in fashion, Frankfurt and Zurich in financial services, Amsterdam and Munich and Rome in cultural tourism – and could offer a better ambience than the bigger global cities.

There is therefore an entire system of major European cities, perhaps 40 or 50 in number, comprising all the national capitals and also a number of provincial capitals within the larger nation-states, which in some sense compete in the provision of higher-level international services. Over the half-century since 1950, many have proved highly dynamic in population terms, attracting migrants from the rural areas of their countries and also guest workers from abroad. As a result, complex patterns of internal migration have come to occur, resulting in a very fine-grained process of social differentiation: the inner cities are occupied both by low-income foreign immigrants and by gentrifying younger single people and childless couples; the outer cities are occupied by middle-income blue- and white-collar workers but also by large enclaves of low-income workers ghettoised in large public housing estates built in the 1960s, the expanding rural fringes contain both gentrified small towns and villages, invaded by high-income refugees from the inner cities, and also places with a more modest social and economic position, in which middle-income in-migrants live side by side with the indigenous population, some of them struggling as in-migration inflates local housing markets.

Flows, Corridors and Blue Bananas

This is a pattern that is now occurring widely around the major European capitals, and is just beginning to appear in Eastern Europe after nearly a decade of economic liberalisation.[18] To varying degrees, it envelops wide rings at increasing distances from the core cities; around London, the extreme case in all Europe and one of the most extreme cases in the world, deconcentration has proceeded so far that the zone of maximum population growth is now 100 miles and more distant.[19] Particularly along main transportation corridors where longer-distance movement by car or train is easier, it is now producing coalescence and interfusion of the outer commuter fields of different major cities, as between London and Milton Keynes and Northampton and Coventry and Birmingham. The so-called linear megalopolis, which Jean Gottmann postulated for the United States in the 1960s,[20] may now have become a general model for the functional relations in urbanised regions around the world.

Roger Brunet's notorious Blue Banana, published in his analysis of European cities in 1989,[21] is a metaphorical expression of it. However, there really is no evidence in Brunet's report as to what is happening inside this 1,000-mile-long piece of fruit stretching from Birmingham to Milan. One can postulate a series of interlocking functional city regions, in which commuter fields, newspaper circulation fields, TV and radio station catchments, all begin to overlap. And some of these can cross international borders, which in any case have disappeared since implementation of the Schengen agreement: on Saturdays Dutch people travel to the giant regional shopping centre at Oberhausen; on Sundays, when restrictive German trading hours frustrate the customers, there is a reverse flow out of the Ruhr into Rotterdam or Utrecht. But always, these relationships are limited so far by the surviving barriers of language and culture; it will take more than Schengen to erode those.

The Central Contradiction of Regional Planning

How does that relate to the central question? It relates through the complex politics of guiding the process of regional growth and change. Almost everywhere in Europe, there is now the same set of tensions between the pressures to try to rebuild shattered urban economies, on the one hand, and to control the processes of decentralisation, on the other. The UK was first into this process and hopefully will be first out of it. Well over 20 years ago, as we have seen it became evident that there was a need to rebuild urban economies around new sources of growth, above all in advanced services. Exactly the same processes are now impinging on cities all over mainland Europe, bringing acute economic and social pressures: in Brussels, in the Ruhrgebiet, in Piedmont.

At the same time, the forces of outward decentralisation are meeting resistance: principled resistance in the form of environmentalists who are concerned at the implications for sustainability, less principled in the case of wealthy ruralites who want to pull up their Nimby drawbridges. And there may well be, as there has been in the past, an alliance between these people and the political leaders in the cities; it is a very logical and a very easy course of action to march under a common banner of urban containment and urban compaction, coupled with urban regeneration.

Nevertheless, the outward pressures are too strong, and they will not be resisted. Powerful demographic and social and economic changes will ensure some counter-movement: the increasing numbers of one-person households: the student population in the urban universities; the attractions of urban living for double-income-no-kids couples; the increasing attractiveness for developers of converting old warehouse and office buildings into apartment complexes, dramatically illustrated in London Docklands and now all around the fringes of the City of London. But, they will be far outweighed by the counter-movement. Again, one can argue that there are policy initiatives that surely should be taken to counter some of the more obvious causes of that counter-movement out of the cities, particularly of the conventional nuclear families with children which still account for the majority of all households in the country; notably, the improvement of standards in the worst inner-city schools. But it will take time, and it will take resources that we do not seem to have, at least in the short term.

I want to stress that this calls out, not for the abandonment of planning, but on the contrary for planning on a large strategic scale: edge city may be a reality, but it does not have to have the physical expression that one sees in the most spectacularly unplanned American instances. The problem, as ever in planning, is to accept the trends but then seek to manipulate them so as to achieve a future that works better, and achieves a more agreeable pattern of living, for everyone.

If so, the central problem for the planning of the city regions will be political with a small 'p', and sometimes with a large 'P' too. It will consist in devising regional administrations large enough to provide adequately and coherently for an orderly process of decentralisation around the great cities and conurbations. This is already almost but perhaps not quite impossible around London, just still possible elsewhere. Only such regional units will be able to perform the balancing acts necessary to accommodate the growth in a sensible and sustainable way – which means in reasonably self-contained, mixed-use units along strong public transport lines. They will need to represent everyone in the region, so that local interests do not feel they are being swamped; but they will have to be strong enough to take unpopular decisions. They may also need to be supplemented by implementation mechanisms like the new town development corporations and their linear successors the urban development corporations: quangos set up with the ability to acquire land and to promote development reasonably quickly, even at some cost in local democracy.

There is a 50-year experience here, first of the English new town development corporations in the immediate post-war years, then of the urban development corporations of the 1980s, and we know that in neither case were the relationships with directly-elected local authorities particularly smooth. There is always a need, in this process, to represent the unrepresented: the people who are not here now and so can take no part in the processes of local democracy, but who want to be here. It seems to me that all our experience in England and in Scotland suggests that the only way out of this dilemma is through strong elected regional authorities plus some limited-life quangos, unelected but with strong local representation.

The Relevance for Belfast

How are these lessons to be applied to the planning of the Belfast city region? On a favourable peace scenario, Belfast should be vigorously competing for investment and for recognition with its peers in the European urban hierarchy: small national capitals and provincial capitals in what the 'Europe 2000+' report calls the Atlantic Arc of Europe, places like Dublin and Glasgow and Liverpool and Manchester.[22] Like its equivalents in Britain, it will need to establish a market niche, a speciality, which makes it distinctively different. I cannot say what that should be: it could be popular music, it could be poetry, and it could be a commemoration of the city's very special and tragic history. At the same time, the city will need to define its own place within the wider region, which is surely the provision of those very special and growing services that cannot be produced elsewhere. Defining and assisting such optimal roles is what regional planning is about – which is one reason, though far from the only one, why it is worth doing.

To achieve this, it must employ instruments both of promotion and of regulation. As well as discouraging or prohibiting development in some places (like green belts) it encourages it in other places where that development might not naturally happen. But that process must not be too unnatural: as I have already tried to argue, good regional planning consists in bending very subtly the natural forces of change, driven by market forces or social preferences, so as to achieve a more nearly optimal pattern of development.

Fiscal instruments can play a part in this process of manipulation; the problem is that usually they are defined and levied at higher stages of government, especially in a centralised nation-state like the UK. For instance, it might be a good principle to try to charge motorists more for driving single-occupancy cars at congested peak times into the city centre, and then deploy the proceeds to bolster the public transport system. Insofar as Northern Ireland might be allowed to go its own way in some respects, that could be a major advantage in trying to develop innovative policies.

The city has suffered population losses on a huge scale over the last quarter century; though very special political circumstances may have played a role, the trend is similar to that in many similar cities in the mainland UK. The losses are bound to bottom out eventually, save for some unusual catastrophe, and − given that there evidently is brownfield land within the city limits − they could easily reverse. Nonetheless, I would support the general conclusion that brownfield land is unlikely to account for more than 40 per cent of total demand, and could well be lower.

It is welcome news that the Belfast City Council has officially accepted the fact that the city has thinned out, and that this in itself is no bad thing. The important fact is that a city with some 300,000 people is at the lower end of that level in the European urban hierarchy that has shown such dynamism in recent decades, a level that also includes great provincial cities of Germany such as Hanover and Stuttgart. Such a city, set within an expanding city region of up to one million people, is as near-optimal a form of urban organisation as we know in Europe: it can provide the services appropriate to a major provincial capital city, while avoiding the stresses of congestion which afflict larger places (and here, a comparison with Dublin is instructive) and providing a variety of lifestyles to suit all tastes and all pockets.

There is indeed a case for deconcentrating some of those old inner working-class communities, which were the locations of some of the worst housing conditions in the United Kingdom, and where so much of the sectarian bitterness is concentrated; there is a hope at least for a reintegration of different groups in the middle-class suburbs, while new mixed communities of younger people in smaller households are concentrated near the city centre, especially around the city's universities. A worry was expressed that the result of this process could be the kind of ghettoisation observable in the worst American cities. I think it unlikely: as William Julius Wilson has pointed out, that was a result of the out-migration of the Afro-American middle class and the unusual concentration of a number of interrelated social pathologies (long-term structural unemployment, under-education, poor lone parenthood, drug abuse, crime) in the inner cities.[23]

I think it is more instructive to compare Belfast with some urban neighbourhoods on the European mainland, for instance the *Grands Ensembles* of the Parisian *banlieue,* where sectarian ghettoisation is becoming the rule, but where problems so far are nowhere near the intensity of those in the worst American ghettos.[24]

Finally, the basic geography of Northern Ireland suggests strongly that there is in reality only one city region for planning purposes. Of course, Londonderry is a distinct centre in its own right; but it does not command a region sufficiently large to act as a logical planning unit. Population has spread out from Belfast up to 30 miles away, which represents half the average distance from the City Hall to the border and the sea; all experience of other places suggests that, particularly if the peace process attracts in-movement of people and investment, this radius will soon increase. So we are left with the Department of the Environment as the logical regional planning unit, and that raises the problem of the democratic deficit in Northern Ireland politics.

The fact is that during all those years of the Troubles, the planning process has served very well, and in a peaceful future, Northern Ireland could do even better. Generous infrastructure investment, particularly in motorways and trunk roads, coupled with maintenance of the green belt, have provided the basis for a polycentric city-regional structure which, as it evolves, could provide a model for the cities of Britain and for Europe generally. Belfast's civic leaders seem to be displaying a degree of consensus which is rare in mainland UK, and the place is so far relatively free of the rampant Nimbyism which clouds all planning debate over large parts of Southern and Central England. On that basis, Northern Ireland has a good chance of showing the rest of us how to plan a model of the liveable and sustainable city region.

Notes

1. GB Royal Commission on Local Government in England 1966–1969 (1969), 'Report' (The 'Redcliffe-Maud' Report) (Cmnd 4040), HMSO, London.
2. Ibid.
3. GB Royal Commission on Local Government in England 1966–1969 (1969), 'Report' (The 'Redcliffe-Maud' Report).
4. Hall, P. (1969), 'Geography: Illogical? (The Maud Report Examined)', *New Society*, 19 June, pp. 954–5.
5. Ibid.
6. GB Royal Commission on Local Government in Scotland 1966–69 (1969), 'Report' (The 'Wheatley' Report) (Cmnd 4150), HMSO, London.
7. Breheny, M. and Hall, P. (eds) (1996), 'The People – Where Will They Go? National Report of the TCPA Regional Inquiry into Housing Need and Provision in England', Town and Country Planning Association, London; Breheny, M. and Rockwood, R. (1993), 'Planning the Sustainable City Region', in Blowers, A. (ed.), *Planning for a Sustainable Environment*, Earthscan, London,

pp. 150–89; Hall, P. (1996), *The People – Where Will They Go?* (The Denman Lectures, 18), University of Cambridge, Department of Land Economy, Cambridge.

8. Dillon, D., Weiss, S. and Hait, P. (1989), 'Supersuburbs', *Planning*, 55, pp. 7–21; Garreau, J. (1991), *Edge City: Life on the New Frontier*, Doubleday, New York.

9. Gordon, P. and Richardson, H.W. (1996), 'Employment Decentralization in US Metropolitan Areas: Is Los Angeles the Outlier or the Norm?', *Environment and Planning, A*, 28, pp. 1727–43.

10. Webber, M.M. (1964), 'The Urban Place and the Nonplace Urban Realm', in Webber, M.M. et al., *Explorations into Urban Structure*, University of Pennsylvania Press, Philadelphia, pp. 79–153; Webber, M.M. (1963), 'Order in Diversity: Community without Propinquity', in Wingo, L. et al., *Cities and Space. The Future Use of Urban Land*, Johns Hopkins University Press, Baltimore, pp. 23–54.

11. Webber, M.M. (1964) 'The Urban Place and the Nonplace Urban Realm'.

12. Ibid.

13. Castells, M. (1996), *The Information Age: Economy, Society and Culture, Vol. 1, The Rise of the Network Society*, Blackwell, Oxford.

14. Graham, S. and Marvin, S. (1996) *Telecommunications and the City: Electronic Spaces, Urban Places*, Routledge, London.

15. Sassen, S. (1991) *The Global City: New York, London, Tokyo*, Princeton University Press, Princeton.

16. Alexander, C. (1965), 'A City is Not a Tree', *Architectural Forum*, Vol. 122, No. 1, pp. 58–61; No. 2, pp. 58–62. Reprinted (1996), in Le Gates, R. and Stout, F. (eds), *The City Reader*, Routledge, London, pp. 118–31.

17. GB Government Office for London (1996), 'Four World Cities: A Comparative Study of London, Paris, New York and Tokyo', Llewelyn Davies Planning, London.

18. Borgegard, L-E., Hall, P. and Musterd, S. (eds) (1998), *Migration, Mobility and Metropolitan Change in a Dynamic Society*, Belhaven, London.

19. Hall, P. (1989), *London 2001*, Unwin Hyman, London.

20. Gottmann, J. (1961), *Megalopolis. The Urbanised Northeastern Seaboard of the United States*, Twentieth Century Fund, New York.

21. Brunet, R. et al. (1989), *Les Villes 'Europdenes'. Rapport pour la DATAR*, La Documentation Française, Paris.

22. European Commission (1994), 'Europe 2000+: Cooperation for European Territorial Development', Office for Official Publications for the European Communities, Luxembourg.

23. Wilson, W.J. (1987), *The Truly Disadvantaged: The Inner City, the Underclass, and Public Policy*, University of Chicago Press, Chicago; Wilson W.J. (1996), *When Work Disappears: The World of the New Urban Poor*, Knopf, New York.
24. Wacquant, L.J.D. (1995), 'The Comparative Structure and Experience of Urban Exclusion: "Race", Class and Space in Chicago and Paris', in McFate, K., Lawson, R. and Wilson, W.J. (eds), *Poverty, Inequality and the Future of Social Policy: Western States in the New World Order*, Russell Sage Foundation, New York, pp. 543–70.

4 The Just City and the Efficient City

Wim Wievel and Joseph Persky

If Belfast were Chicago, then it would have:

- An Irish Catholic mayor named Richard Daley.
- The weather in the summer would be 75 degrees and sunny.
- There would be about one job located in the city for every two residents – man, woman, or child. That's a lot of jobs; right now in Belfast it is only one job for every three residents. But suburbanites would hold four out of ten of these jobs.
- The official unemployment rate would be only about 6 per cent but the differences between neighbourhoods would be vast. In some neighbourhoods the percentage of working age people with jobs would be three times as high as in poor neighbourhoods – 75 per cent compared to 25 per cent!
- Almost six out of ten people would be Protestants, and four out of ten Catholics, with small numbers of Jews, Muslims and other religions.
- More strikingly, 40 per cent of the population would be black, 25 per cent Hispanic, and only 35 per cent white.
- You would have about 160 murders a year.
- The median household income would be about $30,000 (or £20,000). But the official poverty level for a family of four would be about £8,000. And, 28 per cent of your population would be living *below that* level.
- Six out of ten children would graduate with a high school diploma.
- Instead of one-third of the housing stock being owned publicly, only about 4 per cent would be.

Both cities – Belfast, Chicago – have their problems. In recent years some well-known economists and political commentators have characterised cities as economically and politically irrelevant. Urban policy has been neglected by central governments both here and in the

United States. Cities have been seen only for their problems, as the garbage cans of society, with crime, poorly educated residents, and deteriorating infrastructure.

Cities are still the most creative, most productive and most vibrant places. With additional investment, they can be even more so. With the largest number of under-utilised people, the largest stock of usable or reparable infrastructure, and the biggest supply of conveniently located land, there are economic, not just moral or liberal reasons to focus on cities. This chapter will discuss six main points:[1]

1. In the new global marketplace, national economies are evolving towards a heightened reliance on dynamic, growing cities. High-paying service jobs in the new information economy are attracted to cities. These jobs figure importantly in a country's international competitiveness.
2. The benefits of what economists call 'agglomeration' – the geographic concentration of many and diverse types of workers and firms – continue to enhance the value of doing business in the city.
3. Central cities and their neighbouring suburbs and smaller cities are woven into highly integrated regional, metropolitan economies. Cities provide locations for high-paying jobs held by residents of the suburbs. They also provide cultural, medical, recreational and educational facilities heavily patronised by non-residents.
4. The trend of the past 40 years towards the continual dispersal of people and jobs to outlying suburbs is increasingly inefficient and counter-productive for a country's and region's prosperity. The suburbs are strained by their growing economic and social roles.
5. Conditions are ripe for rejuvenating the ability of cities to provide employment and homes. In cities can be found a vast stock of private and public capital, as well as workers.
6. Concerted government actions and private sector participation is necessary to jump-start and sustain economic growth in cities. The crucial deficiencies all relate to traditional government roles in infrastructure, education, worker retraining and action against poverty. At the same time, public commitments to such endeavours will advance private enterprise throughout metropolitan regions.

The labour market of cities shows that cities are the key source of high-wage employment based in high-productivity industries. Many relatively poor workers live in central cities. But the earnings of people who work in the central cities are considerably higher on average than the earnings of workers in suburban firms.

In a sample of 14 large US metropolitan areas, the wages of central city jobs averaged 20 per cent higher than those of suburban jobs. Moreover, this earnings gap has been widening. Jobs downtown must be productive to support the cost of a central location, and productive jobs can command higher wages.

The high pay of city jobs has historically enticed suburban residents to commute to the city. For instance, in Chicago, 35 per cent of all jobs in the city are held by suburbanites, but they earn 47 per cent of all wages and salaries. Although it is true that workers commute both ways across the city boundary, the high wages of jobs held by well-educated suburbanites channels a net flow of earnings out of the cities.

Suburban families are intricately intertwined with cities in other ways. A recent survey of Americans living outside of the 100 largest cities – but within 20 miles of them – found that about half of the households had at least one member working in the city. 67 per cent depend on the city for major medical care and 43 per cent had members either attending or planning to attend a city-based college or university.

Even those suburbanites who think they are not connected to the city might bear in mind that much of the income of their neighbours, and therefore the local retail sales, property taxes and real estate values, are supported by income earned in the city. For Chicago's suburban areas, 20 per cent of all wages and salaries comes from central city jobs.

Research has shown that cities and their associated peripheral areas are in the same economic boat. Prosperous cities are associated with prosperous suburbs, and suburbs grow near cities that grow. Economic activities in one part of a metropolitan area positively affect the remainder of that area. For instance, the growth of service firms in the cities reduces costs to suburban manufacturing plants that draw upon these services. In the same vein, a new industrial plant in the suburbs increases the demand for services supplied by firms located in the cities.

Data on 56 US metro areas also show a strong correlation between metro job growth and the ratio of central city to suburban income. Employment grew most where income disparities between the central city and the suburbs were lowest.

What distinguishes a city in economic terms? The unique characteristics of a city include its high density and its large number and variety of firms, workers and cultural and social activities, known as 'agglomeration economies'. High density facilitates the rapid exchange of information, thereby increasing productivity for a broad range of economic activities. It also reduces the cost of providing transportation and other public services such as health care and utilities.

Because of worldwide economic changes, the advantages of density have resurfaced during the past 20 years. Density makes it possible for urban jobs to pay high wages. It has spurred the rapid growth of downtown areas. Density may even breathe new life into urban manufacturing districts that would otherwise be given up for lost. Urban jobs generate technological and cultural innovation and create a large share of national wealth. Jobs in the central cities of large metropolitan areas in the USA garner 37.7 per cent of nation-wide earnings, while they constitute 32.2 per cent of all jobs. On the average, these jobs pay higher wages than jobs in suburbs. Earnings in smaller cities follow, while non-metropolitan areas bring up the rear.

The cities' high earnings result, not surprisingly, from a concentration of high productivity industries, such as producer services and information-intensive industries. Examples include such activities as business headquarters, finance and insurance, business services, legal services and education. But it is true even *within industries*. The earnings of city workers in finance, insurance and real estate are far higher than those of their counterparts in the suburbs.

Why have we seen the growth of these high-paying service jobs in cities? Such fields as law, finance, advertising, data processing and accounting have spawned new areas of specialisation in the last ten years. Many firms have found it economical to farm out specialised functions that were formerly handled by in-house generalists. This process facilitated the development of comparatively small, highly efficient business firms. By locating closely together in compact and dense downtowns, they are able to realise the economies of agglomeration that I mentioned before. In other words, by locating in the large cities these firms can gain access to more corporate customers and can find a greater variety of suppliers.

Along with density, *diversity* in cities and metropolitan areas promotes economic growth. The greater variety of industries a city has, the more rapidly it grows. The main reason for this is the cross-fertilisation of ideas across industries, speeding up innovation, as products and production processes from one industry find new applications in another. Some of these benefits can occur even though firms are not located closely together. But it turns out they are greater when firms are closer. The loss of urban density in past decades may have reduced the growth of manufacturing output by as much as a third.

The size and density of cities confers unique economic advantages that play an essential role in regional economies. The unplanned dispersal of jobs and people over an ever-growing suburban area adds to costs in the economy which no individual firm, worker or local government has the means or incentive to counteract. It is in our best interest to ensure that employment and households are located in such a way as to maximise productivity.

So let's talk about the different parts of the metro area. In the past 25 years, the central business districts of many cities have been growing. Private firms and individuals have made massive investments in downtown. The eagerness of private investors to add to the stock of downtown capital is a testimony to the enhanced productivity of central locations. But this private investment record also points to the importance of the public sector in nurturing the growth and renewal of cities. Urban renewal and tax laws helped this process. Public initiative was necessary to start the process and ongoing public care is required to manage the downtown environment.

In the meantime, what has happened in the suburbs? Dispersing people and jobs over a wide area creates significant economic costs as well as benefits. At some point the costs outrun the benefits. The suburban expansion of the post-Second World War period has now run up against significant limits. The inner ring of suburbs increasingly resembles city neighbourhoods. Rather than solving the problems of cities, we are simply recreating them in new places. Between 1970 and 1990, in Chicago, the population increased by 4 per cent, but residential land use increased by 46 per cent and corporate and industrial land use increased by 74 per cent. Other US cities in the Northeast and Midwest show the same pattern. The costs associated with that in terms of providing infrastructure and transportation are considerable.

The outer ring of suburbs has grown remarkably over the last two decades, but something new is happening now. Suburban communities are now calling for relief from the very growth they have sought for so long. They have discovered that unchecked and unplanned business growth is expensive. Creating and maintaining the infrastructure to handle a system of remote employment centres is too expensive. With considerable effort, crowded suburban areas could be helped by massive investment in public infrastructure, but to expand much further into the hinterlands will prove uneconomic both to the public and private sectors and to city and suburb. Future metropolitan growth would better take the form of infilling or 'reconcentration'.

Can a case be made on the grounds of economic efficiency for policies which encourage central city and inner suburban development while discouraging the continuing expansion of the outer suburbs? In our own work, studying the social, public and private costs and benefits of suburban development compared to central city development, we have looked at the reasons why a company locates on the fringe of metropolitan areas. It is clear that such moves impose very high social costs, and costs to the public sector. This includes such costs as:

1. Greater congestion as more workers drive, and create slow-downs for others.
2. The associated costs of increased accidents and air pollution.
3. The loss to society of having potentially productive labour go unused. This is a somewhat complicated, but very important point. If a firm locates in the central city, its jobs are likely to be filled by workers from low-income households who would otherwise be unemployed. Their employment is a gain to the economy. On the

other hand, suburbanites, who are likely to have attractive alter-
natives anyway, in the form of other employment or further
education, will hold more of the jobs if a firm locates in the outer
suburbs. Thus, their employment is less of a net gain to society.

4. There are also social costs associated with the loss of open space
   if a firm locates on the suburban edge, and with the possible
   abandonment of housing in the central city as workers there have
   fewer jobs and less purchasing power.

5. There are also direct costs to the public sector for providing
   highways, education and other services. Companies and residents
   in the central city pay a higher share of these costs than is the case
   in the suburbs, where other residents, as well as the state and
   national governments end up subsidising the new development.

All of these costs are of course partly offset by gains. Because of the
availability of relatively skilled labour at low costs, especially the female
labour force, suburban firms can often produce more efficiently. And
suburban development creates gains in land value. On balance, what
we see is that there are very large public and social costs, which are
only partially offset by the private gains.

This conclusion reinforces the powerful distributional or moral
considerations that already argue for government efforts to strengthen
central city economies. What is new, is that from an efficiency
standpoint, the current pattern of sprawl carries large costs with it, and
changing that pattern may in fact be efficient. Rebuilding downtowns
to take advantage of new economic functions is one way of changing
the pattern of sprawl.

City Neighbourhoods

Is there a productive role for the neighbourhoods in the age of the global
economy? The answer is an emphatic *yes*, for several reasons.

1. Existing commercial and business centres in the cities' neighbourhoods start with tremendous built-in advantages. They lie on
   the nodes of public transportation systems whose ridership can be
   easily expanded. Many of them enjoy convenient access to the web
   of highways originally built for suburban commuters. Many have
   affordable office space available in existing structures.

2. Many people in the cities' labour force also live there because they
   cannot easily afford to drive a car or to own a home. Rental
   apartments and public transportation have historically provided a
   better quality of life for these workers at lower cost. The largest

supply of rental housing and the best access to public transportation are still found in the working-class and middle-class neighbourhoods of our cities.

3. City neighbourhoods enjoy proximity to the newly revived core of the central business districts. Thanks to improved transport and communication in the cities, these neighbourhoods are highly accessible, making them more feasible sites for a range of back-office and secondary service functions.

4. Finally, the neighbourhoods have always generated new entrepreneurs, many of them immigrants, eager to profit from these advantages. Many cities boast an emerging cadre of neighbourhood development organisations, with experience in assembling urban land and negotiating with an array of neighbourhood, city hall and private investor interests.

Given all these advantages, why have formerly thriving and busy neighbourhoods of large cities been steadily thinning out? For decades the public and private capital of these areas have been allowed to deteriorate, along a course similar to that of the old downtowns. As long as suburban development remained cheap, these older areas suffered losses in employment and population. However, with the increasing inefficiency of gridlocked suburbs and the renewed vitality of the nearby downtown, neighbourhoods are ripe for redevelopment. As with downtown, such redevelopment will require large public reinvestment. These investments will pay off. The underlying logic of economic geography is on their side.

Of course, retaining and attracting residents and businesses back into the central city has been a goal of some central government, local and community-based programmes for at least 30 years. It has also been subject to criticism for many years. One strand of critique argues that neighbourhood revitalisation efforts may increase segregation and isolation by keeping (minority) poor from obtaining opportunities to move out. Another argument posits that most of these programmes are ineffective and do not improve conditions for low-income residents. For instance, Nicholas Leman[2] argues that community development organisations have had some success in creating new housing but have not moved residents into jobs. Others have analysed cities that are widely considered to have revitalised their downtowns and found that job opportunity for low and moderate income residents had not increased.

The shortcomings of these efforts may reflect less their inherent limitations than the fact that they have been poorly funded and are up against very strong private incentives working toward deconcentration. One reason they have been funded poorly is that they have been seen as 'do-good' programmes. But, as we have argued, they can in fact contribute to economic efficiency. Looked at that way, well-designed efforts to attract businesses and households back to cities are far less expensive than their critics have suggested. Such programmes not only achieve desirable distributional results, but may also improve efficiency. Indeed, in Chicago we have recently seen increased interest from private developers in central city development for housing, retail, office and even industrial space.

Public efforts to rebuild neighbourhoods must focus on rebuilding the infrastructure and educational systems of the city, refitting them for new service employment as well as high-skilled manufacturing jobs. A key component of this effort is the improvement of the urban labour force. The urban labour force has received a lot of bad press. It has been called under-prepared, mismatched and lacking in skills. There is no denying that cities contain the largest concentrations of the unemployed, many of whom lack skills and work experience. These problems require serious attention, but they are only part of the picture. The sheer size of the urban labour force makes it the repository of a huge variety of uniquely special skills. This large and diverse labour force remains attractive to a wide range of productive firms.

One source of illumination on the job-readiness of city workers of all races is research on US blacks in the labour force. William Julius Wilson[3] has pointed out that dramatic progress occurs in the metropolitan areas with the tightest labour markets. During recessions, employment rates of young black males may be as low as 30 per cent, but they grow to 70 per cent in cities with tight labour markets. Apparently, once the labour market gets tight, employers find a way to overcome all of the supposed barriers in skills. Since employment rates go up and down so much with the general economy, there are less grounds for suspecting that there are any meaningful psychological or cultural barriers to the entry of the poor into the labour market.

There has been some exaggeration of the skill requirements for the workforce of the future. Terms such as 'the workforce crisis' and the 'knowledge gap' have been widely used in the media. In 1988, 21.9 per cent of the US workforce had a college degree. At that time, it was projected that 22.9 per cent of the total labour force will need to have a college degree by the year 2000. A 1 percentage point change over twelve years in the proportion of the workforce that will need a college degree hardly justifies headlines and cover stories. It certainly does not imply the obsolescence of workers with less formal education.

People lose sight of the fact that high school completion rates in the USA continue at or near all-time highs, although it is true that drop-out rates among minority youth in public school systems remain unacceptably high. The skill requirements of the near future have been exaggerated and a concerted programme of investment in basic human capital can yield impressive results. But such an effort must be concentrated in low-income areas where the bulk of the high school drop-outs live. As high school graduates, they will have higher employment rates and higher earnings. Furthermore, research on inner-city youth shows that an increase in the number of years in school decreases participation in crime. In addition, an increase in school performance increases wages, decreases the likelihood of dropping out, and improves work habits.

Our cities' potential will not be entirely fulfilled until they succeed in providing more attractive places to live, as well as employment. For many years now, some cities have had difficulty maintaining their appeal for middle-class residents. The long-run viability of cities depends on policies that recognise and strengthen the vital economic contribution of the working poor, and provide for those unable to work. But they also have to revitalise the attractiveness of cities for the middle class. Providing middle-class housing, good schools, and doing a better job of dealing with poverty are critical to this. Dealing with urban poverty is important not only because poverty represents a direct waste of human resources, but also because widespread urban poverty contributes to the fiscal stress, troubled school systems, and crime that oppress the poor, diminish the general quality of life, and make the middle class move out.

Europe is far ahead of the USA in dealing with poverty. Research by Rebecca Blank,[4] at Northwestern University, shows that market forces alone would produce a similar rate of poverty in Western Europe as in the USA. But European social programmes reduce poverty rates to a third or a quarter of those in the United States. European governments offer higher cash allowances for families with children, higher subsistence payments, rental subsidies and more health care than in the United States. Lower poverty rates have helped Western European cities remain more attractive and viable living environments, rather than repositories of social problems. In doing so, they sustain their international economic competitiveness as well. The UK of course has moved away from some of the aspects of the general Western European system, but is still ahead, as we would call it, of the USA.

So what needs to be done? Obviously, the policy prescriptions take on a different form in Belfast than in Chicago, and we would not presume to go into detail for you. The most important point is the notion that dealing with the issues we have raised is not just morally right, but also economically productive, that the *just* city is also an *efficient* city. The agenda includes such items as:

1. rehabilitation of neighbourhood and inner-ring infrastructure, as Belfast has been doing on an impressive scale in the rebuilding of public sector housing;

2. preparation of the workforce, focusing on early childhood and School to Work programmes, and particularly inner-city drop-out problems. The USA and Northern Ireland still have a lot to do in this regard;
3. improvement of the urban quality of life by assistance to the poor and central government assistance to cities dealing with multiple problems. There is far more of this in Northern Ireland than in the USA;
4. ensuring that affordable rental housing and home ownership are available in cities, including some programmes aimed at the middle class. Again, Northern Ireland is far ahead of the USA in this regard;
5. implementation of other programmes that counteract sprawl, mitigate its effects, or more fairly distribute its costs and benefits. This includes programmes such as regional impact fees for new development; regional tax base sharing; reverse commuting; requiring affordable housing in the suburbs; growth management; congestion pricing on highways, etc.

In certain ways, Northern Ireland has many programmes like this in place; far more than the USA does. Thus, the USA should not be taken as a model. What remains to be seen is whether all these great programmes can be sustained.

Arguably, the economy of Belfast has an artificial, fluffed-up quality; it can perhaps be seen as a war economy. Every programme and organisation has funds from the European Union, the USA or London. How much of Belfast's middle-class and working people are sustained by these funds that come in to help deal with the crisis? And how many in turn sustain the retail stores, schoolteachers, construction workers, etc.? It is not clear what Belfast's competitive niche is, once being one of the 'sick men of Europe' stops paying the rent. The current economy is based on political considerations, not economic ones. How long can that be sustained?

If the current funds are being used to invest wisely in the development of physical and human infrastructure, then the current dependence will lay the groundwork for future growth. However, the end of subsidies, once it comes, will no doubt lead to major upheaval in the non-profit sector.

Finally, to get anywhere with any of these programmes, along with these policies, there needs to be renewal of civic spirit, of the sense of shared destiny of those in a metropolitan area. While Belfast has its sectarian fault line, we in Chicago have our own problems with this, largely around racial lines. There is increasing evidence that civic or social capital, in the form of trust, the existence of partnerships and community, make a difference to the well-being of cities and countries.

The existence of such bonds makes people more likely to recognise their common fate, and therefore be willing to forgo short-term gain for long-term well-being. It also makes it easier to implement programmes, to develop the consensus to move forward. This is not a naive call for 'why can't we all get along', as Rodney King said. True partnerships are unattainable unless the realities of power are addressed first, and the different interests people have are acknowledged. Working together like this is the *right* thing to do. It has been suggested here that it is also a smart and *efficient* thing to do.

Notes

1. Persky, Joseph, Sclarr, Elliott and Wievel, Wim (1991), *Does America Need Cities? An Urban Investment Strategy for National Prosperity*, Economic Policy Unit, Washington, DC.
2. Leman, Nicholas (1994), 'The Myth of Community Development', *New York Times Magazine*, 9 January, p. 27.
3. Wilson, William Julius (1977), *When Work Disappears*, University of Chicago Press, Chicago.
4. Blank, Rebecca, cited in 'In debate on US poverty, 2 studies find an argument on who is to blame', *New York Times*, 29 October 1991.

5 Sustainable Cities

Frank Gaffikin and Mike Morrissey

The simplest definition of sustainability comes from the 1987 Brundtland Report,[1] which says that development must be sustainable 'to ensure that it meets the needs of the present without compromising the ability of future generations to meet their own needs'. Another stark explanation suggests:[2]

> Human economic activity is taking resources faster than the planet can replenish them and producing wastes faster than the planet can absorb them. If this continues, it will destroy the planet's ability to support human life.

The term *development* infers human *progress*. Thus, for instance, economic *development* is not the same necessarily as economic *growth*, since some forms of growth may be harmful to human welfare and progress. In this respect, there may have to be *trade-offs* between growth and environmental protection, with emphasis on those activities that contribute to *both* development and growth.

These concerns have been around for decades – if only at the simple level of how a 'throw away' consumer society could last, when newly developing countries were keen to join the act. However, they have received greater coherence and attention since the energy debate sparked by the 'oil crisis' in the mid-1970s. A new urgency was generated by a series of conferences and reports in the 1980s, amid dire predictions about acid rain and global warming. In short, we are over two decades into the serious, high-level, international debate, and it is reasonable to ask what progress has been made in achieving a new approach to the built and natural environment. A key step came in 1987 with the World Commission on Environment and Development (the Brundtland Report). Up to then, there had been reports on *development* in relation to world poverty, and reports on the *environment*. This was an attempt to link the two, and to show that they did not need to be adversaries.

Many critics charge that the usual definitions of sustainable development are bland, and offer no practical guidance to policy. The current challenge is to detail feasible tasks that move beyond mantras and exhortations. A starting point here is to break down the term *sustainable development* into separate though linked dimensions:[3]

1. Futurity – thinking of the long-term impact of our economic activity, for instance on the ability of future generations to meet their needs. In short, the call here is to regard ourselves as *stewards* rather than owners of the earth's resources.
2. Inter-generational equity – *fairness to the next generation* demands that we pass on to them the chance 'to experience the same level of well-being from the use of the natural environment as the present generation'.[4] This view argues that 'pursuing policies that imperil the welfare of future generations, who are unrepresented in any political or economic forum, is unfair'.[5]
3. Current social justice – this relates to equity *within* the current generation within and among societies across the world. Poor people, confined to squalid habitats, can make inefficient use of the environment because they lack the means to meet their basic needs and lack the incentive to see the environment as an asset that gives quality to their lives. A simple example is of a family with a leaking roof that it cannot afford to repair. Instead, unnecessary energy is exhausted to maintain heat in the home. More generally, the 'social diseases' of deprivation – educational under-attainment, ill-health, economic insecurity – mean that the poor are ill-equipped to avail of a good environment. In these terms, the *social* damage of poverty is matched by its *environmental* damage.
4. Environmental costs in economic appraisal – orthodox evaluation of the *financial viability* of projects has tended to exclude calculation of environmental costs and benefits. Environmental impact assessment needs to be integrated into economic appraisal.
5. Quality and quantity of economic growth – figures for growth need to measure the *quality* as well as *quantity* of economic gain. Presently, Gross Domestic Product (GDP) lumps together all economic activity, even that which reduces the quality of life, or that which is needed to amend the harm done by other economic activity.
6. Environmental capacities – waste can be absorbed as long as deposits do not surpass certain thresholds. Beyond these limits, environmental resources are stretched to a point that threatens a ratchet decline in the capacity of the biosphere. We cannot live beyond 'the world's ecological means'.[6]

Environmental assets are central to all social and economic life. Sometimes referred to as *the stock of natural capital,* these assets provide:[7] a supply of natural resources for use in the economy – water, soil quality, forest and other biomass, genetic diversity, etc.; a means of absorbing waste effects from the economic process – rivers, seas, land-based waste sites, atmosphere, etc.; a means of enhancing our quality of life – our aesthetic and spiritual relationship to nature includes wildlife, countryside, etc. Neglected or abused environments can lead to ill-health, stress, social unrest, etc.; a means of creating business and job opportunities in leisure and tourism, and a set of life support systems – the general ecosystem.

The Difficult Goal of Sustainable Cities

The world is urbanising, a process starkly evident in the growth of mega cities, particularly in Latin America and Asia. Any credible strategy to address this agenda has to respond to the urban pressures on the environment. As noted by Tim Hall:[8]

Cities are the major consumers of the world's non-renewable energy resources; they are also the world's major producers of pollution and waste. The city is also (and is likely to continue to be) the locus of both major population migration and population growth. Much of the current environmental 'crisis' is seen as either directly or indirectly attributable to cities.

In outlining a number of scenarios for future cities, Tim Hall identifies the problem of sustainability they face. The *global* city refers to those most connected to the increasingly integrated world economy such as the world's financial system. Such cities are vulnerable to the instability of this new international finance and are prone to the deep internal social, economic and spatial inequalities. The *competitive* city is given to favouring property flagship schemes and other speculative regeneration initiatives, designed in part to re-image place. Since these projects rely on substantial public investment, such spending can detract from the resources needed by public services and lead to the 'wasteful duplication of facilities'.[9]

The *electronic* city tied to the telecommunications revolution may offer scope for greater sustainability insofar as the related 'decentralisation of employment and the development of telecommuting is likely to reduce the volume of centre–suburb commuting, make journeys more flexible with regard to time, and ease the burden on urban transport infrastructure during rush hours'.[10] However, there is a great potential for new inequalities to be generated. The most significant telecommunication network nodes may well be concentrated in the large global cities and in certain spaces within cities, excluding the 'information underclass'. The *edge* city, whatever its long-term capacity for environmental self-sustainability, tends to be socially exclusive, favouring an affluent community keen to 'gate' its settlement from lower income groups from the central city. Finally, the *creative* city, as our discussion elsewhere notes, is one that invests in and draws upon creative and innovative forces in the city: artists, educators, architects, designers, social and business entrepreneurs, to discover new responses to urban change.

In all of these scenarios, one dimension of sustainability needs to be addressed – that of the capacity of the ecosystem to absorb the production process. Even allowing for some 'de-materialisation' of production, with the increasing role of financial, information and cultural industries, the environmental impacts of urban living remain a formidable challenge. One approach is to adopt a 'carrot and stick' policy that rewards prudent use of the environment and penalises abuse. This would include charging for the use of environmental assets that tend to be indulged as free and readily available, like water; and taxing emissions that degrade the environment. The revenue generated would allow for reductions of taxes on labour, thereby stimulating the urban labour market. It is argued that this favours labour-intensive production over energy-intensive forms of production. The 'charges should be used to provide incentives for polluters to abate pollution'.[11]

One such often mentioned is the *carbon tax*, designed to curb the greenhouse gases that are thought to contribute to global warming. The notion is that the tax would be graduated to reflect the level of carbon gas in a fuel: for instance, coal has more than oil, and oil has more than natural gas. But, the distributional nature of such taxation is problematic. For instance, the cost might not necessarily be absorbed by the producer, but rather be transferred to the consumer in higher prices. For the poorest consumers tied to a particular form of domestic heating and cooking, higher prices would amount to regressive taxation. Thus, the principle of equity would be infringed. Moreover, though the urban systems of advanced industrial societies particularly have long imposed an acute environmental burden, the problem of environmental degradation is an *international* one. It cannot be tackled by tax and incentive systems in one country. Besides, no one country is prepared to levy such taxes unilaterally, fearing that the related higher production costs will impair competitiveness. Thus, solutions have to be global in reach.

This, in turn, implies that enough countries have to agree not only whether to tax, but also what *form* of tax (graduated? progressive? etc.) and what *level* of tax. Tax harmonisation across the world would be problematic given different levels of development. But, great variation in pollution tax levels would put some countries at a trading and investment disadvantage. Yet, developing countries are not inclined to heed homilies from the rich West about controlling urban development when they see their current expansion in this regard as simply 'catching up'.

Accordingly, the achievement of the sustainable city remains an elusive goal. Part of the difficulty is that the environmentalists are not themselves of one mind. For instance, some focus on *human welfare* whereas others insist that a balanced ecosystem demands concern about *all living organisms*, and an appreciation of their interdependence. Some continue to look to *science* for the answers, such as the capacity to generate substitute clean fuels, the non-pollutant car, 'safe' nuclear energy, etc. Others attribute current problems to the over-weening arrogance of science that it could command the physical and natural world to human will. Some continue to hold that it is possible to pursue ever-rising economic prosperity alongside greater environmental concern. Others insist that there are *'limits to growth'* and that there is a 'trade-off' between economic growth and quality of life.

Some believe that environmental protection can be secured by using *the market* – the pricing/taxing approach already mentioned. Others argue that the market is an instrument of short-termism, concerned about immediate investment yield. It will never allow for the *negative externalities* of production. They argue for more government 'command and control' measures, and a *cultural* shift away from consumerism. Critics of such regulation suggest that it is inimical to a more market-driven global economy and would impose competitive disadvantage.

Defining the Sustainable City

Some new initiatives in this field elsewhere acknowledge a wider definition. They refer to the concept of 'sustainable communities', meaning that development should be viable not just in an *economic* and *environmental* sense, but also in a *social* sense. The latest government thinking in Britain endorses this understanding.[12] An example of this more integrated approach is 'Planning the Sustainable City Region: Manchester 2020'. It suggests that there are three criteria for effective strategies in this regard:[13]

- the *containment of spatial growth* in order to achieve a compact settlement form, involving a reduction in energy demand by deploying transportation and communication systems designed to minimise transport distance for people and goods. This implies mixed land use to bring into the best proximity where people live, work, shop, and leisure, thereby offering the best means to secure cohesion, efficiency and viability, while protecting the quality of both the built environment and its hinterland;

- the *reorganisation of aspects such as 'the physical metabolism'* to ensure higher standards of services such as shelter and mobility, while mindful of minimising harmful environmental impacts within viable local and global capacity; and
- the *integration of the economic, environmental and social dimensions* to development, including an appraisal of new industrial and commercial developments in terms not only of jobs and investment, but also on energy use and pollution. It also involves the promotion of energy-efficient heating, cooling and insulation systems in both urban housing and workplace.

To give a flavour of the many and mixed steps advocated for sustainable communities, the following 20 provide some examples.[14] The important point is that the total effect of this kind of combined strategy is greater than the sum of the parts:

1. optimising the use of vacant and derelict land;
2. clustering of higher densities around local settlement centres and public transport nodes;
3. protecting precious capital in built and natural heritage;
4. upgrading buildings to best practice energy use, with renovation and maintenance based on 'low impact green' materials; and with all buildings being monitored for environmental health hazards;
5. ensuring all new building to energy rating NHER 10 or commercial equivalent;
6. reducing the need for travel to work, amenities and services;
7. promoting new clean smart technologies in transport;
8. designing neighbourhoods for pedestrian and cyclist priority;
9. providing flexible integrated public transport to compete with the car and to facilitate intermodal travel;
10. greening of the city and town, with increasing networks of greenways and wildlife habitats, and doubling biodiversity and biomass on open land in agriculture, woodlands and freshwaters, with community forests to stretch to one-third of urban fringe;
11. promoting organic and low impact food production;
12. defining minimum standards in waste and pollution strategies, e.g. for human health impact as one statistical fatality per million;
13. containing transport emissions by previously mentioned transport policies;

14. moving waste management 'up the hierarchy' by promoting its reuse at source by producers; targeting up to 50 per cent of household/commercial waste to be reused, recycled or composted;
15. promoting renewable energy sources to meet up to 10 per cent of local need;
16. providing infrastructure for linked heat and power across all inner and industrial areas;
17. changing lifestyles to cut the environmental costs of consumption;
18. supporting community-based social and economic networks;
19. promoting the social economy; and
20. developing civic awareness and involvement.

The Sustainable City: The US experience

Wievel and Persky remind us that the uncontrolled sprawl of the US urban experience has brought a series of both social and economic problems. Looking to this experience in the USA suggests that the goal of sustainable settlement can often be in conflict with that of dispersed development. There have been three waves of such dispersal within US regions. The first was in the post-war period when a substantial suburbanisation of residence and to some extent industry occurred, followed since the 1960s by the 'malling' of the suburbs with significant out-of-town retail complexes; followed since the 1970s by the suburbanisation of offices, two-thirds of which are now in such centres. These patterns reinforced each other with, for example, more of an office workforce creating demand for more suburban housing and retailing, producing in some instances a scale of development referred to as 'edge cities'.[15]

These processes were the outcome of 'push' factors from central cities, such as congestion, pollution, noise, crime and grime, together with 'pull' factors in the suburbs, such as the facility of under-priced car use, good supply of relatively cheap land, public policies which subsidised housing and highways, technology changes from the telephone onwards which minimised the effect of distance, and the desire by employers for low-rise offices which allowed for more efficient employee interaction.

But the result was a depletion of resources and investment in central cities; an increased use and cost of energy and pollution; and a deepening social and racial rift as a white middle-class flight from the cities' further ghettoised lower income groups in declining urban areas. Once the pattern was set, it tended to spiral, with demoralisation and poverty in the city streets spilling over into low attainment in the underfunded public schools, the poor performance of which was a further inducement to middle-class parents to leave. In other words, the USA experienced a twin process of sprawl and segregation.[16]

Of course, not all the problems fell to the cities. The rural areas suffered an incursion. People who moved to the suburbs for the quiet life with open greenery discovered, as the demand for such development rose, increasing density and traffic congestion, long commutes to work, and rising crime and other features of city life they imagined they had escaped. To redress the harmful effects of these trends, current effort in many US regions is targeted at what some refer to as 'sensible growth', the goals of which include the following:[17]

- exercising good stewardship of the land by protecting open space for public use;
- deploying scarce infrastructure spending prudently by emphasising reinvestment over expansion;
- reducing the almost total reliance on the car, creating walkable communities with convenient access to retail, employment, services and alternative transport modes; and
- providing greater housing choice in socially mixed and mixed use neighbourhoods.

A series of studies are now questioning who pays for the existing pattern, which fragments city and suburb.[18] As one publication put it in relation to sprawling development:[19]

There are questions as to whether new buyers ultimately pay all the costs associated with the development and whether various public subsidies fuel dispersion and distort the private market.

This suggests that the goal of sustainable communities requires a comprehensive social cost–benefit analysis of major development, whereby the question of who pays what for what benefit for whom is clearly discernible. In one of the definitive books about this issue, Downs has suggested that existing patterns of urban growth in the USA, by effectively concentrating the poorest families in the most depressed spaces, are largely responsible for the four great social problems that beset the country. These are: rising rates of crime and violence, increased child poverty, low attaining public education, and a weak attachment of the deprived to the mainstream workforce.[20] While these are national in their scope, they are most acute in inner-urban areas, where they operate as linked multiple deprivation. Without redress of these mainly urban maladies, he regards the whole US system as unsustainable in terms of political legitimacy, economic efficiency and personal security.

However, tackling this long-standing pattern confronts the apparent desire of most Americans 'to live in neighbourhoods occupied primarily by households with incomes equal to or higher than their own, similar cultural values and outlooks, and similar racial or ethnic backgrounds'.[21] As we outlined earlier, US urban policy has steadily eroded the financial support from central government to cities. Thus, cities have become more reliant on the local generation of public revenue. Yet, the poorest ones that have lost their potential middle class to surrounding suburbs and edge cities face a conundrum. To attract and retain business, they feel obliged to offer tax concessions. Yet, these can reduce the public funds available for services to their deprived constituents. On the other hand, the surrounding hinterland contains the wealthiest residents and thus the higher local tax base. Yet, although such a favourable tax regime could afford redistributive policies, these are the very areas resistant to the migration of low-income families and public policies supportive of them. Downs concludes that in the interests of equity 'growth-related policies should be designed so that people making specific choices under those policies must bear private marginal costs equivalent to the social marginal costs resulting from their choices'.[22] As Wievel and Persky admit, one of the ways to achieve this – greater metropolitan governance – is resisted in the USA by formidable vested interests. The question is whether there is a more favourable climate for such a city region focus in the UK.

Locating the Urban in a Regional Context

UK regional planning in the past was largely reactive. True, besides an ability to exhort and cajole, it could also deploy a mix of regulation and subsidy to support a more even development pattern across all regions. But this kind of 'indicative planning' fell short of a capacity to make the plan happen. Rather, the plan's fulfilment was dependent on a myriad of largely disconnected decisions by corporations, public and voluntary bodies, many of which stakeholders had little hand in the plan's authorship.

Moreover, urban and regional policies were never well linked. In both contexts, traditional land use planning often failed to achieve an integration of the social, economic and environmental dimensions. But recently there has been new thinking in Britain about regional development. There, government has outlined in its document, 'Modernising Planning',[23] the basis for achieving greater legitimacy and transparency in the system. According to this policy statement, regional planning should:

- be based on a partnership with all the key stakeholders in the region from an early formative stage;
- provide the framework for tackling regional and sub-regional issues difficult for any individual local authorities to resolve;

- be 'sufficiently prescriptive' to set the location of significant development;
- include an integrated transport strategy;
- facilitate the regional economic strategies of the new Regional Development Agencies (RDAs);
- offer a framework for bids for EU financial support; and
- be consistent with EU approaches to spatial planning (e.g. the European Spatial Development Perspective).

Central to this new planning then is that it be set in a *European context*; that it moves beyond development control to a more *proactive development strategy*; that it is based on *inclusive partnerships*; that it offers an *integrated solution* that binds the different aspects of a city region's well-being – the economic, social, environmental, educational, etc.; and that it goes beyond the aspirational to include the *resource and institutional means of the plan's delivery*.

Specifically, the new regional agenda in Britain extols the role of 'Regional Chambers', comprising a diverse range of interests that go beyond just the local governments. Such bodies would be designed to lend a wide regional ownership to the process. This conforms to current thinking about reinventing governance,[24] whereby decision-making goes beyond traditional politics to include an active citizenship keen to share responsibility for social progress.

In this respect, effective urban and region development requires a dense and sophisticated network of social organisations outside of government. Compelling evidence from successful regions elsewhere shows that such institutional richness, if properly tapped, can be a pivotal development resource.[25] Indeed, the social wealth generated by a learning creative networked society is a necessary complement to material wealth creation, especially if 'quality of life' and social solidarity are to be embedded as core values.

Thus, while urban and regional planning often needs a lead government agency, it is critical that the process is not only embedded at an interdepartmental level within government, but is also inclusive of wider civil society. Perhaps, to give full expression to this new approach, the composition of any city-regional planning team should be extended beyond the planning service, while the plan is still at a formative stage. Operating as an interdisciplinary team of planners, economists, health managers, educationalists, community developers, and so on, and drawing in expertise from outside government, such a broader body could facilitate a multi-agency and cross-sectoral perspective.

Permitting those agencies that can help deliver the plan to help shape it in the first instance is one part of improving implementation. Another is to recognise that an imaginative mix of regulation and incentives is needed to encourage development to accord with a 'sustainable' strategy. Interestingly, 'Modernising Planning', in addressing new measures to improve delivery, highlights the need for innovative and experimental use of economic instruments such as tradable permits, tax and financial incentives to realise policy objectives. These would be part of a proactive engagement with stakeholders, who in return would be expected to offer clear planning gain agreements: 'Our aim here is not just to ensure that such agreements reflect external costs but to speed up decision making by requiring obligations to be more predictable and transparent.'[26]

For instance, a strategy for a city region, based on principles of compactness, sustainability, proximity, equity and efficiency may consider a package such as the following:[27]

- greater planning 'restriction' in greenfield sites, and greater planning 'facilitation' in urban and rural settlements;
- tax credits for clearing contaminated land and further credits for building socially mixed housing on such brownfield sites;
- tax credits for multiple occupancy, and residential use of commercial property, provided these comply with proper dwelling standards;
- removal of VAT from conversions to encourage refurbishment as an alternative to moving to larger newly built property outside existing settlements;
- tax credits for those families giving up car ownership, together with affordable annual season tickets for an integrated public transport;
- provision of affordable housing in the countryside, with preference to local need, and to construction being undertaken by a consortium of local housing associations and local authority housing bodies, capable of bringing a sensitivity to the local place, and to employing local labour;
- to help pay for such financial inducements, a land development tax on use of greenfield sites; and
- increased tax burden on car use in urban areas, including selective road tolls, and higher parking costs.

Conclusion

It has been argued here that sustainable urban development needs to pay regard to environmental impacts. It needs to be set in a wider regional frame; and it needs to be inclusive of all sections of the population. Yet, this approach confronts any number of tensions. For example, on the basis of efficiency and environmental impact, it makes great sense to concentrate new development in areas that have surplus capacity in terms of physical and social infrastructure. However, it could be argued that some areas with such capacity are the beneficiaries of previous planning decisions biased towards already well-developed areas. To grant them further scope for growth may be seen as reinforcing uneven development. In other words, an equity agenda would argue that planning does not start from a level playing field, where all parts of a city region have the same opportunity for bidding for development. Previous rounds of investment in infrastructure favour some areas over others, and the relatively neglected areas may make a good case for saying 'it is now our turn'.

In similar vein, it makes sense in terms of efficiency and economy to increase density levels in existing settlements. But, one of the 'push' factors out of towns and cities is the concentration of the built environment and limited green open space. So, if we want to extol town/city living as offering quality of life, the degree of land intensification has to be watched carefully. Increasingly, new housing development rests with private developers. Yet, to attain other goals of proximity, sustainability and equity, it means that developers are going to face impositions such as planning agreements. How is this balance between intervention and the market going to be struck to protect the general public good?

Our argument here is that the sustainable city has to be concerned about the five Es: *Efficiency; Economy; Equity; Environment* and *Empowerment*. And it is the latter dimension – empowering diverse stakeholders to get involved – which underpins the others. Trade-offs between conflicting goals, weighting among the goals, phasing the investment needed – all these and more need to be subject to debate and engagement in a wide political process that includes the citizen.

Notes

1. World Commission on Environment and Development (WCED) (1987), *Our Common Future*, Oxford University Press, Oxford.
2. Stewart, J. and Hams, T. (1992), *Local Government for Sustainable Development*, LGMB, Luton.
3. Stoker, G. and Young, S. (1993), *Cities in the 1990s: Local Choice for a Balanced Strategy*, Longman, Harlow.
4. Jacobs, M. (1990) *Sustainable Development: Greening the Economy*, Fabian Tract 538, Fabian Society, London.
5. Repetto, R. (1986), *World Enough and Time*, Yale University Press, New Haven.
6. World Commission on Environment and Development (1987), *Our Common Future*, Oxford University Press, London.

7. Pearce, D. (1992), 'Economics, Equity and Sustainable Development', in Ekins, P. and Max-Neef, M. (eds), *Real Life Economics: Understanding Wealth Creation*, Routledge, London.

8. Hall, T. (1998), *Urban Geography*, Routledge, London and New York, p. 158.

9. Ibid., p. 161.

10. Ibid.

11. Pearce, D., Markandya, A. and Barbier, E. (1990), *Blueprint for a Green Economy*, Earthscan Publications, London, p. 162.

12. Department of Environment, Transport and the Regions (DETR) (December 1997), 'Modernising Planning: A Policy Statement by the Minister for the Regions, Regeneration and Planning', DETR, London.

13. Town and Country Planning Association and Centre for Employment Research, Manchester Metropolitan University, (1998) 'Planning the Sustainable City Region: Manchester 2020: An Inquiry into the Prospects for Integrated Sustainable Development in a Major Conurbation'.

14. Ibid.

15. Johnson, E (August 1996), *The Dispersed and Segregated Metropolis*, Published Essay for the Commercial Club of Chicago, Chicago.

16. Frieden, B. and Sagalyn, L. (1989), *Downtown, INC: How America Rebuilds Cities*, MIT Press, Cambridge, Massachusetts.

17. Campaign for Sensible Growth (January 1998), *Growing Sensibly: A Guidebook of Best Development Practice in the Chicago Region*, Metropolitan Planning Council, Chicago.

18. See, for example, Bank of America and the Resources Agency (1994), *California at the Crossroads: The Costs of Sprawling Land Use Patterns*, Los Angeles.

19. Campaign for Sensible Growth (January 1998), *Growing Sensibly: A Guidebook of Best Development Practice in the Chicago Region*, p. 1.

20. Downs, A. (1994), *New Visions for Metropolitan America*, The Brookings Institute, Washington, DC, and the Lincoln Institute of Land Policy, Cambridge, Massachusetts.

21. Ibid., p. 19.

22. Ibid., p. 32.

23. Department of Environment, Transport and the Regions (DETR) (January 1998), 'Modernising Planning: A Policy Statement by the Minister for the Regions, Regeneration and Planning', DETR, London.

24. For example, in an urban context, see Healey, P. et al. (eds.), (1995), *Managing Cities: The New Urban Context*, Wiley, Chichester.

25. See Dunford, M. and Hudson, R. (December 1996), *Successful European Regions: Northern Ireland Learning from Others*, Research Monograph 3, Northern Ireland Economic Council, Belfast.
26. Department of Environment, Transport and the Regions (DETR) (1998), 'Modernising Planning: A Policy Statement by the Minister for the Regions, Regeneration and Planning', p. 11.
27. Based on Bilton, M. (5 April 1998), 'Demolition Job: Why Government Plans for 4,000,000 Humans Don't Add Up', *Sunday Times Magazine*, pp. 26–31.

6 Urban Regeneration: Lessons from Europe and the UK

Michael Parkinson

This chapter draws upon four strands of my work: a study of European cities for DG XVI; an evaluation for the Department of the Environment (DoE) on Action for Cities – looking back at the last ten years' work; an assessment for the DoE of City Challenge – looking forward to the next five years; and my role acting as adviser to the House of Commons Environment Select Committee.

I will:

- look at what has been happening in Europe in the last ten years and discuss the rise of the entrepreneurial city;
- look at Britain in that wider context and assess the impact of urban policy during the past 15 years;
- discuss new developments and some crucial features of the new policies like City Challenge and the Single Regeneration Budget; and
- ask how some of the Labour government's new concerns may fit into this.

Lessons from Europe – the Rise of the Entrepreneurial City

There are four key questions raised by the European experience:

- what has been happening to the European economy?
- what impact has economic change had upon spatial arrangements?
- how are cities and regions responding?
- what are the outstanding economic social and environmental challenges – involving government, private sector and communities?

In turn, major themes are raised by such considerations: the role of internationalisation – which is deepening and quickening; the impact of economic restructuring – which is continuing; the reality of growing competition – between firms, nations, regions, cities; and the uneven development – between groups and areas – generated in the process. To begin with, the following features of European cities are notable:

The Heterogeneity of the European Urban Experience

Despite some signs of convergence, substantial differences in the historical, institutional, economic, social and environmental contexts still pertain. Their problems and opportunities are different. In simple terms, Copenhagen is not Seville. Glasgow is not Thessalonica. Liverpool is not Madrid or Frankfurt or Athens. Peripheral cities on the edge differ from those nearer to the economic core. Clearly, declining cities are not facing the opportunities – or costs – of expansion.

The Dynamic Nature of the New European Urban System

The European urban system is one of rapid change with the emergence of new functions, roles and relationships. In the past, national contexts mattered. Now the European context matters. City leaders, in seeking new economic niches and functions for their cities, are making strategic alliances and coalitions: to trade; to exchange ideas, experience best practice; to promote local economic development; to get resources for, and to promote, the agenda of cities. The most dynamic cities in Europe have been the most active players in such networks. Barcelona, Montpellier, Lyon, Rotterdam come to mind on the continent. Nearer to home, Manchester, Birmingham and Glasgow stand out. In such places, the first indications of the entrepreneurial city have been evident.

Contradictory Trends – Competition and Social Cohesion

Despite collaboration and complementarity through networks, a crucial feature of urban change during the 1990s was competition between cities seeking economic success. This drove change rapidly during the 1980s and will do so even more rapidly during the 1990s. This is not merely because of the Single Market but the speeding up of economic internationalisation. The implication is that there will be winners and losers – between and within cities. Some cities and some groups will flourish – others may be left behind.

Much of the focus has been on economic competitiveness. But the key feature is social cohesion. Economic growth at the expense of growing inequality is unstable. Leaders need to develop strategies to reconcile growth and equity – to include the excluded.

Strategic choices by leaders matter. Cities are constrained by history, by location, by economic structure. But choices have to be made. Leadership is a crucial feature in the economic trajectory of cities. The market matters but state matters also. Economics matter but so do politics. Leadership is one of the threads pulling all successful urban development together. It helps answer the question, why do cities in similar circumstances behave differently?

European Cities Towards 2000

A series of critical questions can be posed about the future of the European city. For instance, is it going to experience greater stability or instability? The world of the 1990s has been a rapidly changing one. Yet, in some ways, it has become more stable. The driving forces of change in the period from the 1950s to the mid-1980s may have slowed down. The economic transformation from manufacturing-based to service sector-based economy has been substantially achieved. Migration from outside to inside community, from the periphery to centre, from rural to urban areas has slowed down. Demographic change has slowed down. The rapid birth rates especially in southern European countries and cities which fuelled labour market growth is declining. Northern Europe has a declining and ageing population. This brings different pressures. The growth of smaller and medium sized cities has slowed. The rapid decline of large cities is slowing. But there are new sources of instability. The service sector economy is inherently unstable. Cities which boomed on financial services in the 1980s, have been struggling in the 1990s. Traditional migration has declined. But the nature, scale or consequences of legal and illegal migration from the Maghreb and eastern countries into Germany and beyond is unclear. The barriers are now going up, compounding the problems of earlier generations of migrants and ethnic minorities who are still struggling to be integrated into the economic and social mainstream. There is a wider trend. The spatial impact of economic change has been highly uneven with the economic marginalisation, social exclusion and physical segregation of vulnerable and marginal groups.

Another question worth posing is whether cities are coming back, and experiencing a reurbanisation. In the 1950s and 1960s big cities grew. In the 1970s medium-sized cities grew, while larger cities declined. Something happened in the mid-1980s. The second part of the decline looks different from the first. The rapid growth of smaller and medium-sized cities dropped. Also many big cities have stopped declining. Since 1987 all the big German cities have grown and not only because of migration. After a decade and a half of population loss, Rotterdam, Amsterdam, Brussels, Milan, Paris, possibly even London grew. At least the rate of decline has been slowing down. It may be a blip on a secular trend of decline – or maybe something else.

Yet another issue concerns the extent to which cities are experiencing sustainable economic growth. Many cities showed great capacity to recover or grow during the late 1980s. This applied to both the traditional cities in the old core – Rotterdam, Hamburg, Dortmund and to the dynamic cities in the new core, the Mediterranean crescent. Problematic cities remained in the periphery – such as Seville and Rennes. Cities are finding new niches and the accumulation of intellectual, economic and physical assets provide the source of innovation. Many are developing new diversified economic development strategies.

In this respect, a new culture of enterprise is necessary. Arguably, the entrepreneurial city is the connection between demographic resurgence and economic recovery. This has involved imaginative institutional and political responses to economic change. In the last ten years we have seen the emergence of the urban issue on the European agenda. The city has been viewed not just as an economic welfare case, as a source of problems. Rather, the main perspective has been on regarding the city in terms of assets not liabilities, a place of new opportunities. Such a view is not the exclusive insight of Europe. Indeed, it is becoming the credo of all industrial cities seeking to remake their viability.

As such, this drive is really reinventing the old role of the city as the basis for 'the wealth of nations'. In its most acute form, we are even seeing the return of the 'city state' – cities capable of a fair degree of autonomy from their own national authority in dealing with the wider world. The entrepreneurial city, as a conscious mobilisation of local resources in a sustained strategy for economic recovery, has been driven by:

- the scale of international forces on the local economy;
- an inability to rely upon traditional solutions;
- the limitations of regional policy – both in national and European Community guise;
- the dynamic within Europe for greater integration and success, based on economic competition; and within Europe, the push to more
- decentralisation and regionalism.

Virtually all European countries are strengthening or inventing regional and local institutions. Germany has always been federal. But Spain

France, Belgium and Italy are actively encouraging it. There are four exceptions – Greece, the Republic of Ireland, Portugal and the United Kingdom. For the most part, they have been going in the opposite direction. Decentralisation has given new political space and new responsibilities – if not always resources. Within this pattern, urban leaders become key players. And, it is a game worth playing. Decentralisation has reinvigorated cities and regions. Maragal, Michel Noir, Georges Freche, Pierre Mauroy in Lille are national and European players. But in the UK we have weakened our cities and made local leadership less relevant. And yet we ask our civic leaders to rise to the new challenges.

A key task here is the promotion of the competitive city. What are the characteristics of urban economic competitiveness? The criteria are simple but still compelling. Entrepreneurial cities and regions have more rather than less of the following characteristics:

1. economic diversity in manufacturing and services sector preferably in the high value-added and in the exporting or import substitution sectors;
2. a supply of skilled human capital. The successful cities and regions will be those who have the people who can operate successfully in the knowledge and information-based industries where we will have to compete in the future;
3. the right institutional networks. Competitive cities and regions need a range of links between institutions of higher education, research institutions, private industry and government to exploit the intellectual knowledge of skilled people;
4. the right environment. Cities are for living in as well as working in. Competitive cities need the economic, social, environmental and cultural conditions which will attract and retain a potentially mobile workforce. This clearly means the right physical environment. But it also means the right cultural environment as well as the right economic and social environment. Economic prosperity cannot be sustained on a sea of vast inequality. Social cohesion and economic competitiveness are mutually sustaining not mutually exclusive;
5. good communications. Partly this means physical communication – roads, airports, railroad links and electronic communications. But communication is partly a cultural process, a question of attitude. Entrepreneurial cities and regions need an international strategy, their own 'foreign policy' if you like. They need to determine which wider markets they will play in. This underlines the importance of international networking;
6. the institutional capacity to mobilise public, private and community resources in the long-term to deliver agreed economic and social

development strategies. In this respect, process is almost as important as product for the entrepreneurial city and region.

Lessons from Urban Regeneration in the UK

Designing urban policy has posed a series of key questions to governments in the UK. For instance, what is the target of the policy – exclusively 'inner-city problems' or wider urban challenges?

- Is the problem economic, social, or environmental – or some combination of all three?
- What is the right balance of power and responsibility between national and local government?
- What is the best mix of public, private and community intervention?
- Should social need or economic opportunity determine policy priorities and the flow of public resources to cities?
- How can government best achieve an integrated approach to a multi-faceted set of problems?
- How can government get the best out of other partners?
- Are competition and partnership mutually reinforcing – or mutually exclusive – ways of delivering urban policy?

Different governments have answered these questions in different ways, adopting different approaches. Five main periods have been discernible.

1. 1968–74: This was typified by 'the pathology of the ghetto', a view that the problem of urban decline was restricted to certain geographical, largely inner-city, pockets, and its solution lay mainly in rehabilitating local capacities for self-help and better adaption to mainstream social and economic life.
2. 1974–79: This saw the creation of inner-city partnerships, particularly in the major urban centres. Slowly, the problem was being redefined in terms of structural economic change rather than being trapped in narrow notions of anti-poverty welfarism. Yet, the requisite resources for carrying through any such reconception into significant practical intervention were unavailable.
3. 1979–92: The age of Thatcher promoted private sector-led entrepreneurialism, with great emphasis on property-based regeneration. Nevertheless, many features of the by now long-standing 'compensatory' type of urban programmes remained, whereby symptoms of decline were eased, without any fundamental redress of the economic roots of the problem.

4. 1992–97: In the Major years, urban policy balanced between partnership and competition. Less hostility to the role of local government alongside a streamlining of resource allocation under the Single Regeneration Budget marked this period, rather than any innovative policy initiative.
5. 1997–present: There has been a leap in the dark, with different policies for different parts of the country. It remains unclear how, where and when they will collide or connect. In the 'Celtic fringe' there is devolution. In the northern periphery, there is the beginning of regionalisation. In the southern heartland, there are strategic authorities, and for London an elected mayor. Throughout the country, alongside labour market initiatives like the New Deal, there have been signs of a redefined scope for local government, within a framework which extols cross-sectoral partnerships.

As a consequence of all these changes, urban policy in the late 1990s in Britain is being implemented in the context of: constrained public resources; a high degree of fragmentation among local service providers; a reduced executive role for local government; a national urban policy agenda which goes beyond physical change but is only indirectly linked to the mainstream programmes that impact most heavily on cities financially; a new quasi-prefectoral role for regional government departments; central government policies which increasingly allocate resources through competitive bidding and reward areas that display a high degree of public entrepreneurialism and partnership; and a growing role for the European Commission.

The New Urban Entrepreneurialism 1979–92

Until the late 1960s Britain did not have an explicit national urban policy. From then until 1979, urban policy under both political parties in Britain rested on two shared assumptions. First, it was to provide social and welfare services to victims of economic change in the inner cities. It was less concerned to create wealth in those areas. Secondly, the private sector was seen to be the cause of many inner-city problems, whereas the public sector was considered the solution.

In the 1980s, the public sector became the problem and the private sector the solution. Markets replaced politics as the primary response to urban decline. The values of urban entrepreneurialism replaced those of public intervention. Investment in physical capital replaced investment in social capital. Wealth creation replaced the distribution of welfare, and central state power was increased at the expense of local authorities.

Between 1979 and 1993, government radically restructured and restricted the way in which it financed cities. Eliminating a complete tier of elected government, the Metropolitan County Councils in the six largest urban areas, it sought to privatise the delivery of many local authority services.

The Impact of Urban Entrepreneurialism

Assessing the impact of these policies, several features are worth noting. The resources of the Urban Programme have been limited. Expenditure on all programmes which affect cities was estimated at £4 billion of total spend of £200 billion by government. The Urban Programme in 1993–94 was £1.01 billion. It rose throughout the 1980s. But the figures for 1996–97 indicated a reduction to £800 million. Whatever impact government policy has had in the past, expenditure cuts suggest it will be reduced in future. Indeed, urban funding in general has been in decline. The major sources of funding for cities remains the Rate Support Grant and the Housing Investment Programmes, both substantially reduced during the decade – from 90 per cent to 70 per cent of expenditure in large cities.

Smaller cities have tended to benefit while larger cities have tended to lose. Urban policy did improve the position of the 57 cities in greatest need. It reduced unemployment, attracted younger residents and raised demand for private housing in those cities. But the seven largest cities in the country have not shared in this relative progress. Indeed, there has been intensification of economic distress at the heart of the biggest cities which have continued to deteriorate. Increasing polarisation between city residents in the deprived central areas in the larger cities and those who live in either smaller or less deprived cities has marked this period.

There has continued to be a lack of co-ordination among the policies and efforts of the different government departments whose work impacts upon cities. Some government departments operate with different spatial priorities – for example the wider region as opposed to the city. Others have no spatial priorities, and hence no overt commitment to cities at all. At the same time, creating partnership has been elevated as a goal, though the contribution and commitment of the private sectors to that process has been often exaggerated. The government has not provided sustained commitment of public resources and an agreed policy environment, both of which would be essential to attract the private sector into longer term partnerships. Local authorities have been too excluded, neglecting their potential as important facilitators in establishing coalitions to achieve long-term regeneration. Resource cuts have constrained that role. Similarly, local communities have not been given a sufficiently wide role in the regeneration process.

Thus, some main lessons for government emerge from such evaluation. Public–private partnerships and the creation of coalitions of local players are worth while. However, structures and mechanisms which encourage long-term collaborative partnerships are needed. Local authorities in their role as enablers and facilitators should be given greater opportunities, powers and resources. In tandem with this, local communities need to be given greater opportunities to play roles in such coalitions. Greater coherence is needed between the programmes of the different government departments which impact upon the inner cities. To help in this regard, there should be more clarity in the targeting of resources which go to cities. A single urban budget could unite all the resources of the departments which flow into cities, administered at a regional rather than at a national level.

In the early 1990s such criticism, among other pressures, encouraged the government to change policy focus. It made substantial changes to the organisation, financing and priorities of urban policy with the introduction in 1992 of the City Challenge initiative and, even more important, in 1994 the Single Regeneration Budget (SRB). The SRB brought together all government regeneration programmes under a single heading. Critics have two major reservations about these initiatives. They have argued that a competition between local authorities and partners is not the best way of allocating resources to urban areas. They have also observed that the money was not new but found from existing programmes. Despite those two important reservations, City Challenge and the SRB are an important attempt to address some of the key problems of urban policy and have a number of features which differentiate them from the policies of the 1980s.

City Challenge has been the most promising regeneration scheme so far attempted. Widespread support comes from a range of partners for most aspects of its design. They see it as an advance upon previous initiatives particularly because of its partnership basis, its community and private sector involvement, its strategic and targeted approach and its implementation by dedicated multi-disciplinary teams. Moreover, it has been more than meeting its leverage and output targets. In the first three years, the 31 'Challenge projects' had: levered in nearly £1.3 billion of private sector funds; completed/improved nearly 39,200 dwellings; created/preserved over 53,000 jobs; reclaimed/improved nearly 1,900 hectares of derelict land; created/improved over 1,257,400 square metres of floorspace; and promoted nearly 3,150 business start-ups.

In achieving these outputs, competition has offered advantages as a management tool. It has galvanised cross-sectoral involvement, required commitment to future delivery, and produced more positive and imaginative proposals for change. However, for some people competition has been problematic as a basis for allocating urban resources. In particular, it has been regarded as being potentially divisive, penalising those areas without conspicuous development opportunities or capacity to deliver.

The scale of City Challenge resources and its areal targeting has made possible a more strategic integrated approach to regeneration. The programme has allowed developments to occur which required substantial pump priming to take place. It has speeded up development which otherwise would have been more piecemeal. It has triggered further investment and related activity, and it has added value by linking separate programmes, agencies and types of expertise.

City Challenge also has influenced the way in which partner organisations have worked together. Encouraging greater cross-sectoral understanding, it has stimulated more corporate working within local authorities. In terms of efficiency, tighter project management has been evident, while the practice of partnership at programme and project level has helped to bring new alliances in other areas.

Future Policy Issues

Where does urban regeneration policy stand at the end of the 1990s? The focus is upon partnership, spatial targeting, integration and competition with a commitment to economic, social and environmental regeneration. Consensus prevails that progress has been made under the SRB and City Challenge. Local authorities, the private sector, the community sector have welcomed the fact that policy: encourages the integration of departments and funding through partnership, and increasingly a regional approach; adopts an expansive definition of the urban problem, recognising the importance of, and the links between, the economic, social and environmental dimension; recognises that the problems are not narrowly geographically confined; accepts the importance of assessing how policy is performing and how resources are being spent, as well as simply identifying the need that the policy is meant to meet; acknowledges the importance of partnership, whereby the local authority and the local community as well as the national government and the private sector need to be at the table; and endorses the view that many departments affect cities and that they need to be at the same table. In this respect, the SRB in particular has made many departments put their money on the table.

But if those are the virtues of current policy, a number of criticisms have been made. Some are specific to the SRB. But the majority have been faced many times during the past 25 years. In terms of the SRB there is a concern:

- that there is not a sufficiently clear regional strategy to make the selection process transparent or relevant to regional needs;
- that SRB spreads resources too thinly across too many projects within regions, as well as across too many regions, some of which have traditionally not received urban programme funding; and
- that there is a risk that the strategic dimension of the initiative may be lost as the SRB becomes a collection of discrete projects rather than an integrated and strategic approach to a clearly specified area.

Two other outstanding concerns remain, relating to partnership and competition. City Challenge and SRB place partnership at the top of the political agenda. There is clear evidence that partnership is developing. But there are also criticisms that not all partners are equally positioned in the policy. In particular, there is a concern that not only are local communities relatively powerless, but also that the local authorities have lost so many powers and resources that they cannot be equal partners in the regeneration game. City Challenge did empower many communities. But there is a feeling that in the SRB, community groups have lost some ground in the decision-making process.

Reservation also has been expressed about the principle of competition which underpins much current regeneration policy. Competition has been used at least partly to address criticisms of more traditional approaches like the Urban Programme. It was indeed often difficult to see how social need was related to the quality of the programmes and the achievements that were gained from the use of public money. There was a consensus that the traditional Urban Programme needed reinvigorating. In a narrow sense there is evidence that competition has encouraged innovation, collaboration and partnership within particular areas around specific programmes. But as a wider principle of determining priorities and allocating resources, a number of issues remain to be faced.

Competition may have had a beneficial impact upon the winners, but what long-term impact does it have upon losing local authorities, communities and projects? Competition may create excitement and innovation initially but will diminishing returns set in over the years as local authorities find themselves competing in more competitions in more policy areas for declining rewards? How compatible is the competition for nationally allocated funds with the strategic choice of local and regional priorities? Will competition reinforce or undermine the government effort to promote local partnerships? Where should the balance between need and opportunity lie as a source of priorities and the allocation of resources? What should be the relationship between the search to increase economic competitiveness and to reduce social exclusion? What are the limits to the withdrawal of resources from needy areas, communities and projects because they fail to win competitions? In principle, at what point would it stop?

7 Urban Regeneration: The New Policy Agenda

Frank Gaffikin and Mike Morrissey

This chapter elaborates some of the issues raised in Michael Parkinson's overview of policy trends, assessing recent shifts in urban policy and delivery structure in Britain, elsewhere in Europe and in the USA, and examining the key lessons *about urban regeneration* from 30 years of urban programmes.

Certain themes and trends were evident in 1980s urban revitalisation. Among these was the relative emphasis on *downtown* compared to neighbourhood; the fashion for *waterfront development*; the regenerative role of *services*; the increased influence of the private sector, sometimes via new forms of *partnerships*; and the greater use of *place marketing*. But, fundamental to the approach in both the USA and the UK was a dependence on *physical renewal*. Since the 1990s, the agenda has moved on. Strategies that are more comprehensive and integrative are being sought, based on the following lessons:

1. Economic development

- Regeneration based on a few *flagship projects* is 'over-exposed' to the volatility of the property market, and in any case, percolates down very little to the most deprived areas.
- Stable regeneration depends on fine tuning the mix between *indigenous development* and *inward investment*, and in a similar way being *selective* about the sectors which are targeted for growth.
- This selection should be based on a long-term development perspective – what projects are going to *upgrade skills* training of the workforce; introduce *new technologies* and/or *efficient working practices*; bring *management* and *marketing* expertise; *industrially link* with, and *spread good practice* and *technology* to, existing local firms; and require *significant R&D* support?[1]
- Urban economic competitiveness and social cohesion are not mutually exclusive. Cities that are *open for global business* don't have to be *closed to their own most needy neighbourhoods*.

2. Social regeneration

- The Single Regeneration Budget (SRB) has seen the move away from allocation to Urban Priority Areas, designated on the basis of need, to *a system of 'winning and losing' bids*, based on the appeal of submission.
- To avoid needy areas getting left further behind, such an approach would need to be complemented with a systematic effort to *create capacity* in these areas and to provide technical aid in the preparation of bids.
- Labour turnover is more significant than job creation. Thus, *improving employability* of the disadvantaged in the labour market is crucial in helping them avail of these wider opportunities.
- Linking areas of need into *the mainstream economy* needs to become a more key purpose of special urban programmes.

3. Good governance

- Cities need to see their prospects in *the wider context of their hinterland*, and thereby adopt a more metropolitan focus. Consequently, government structures to deliver a co-ordinated development on a larger geographical scale are essential.
- *Complementarity* and *synergy* are critical. Duplication wastes resources, causes confusion and undermines opportunities to rally wide sets of civic constituencies around an ambitious urban vision.
- Local government has had to become more *'entrepreneurial'* in attracting *both* public urban funds and private sector investment.
- This shift from a *managerialist* to an *enterprising* approach in city administration is part of the current fluid nature of local governance, in which new actors like the private sector and community forums are playing a more overt role. This change, though often uneven and confusing, offers new opportunities for *innovative* approaches through new arenas such as partnerships.

Changes in the Policy Context: The Urban Problem: Changes in Definition

In the 1960s, urban programmes were billed as innovative measures to redress a *residual* though trenchant poverty embedded in scattered pockets of inner-urban areas. But in the 1970s, critics disclaimed such *welfare* answers to deepening urban *economic* problems. By the 1980s, official analysis was increasingly in terms of *supply-side* deficits in land and labour, community dependencies, and an overtaxed, overregulated business sector. Policy response to urban 'market failure' was mainly to cut planning red tape, leverage private development and promote community self-help. In 1988, the UK government's 'Action for Cities' document[2] tended to demote local authorities' regeneration role and to elevate that of local business leadership. By then, much of the urban agenda had been devolved to new agencies: for example to Urban Development Corporations or to local bodies by way of Priority Estates Projects and tenant management schemes under Housing Action Trusts (HATs). In all of this, the economic was meant to take priority over the social, and the private sector over the public:[3]

> In 1979 assistance to the private sector from urban programmes was 90 per cent greater than spending on social and community projects, by 1988 this ratio had increased to 500 per cent.

By the 1990s, response to Audit Report critiques about fragmented urban regeneration effort prompted effort at better *co-ordination of administration* and *greater strategic focus* behind funding. The value of *multi-agency partnerships* was affirmed. But there was also a concern to engender a more enterprising local effort at renewal by injecting bids for scarce urban funding with a *competitive* element.

Competitive Bidding

Community Challenge, introduced in 1991, brought with it a competitive aspect, designed to raise the quality and innovation of funding application. Councils were given a renewed role, but they were expected to partner with business and community interests in the production and operation of an area development plan. Selected Urban Priority Authorities (UPAs) were invited to submit. By 1992, 20 out of the 57 UPAs 'won', and shared £750 million over a five-year period. These were not really additional funds, but rather were top-sliced from other programmes.[4] On the downside, this competitive element could be said to: foster rivalry among deprived areas; allocate on criteria other than need; put a gloss of rationality on what is stricter *rationing* within public funding restraint; and promote greater central control over programme content and delivery.[5]

Nevertheless, there is evidence that it has: sharpened the preparation of bids;[6] attempted to minimise overlap of government urban regeneration initiatives; encouraged a holistic perspective on the part of bidding authorities; rewarded those bidders that link their short-to-medium goals to a long-term strategic vision; given a better capacity for development phasing, since it offers five-year, rather than the usual three-year, funding; focused effort away from a large number of small projects spread over 57 priority areas to one with fewer projects under larger budgets; and disciplined performance by specifying targets and outputs.

Yet, of the first winning bids, 'all included the participation of the private sector and most were either in or adjacent to central city areas; they focused overwhelmingly upon infrastructure, and environmental works and site preparation for the private sector'.[7] One evaluation noted that it was widely perceived as 'a 'beauty contest' in which rewards were related to the quality of presentation rather than the strength of the underlying case. Failure in the bid might actually have negative effects on how people work together – leading to recrimination, cynicism and demoralisation.[8]

But the new approach represented advance in terms of its comprehensiveness.[9] By 1993/94, the programme accounted for over a quarter of public spending in inner cities.[10] A central feature was the concern to build '*capabilities of local development organisations*'.[11] Only projects which could demonstrate ongoing viability were chosen, and this sustainability was thought to rest on competent local capacity. One assessment commented that 'City Challenge [had] involved the bidding authorities reaching right down into communities at the neighbourhood level.'[12] Yet, the limited scope for 'grassroots' community influence over these bids was notable.[13]

An example of one City Challenge gives an insight into the approach endorsed by the selection process. Liverpool's five-year programme, in the formerly run-down City Centre East (140 hectares, 900 businesses, over 14,000 jobs), seeks a broad and linked strategy concerned to:[14]

- remove eyesores, stir local pride, improve investor and visitor perceptions: by means, for instance, of creating new quality public open spaces and marking Liverpool's identity as a major European city;
- enhance economic activity, and business confidence;
- create liveable communities in the city centre;
- build community capacity to ensure the basis of further local development beyond the programme;
- improve local people's access to jobs and training; and
- undertake all of this in partnerships, which tap the expertise and resource of community, public agencies and the private sector.

The Single Regeneration Budget

The Single Regeneration Budget was launched in 1994. The lead role was shared between local authorities and the Training and Employment Councils:[15]

The amalgamation of virtually all urban policy measures into the new Single Regeneration Budget and the creation of newly integrated government offices in each of the standard regions to co-ordinate local programmes funded under it represents yet another major development in the institutional context of urban policy.

The new Budget involved 20 programmes from five government departments under ten new Integrated Regional Offices in England.[16] These offices, bringing together the functions of Trade and Industry, Employment, Environment and Transport at a regional level, are meant to provide co-ordination of government action, to help nurture partnerships, and to submit SRB applications to central government. The Budget is designed to offer 'a fund of public money which will complement or attract other resources – public, private or voluntary. It will help to improve local areas and enhance the quality of life of local people by tackling need, stimulating wealth creation and improving competitiveness.'[17] Specifically, bidders are asked to have regard to the following objectives:

- enhance the job prospects, education and skills of residents, with particular regard to equality of opportunity, the young and disadvantaged;
- nurture sustainable growth and wealth generation by making the local economy more competitive;
- improve housing standard, choice, management and maintenance;
- conserve and upgrade the environment and infrastructure, with a premium on quality design;
- promote initiatives which benefit ethnic minorities;
- address crime and create greater community security; and
- improve the quality of life of residents, with special regard to their health, cultural and sports opportunities.

This attempt to overarch diverse urban policy harbours potential for greater *rationalisation*; *coherence*; *simplification*; and *flexible localism*, and allows for *competitive* bids by partnerships for *integrated* urban projects, which maximise *leverage* and *complementarity* with other funding regimes.[18] But it also poses a central problem: its catchment extends beyond the Urban Priority Areas, thereby diffusing funding that could be targeted on need. The Minister proclaimed, 'the government is looking for more effective co-ordination of resources and partnerships that take into account local needs'.[19]

Critics charge that the SRB involves:[20] poor accountability and openness; no extra resources; an inefficiency in encouraging many bids which will receive nothing, thereby wasting the effort of local partnership building and development planning; a possible regressive shift of funding to relatively well-off areas that make competent bids; intra-regional inconsistencies; and incompatibility with other government urban effort. Moreover, while it seems to have rediscovered a leadership role for local government, the argument is made that local councils have been frustrated in such a role by the impact of rate capping, competitive tendering and the growth of local quangos, whose line of responsibility is to Whitehall not Town Hall.

However, a Commons Select Committee report[21] on the first round of the SRB Challenge Fund argued that it had shown its potential to achieve value-for-money; mobilise community and business involvement; integrate diverse government programmes; and create partnerships between local authorities and bodies like the Training and Enterprise Councils. The first two rounds of the Fund together are estimated to create or safeguard half a million jobs, assist 80,000 firms, complete or rehabilitate almost 170,000 homes, and support over 20,000 community organisations.[22]

The Select Committee suggested that:

- The Fund should operate with *minimal bureaucracy* and *clear criteria*. Overall, it approved of the lack of ring-fencing within the Fund.
- The Regional Offices should have *regard to local area plans*, and *consult* annually with local councils, Training and Employment Councils, and others on an appropriate regeneration agenda.
- There was doubt about the *reality of some of the matching funding* 'pledged' by business.
- There were problems for bidding partnerships in *synchronising SRB funding with European funding*, since the two did not always operate in the same cycle.
- The *representativeness* and *functioning* of bidding partnerships should be assessed.
- While allowing for customised responses by particular Regional Offices, *inter-regional disparities* should be addressed in the distribution of funding.
- Localities which had less experience in packaging viable bids should be *helped* to minimise this handicap.
- Full involvement by the community/voluntary sector demanded that it should be given *resources* to ensure its equal participation.

The SRB has not been in practice a single flexible fund open to strategic allocation for new approaches. For instance in one year, amid increasing resource scarcity, nearly 40 per cent was 'spoken for' by Urban Development Corporations, English Partnerships and Housing Action Trusts. But this unified budget has an appeal for the

Treasury. It ensures that any overspend in any particular programme is covered within the grand total.[23]

Revision of the Single Regeneration Budget

In March 1996 a new guidance was issued. The contribution of the voluntary sector is upgraded, and community participation in local renewal is seen as part of the effort to improve quality of life in areas of need. Linked to this, the importance of capacity building to maximise effective involvement is acknowledged. Stressing the need for clearer specification of added value achieved, it asks bidders to quantify targeted groups. The need to enhance private sector contribution is stated, and bidders are urged to avail more of the Private Finance Initiative. Particularly encouraged are schemes which involve joint ventures with business; which give business the chance to lead throughout the phases of design, building, financing and operation (DBFO) of projects; which allow local councils to share facilities with the private sector; which transfer assets like land to the private sector; and which optimise the chance for new private investment and efficient use by business. Variation in partner pledges is recognised. Different types of 'partners' are set: CC (commitment of partners confirmed); E (endorsed but yet to give final commitment); and NYE (not yet endorsed).

In short, public authorities are now faced with a difficult demand. On the one hand, they have to increase the role and competence of voluntary involvement in regeneration, and, on the other, they have to give better incentive for the private sector to take the lead. Possible tensions between these two goals are not acknowledged.

City Pride: An Initiative for Strategic Thinking?

Not all of the recent initiatives have involved new ways of allocating funding. City Pride has involved government calling on London, Birmingham and Manchester to frame their various regeneration drives in a ten-year strategy, which details inputs, sources of inputs, expected outputs, likely partners, etc. Three distinctive features of this initiative pertain. In the first instance, it does not involve any new commitment of government funds. Secondly, it is inviting the cities to devise their strategies in terms of the whole urban area, rather than a series of separate interventions in different parts of the city. Finally, it is encouraging the notion of 'visioning', insofar as it is prompting decision-makers to set a long-term view.

Changes in Funding

For many decades, the main special effort to redress disparities in development among different places was *regional policy*. But from 1981–82 to 1991–92, regional policy spending in Britain decreased by nearly three-quarters (from £1.6 billion to £452.5 million at 1992–93 prices). Meanwhile, *urban policy* spending rose by 240 per cent over the same period (from £303 million to £1.03 billion). The changing share of inner-city spending within the DoE for a ten-year period up to the mid-1990s is seen in Table 7.1. It shows that the Urban Programme declined from three-fifths to one-tenth. Up to the early 1990s, UDC spending accounted for a rising share. Latterly, City Challenge together with English Partnerships (which manages, for example, the City and Derelict Land Grants) have assumed nearly half the budget.

Table 7.1 Share of Inner Cities Expenditure (%)

	1985–86	1987–88	1989–90	1991–92	1993–94	1994–95
Urban Programme	58	51	27	24	17	10
City Challenge	–	–	–	–	22	26
City Grant	5	6	5	4	2	–
Derelict Land Grant	17	16	8	8	11	–
English Partnerships	–	–	–	–	–	22
UDCs and DLR	20	28	58	61	38	36
Task Forces	–	–	2	2	2	2
City Action Teams	–	–	0	1	0	0
Other	0	0	0	0	5	4
Total	100	100	100	100	100	100
£ million	436	483	815	980	993	814

Source: Stewart, M. (1995), 'Public Expenditure Management in Urban Regeneration', in Hambleton, R. and Thomas, H. (eds), *Urban Policy Evaluation: Challenge and Change*, Paul Chapman, London.

Alternative Agendas in Britain

In the 1990s, there has been a series of documents keen to depart from standard urban policy. One such alternative to this policy orthodoxy comes in a report which included Belfast among eight cities studied. It proposes a systematic networking support for community-based regeneration in 200 UK localities which have endured the worst pauperisation and 'hollowing out' of community:[24]

> In all the cities there has been a substantial commitment to diver-
> sifying the local economic base and to the transformation of the city
> centre. ... traditional manufacturing neighbourhoods have become
> relatively poorer as service and commercial sectors have grown and
> city centres regenerated.

This approach elevates focused linked programmes over a series of scattered single-purpose interventions,[25] a path endorsed in the report from the Commission for Social Justice.[26] The latter also called for a National Community Regeneration Agency to help steer, fund and monitor an approach that placed community-based projects at the heart of urban regeneration. A switch in focus from property to people is deemed essential. This, it argues, should be done within better resource-targeting towards the worst-off 250 neighbourhoods. Policy papers from the Centre for Local Economic Strategies (CLES)[27] also have supported greater attention for neighbourhood revitalisation in the whole realm of city renewal, and within this, a greater role for local organisations in the form of Community Regeneration Corporations. Moreover, while the Association of Metropolitan Authorities have sought to reclaim a pivotal role for local government in providing leadership for a broader civic partnership, it has backed the emphasis on empowering local agencies to act effectively in the reshaping of the most impoverished areas.[28]

Much of this has been close to Labour Party thinking. Arguing that 'less than one percent of government urban grant money is presently directed to community-led initiatives',[29] one of its pamphlets favoured a *needs-based* approach, whose basis lay in *community capacity-building* within more *participative* planning, but whose long-term impact demanded *cultural* change within government agencies. This included reallocation of urban funds away from flagship property regeneration into community networks and projects. Another Labour Party document – 'City 2020' (1994) – emphasised that commitment to community-based activity and community empowerment was vital to urban policy.[30] All regeneration funds, it recommended, should come under one *CIVIC Grant*, which should be distributed on the basis of need, not competition.

The View from Scotland

Some of this thinking has been evident in Scotland's urban programmes in the 1980s, which combined conventional espousal of an active private sector[31] with calls for active community participation.[32] More recent Scottish approaches:

- make more explicit the significance of local impact[33]
- set clearer principles for targeting[34]
- situate effort in longer time frames,[35] and
- broaden the partnership concept.[36]

Even in Scotland where the culture for partnerships has taken root earlier, these new structures have been relatively impotent in shaping the significant aspects of urban development. Yet, the policy statement makes plain that 'the main goal of the Partnerships and other similar initiatives will have been achieved when people themselves begin to regard the areas as good places in which to live and bring up their families'.[37]

The European Dimension

There is a growing interest in the European Union in the urban dimension. The Union contains 3,560 towns or cities with more than 10,000 residents; 169 cities of more than 200,000; and 32 of more than 1 million. These 169 cities alone account for nearly six in ten of Europe's urban population. Moreover, many large cities are sited quite close to one another, permitting networks among them. Yet, despite 80 per cent of its population living in cities, the EU has been a long time coming to an urban focus. Certainly, Poverty 2 and 3 addressed issues of deprivation and exclusion relevant to many urban areas. Between 1989 and 1993, a high share of the European Regional Development Fund (ERDF) and the European Social Fund (ESF) spending was devoted to cities in Objective 1 and 2 regions. From its birth in the mid-1970s to the late 1980s, about 85 per cent of the ERDF was spent on infrastructural projects, with an increasing share over time going to the least prosperous regions. In any case, the money has been small. In 1988, the year of their reform into the Structural Funds and the doubling of their resources, ERDF support itself amounted to a mere 0.09 per cent of the EC's GDP.[38]

In terms of other support, the Commission has given modest support to networking the most stricken neighbourhoods in 25 cities under the umbrella of *Quartiers en Crise*. Just under two dozen pilot urban initiatives also have been co-funded by the Commission under Article 10 (of the Regulations relating to ERDF). These have tackled three main aspects: the integration of urban economic and environmental objectives; inner-city/peripheral housing estates whose blight is reinforced by the exclusion of many residents from job and training opportunities; and the restoration of commercial vibrancy to historic urban centres suffering decayed fabric and poor image.

But the most obvious recent advance is the URBAN programme. It supports local partnerships in integrated efforts to improve economic development, social integration, and environmental need in an urban context,[39] and to supplement other effort at promoting social inclusion and cohesion. Between 1994 and 1999, the allocation from the Structural Funds to this Initiative is due to be ECU 600m, of which two-thirds is destined for Objective 1 areas. Thus, a key objective of URBAN, as with the Structural Funds, is to combat exclusion from the labour market: 'URBAN links measures relating to investment with a human resources approach in order to contribute to solutions to the growth of exclusion in certain difficult areas'.[40]

The reform of the Structural Funds has allowed for a clearer and more co-ordinated focus on urban issues:[41]

> This approach is being implemented through the continuation and strengthening of the financial support via the Structural Funds to cities within Objective 1 and Objective 2 regions, through the support for the Urban Pilot Projects and the city networks under the RECITE initiative; by the launch of the new Community Initiative for urban areas (URBAN), which is aiming to promote innovative actions which can be used as examples to be diffused in cities across the EU, and promotion of networks of exchange of experience and co-operation; through the development of further research into urban problems supported by the new Fourth Research Framework programme; ensuring that an urban dimension is introduced to other Community policies, especially those relating to the urban environment; and strengthening the dialogue between cities and their representative organisations in the newly established Committee of the Regions. The Commission is likely to monitor the impacts of Community action on urban areas during this next phase of European policy development.

In the main, the European approach to urban change is an extension of its policy for lagging regions. Reduction of unemployment is seen as key. And achievement here is tied to a long-term strategy: making employment systems more effective, developing the employment potential of small firms, promoting competitive research, implementing the priority trans-European projects, expanding the potential of the information society, and promoting sustainable development which would respect the environment.[42]

Specifically, this agenda links seven key aspects of development, namely the need to:

- improve physical capacity and image – renovation of buildings for economic and social purposes, reclamation of public areas, and the optimum use of derelict and polluted land;

- upgrade the area's connections to trans-European networks – for transport, telecommunications and energy. (This was one of the five priorities identified in the Commission's White Paper on 'Growth, Competitiveness, Employment'.) As part of this exchange, cities are also encouraged to collaborate on ideas and experiences within the field of urban regeneration. An increasing role for such networking of cities has emerged. Largely within the RECITE inter-regional co-operation programme, EC financial support for inter-urban links is open to local/regional authorities of 50,000 or more residents. For instance, the Eurocities network, set up ten years ago, links 'second cities' such as Birmingham. *Quartiers en Crise*, set up in 1989, monitors innovative urban actions, and includes Belfast. The ECOS programme facilitates contact between Western European cities and those in Central and Eastern Europe, while the MED-URDS programme does the same for links with cities in the South Mediterranean;
- enhance human capital – better and more flexible training, education and employment services, targeted towards identified growth sectors. A coherent strategy should include facilitation of employees' adaptation to change in industry and production systems;
- modernise with a broad economic base – which while creating niches of high-value specialisation, does not 'expose' the area to vulnerabilities and volatilities of modern global markets by over-dependence on a particular sector;
- tap sources of local knowledge/expertise – linking higher education and centres of research excellence to optimise innovation and application around high technology;
- offer pathways to social integration – opening access to jobs and training for those excluded by disadvantage, discrimination and disability. Certain groups like the young and long-term unemployed are prioritised;
- create quality social and cultural life and environment – as attraction to outside visitors/investors and as inducement to native talent to stay.

Urban Trends in Europe

The adoption of such policies has to be set against the general urban trends in Europe. The following summarises some key patterns in urban development across the EU.

In the 1970s, smaller towns and cities grew in population and jobs relative to their larger counterparts. Since the 1980s, in most parts of the EU, many large cities – particularly those of over a half a million – have reversed this trend:[43]

> Thus over the 1980s, cities of between 500,000 and 2 million people, tended to increase markedly in all Member States, in the North (in such cities as Amsterdam, Antwerp, Cologne and Dublin) though to an even greater extent in the South (in Palermo, Naples, Thessalonika, Seville and Toulouse, for example).

This growth of large cities is linked to the rapid rate of new product development; the shift from manufacturing to services; from standard to tailored production; and the increasing number of dual-career families where both partners are seeking employment in some proximity. Such changes favour those city regions of a sufficient critical mass capable of offering: a diverse range of jobs; good cultural and leisure amenities; high-speed frequent and flexible transport; efficient communications; good social infrastructure; comprehensive business services; skilled workforce; technical capacities; quality education and training; marketing know-how; and creative resourcefulness.

At the same time, the drawbacks faced by many cities remain in terms of population and investment drain: the relatively high rental and labour costs; the congestion; and the alternative out-of-town sites, whose accessibility has improved with the new transport and telecommunications. Those cities of less than half a million that did grow in the 1980s tended to have some dynamic combination of the following features: *proximity to large city/conurbation* with benefit from its economic dispersal; *quality of life* and distinctiveness in culture, scenic attraction, historical tradition, etc.; *specialisation* in particular growth products/sectors, with strong back-up research and development capacity; and *clustering* of same-size cities in vicinity for mutual networking. Such city regions have been best placed to avail of the new opportunities under the Single Market, including the increase in inward investment. Between 1986 and 1991, the gross inflow of foreign direct investment into the Community from third countries amounted to almost 120 billion ECU. Together with the 150 billion ECU flows between member states during this period, this totalled a substantial source of investment opportunity.[44]

Many of the most secure and best paid new jobs that have come to cities – in finance, business consultancy, legal services, public administration, etc. – are not available to those who have lost jobs amid the contraction of traditional industry. Thus, cities now see increased commuting of high-income groups to city-centre employment, while many who live closest to the city centre remain redundant. The travel patterns involved have contributed to problems with environmental degradation, air quality, noise, accidents, congestion and high energy use. In 1970, under one-fifth of EU cities had one car for every three people. By 1990, over three-quarters of cities were in this position. Dispersal of population and jobs from urban centres to a series of smaller settlements is associated with higher car use.

Such patterns have been linked to widening social inequality. Unemployed and low income families have become ever more segregated together in social housing and/or low-cost urban spaces. Being both spatially contained and socially excluded, more promising horizons seem blocked. This can carry over to low expectation and motivation in education and training and a discouraged attitude to the labour market. These features, and their associated social problems, cannot be redressed by conventional efforts at economic growth alone. Rather, they require intensive and targeted response to the vulnerable areas and populations. Accordingly, across Europe, there are specific urban programmes in many member states: the *Contrats de Ville* in France is a five-year government initiative to link its efforts to tie economic prosperity to social improvement in 187 city districts of greatest need. In the Netherlands, the Social Renewal Programme similarly targets the poorest localities in the main cities.

Unequal development within Europe use to be understood in terms of a dynamic *core* area (embracing 'the golden triangles' of London, Paris, Hamburg and the Manchester–Milan axis, which trends north-west to south-east)[45] in which the conception, control and production functions of the most globally competitive firms were located; and a *peripheral* area, less economically favoured and burdened with old industry and infrastructure. More recently, it has been suggested that the decentralisation of economic activity and population away from traditional metropolitan areas would favour the Alpine and Mediterranean regions, and therein the small but sprouting urban areas around the southern parts of Germany and France and the northern parts of Italy and Spain.

Such simple contrasts are less persuasive in the 1990s. More complex variation is evident. Many urban areas in the Alpine-Mediterranean area have indeed seen growth. But so too have selected cities in the North, particularly those with a low manufacturing tradition. Development has gone beyond the normal vibrant core.

Thus, Parkinson elsewhere has noted *three broad economic spheres* in Europe:

1. the traditional economic heartlands, largely centrally located, undergoing significant industrial dislocation and reorganisation. But their pivotal role endures, centring around their 'control and command' capacities in major firms and sectors, and their global reach in markets;

2. a new core, joining the traditional one, and comprising cities particularly in the Alpine-Mediterranean belt, which has seen growth in new industrial sectors; and

3. the periphery, which includes the poorest areas of Southern Europe and many parts of the Western Spain and France, and much of Ireland and Northern Scotland. These areas are afflicted with a relative dependency on lower level technologies, volatile inward investment largely geared to routine assembly rather than state-of-the-art production, and on an exposed fragile Small-Medium Enterprise (SME) sector.[46]

The issue of unemployment lies at the heart of urban efforts to be both more competitive and socially equitable. While economic growth alone cannot deal with the jobs problem, growth is a key factor. Estimates suggests that growth has to exceed 2.5 per cent a year in Europe simply to keep unemployment from rising. Yet, Europe failed to achieve this target in the early 1990s.[47] What jobs have been created do not readily fill the gap of traditional jobs lost. Of the 9 million additional jobs generated between the mid-1980s and early 1990s, one-third were part-time, of which 80 per cent were taken by women. Thus, 'the regions where employment declined or failed to rise over the period (the 1980s) were mainly old industrial and/or highly urbanised parts of the Community'.[48]

The Europeanisation of Urban Policy

Likely, there will be an increasing *Europeanisation* of urban policy.[49] Europe's contribution has been quite small in finance, but large in influence about policy ideas and structures. Its emphasis has been on seeing the issue in multi-dimensional terms; requiring integrated and multi-facted response from cross-sectoral partnerships; all well monitored and evaluated; and informed by inter-urban networking and exchange.

Clearly, the agenda for urban regeneration in the Single Market is complex. On the one hand, cities have to strive for their *efficient market niche*. At the same time, they have to pay regard to *social cohesion*, whereby they enfranchise their most marginalised.[50] While positioning themselves in a *competitive* advantage to other European cities, they are also encouraged to *network and collaborate* with such cities. In the Single European Act, Article 130A speaks of the need to promote 'economic and social cohesion, increase the impact of Community actions and help to make a reality of the social dimension of the Internal Market'. In the new Europe, great attention is urged towards upgrading *physical infrastructure* and *communications*. Yet, cities also have to invest more in their *human capital*. Encouragement is given to cities identifying a *flexible specialisation*, which distinguishes their global appeal. At the same time, they are warned to *avoid reliance on a few sectors*, which may be subject to rapid decline in the modern world economy. Getting the balance right in these goals also relates to where particular cities are located in the economic arena of Europe.

Northern Ireland's urban areas lie in what has been designated the Atlantic Arc of Europe. The context of this area is seen as one of 'under-employment in a dependent economy, despite the fact that its working population is younger than the Community average and some regions have a highly active Small-Medium Enterprise (SME) base'.[51] As things stand in this Arc, 'most of the forces contributing to development – population, finance, businesses, technology, cultural activities, transport and advanced telecommunications – will tend to be con-centrated in the larger cities (Dublin, Bristol, Rennes, Nantes, Bordeaux, Bilbao and Lisbon). By contrast, there is likely to be a progressive decline in many other areas, especially isolated small and medium-sized towns and old industrial areas.'[52]

This has to be seen in the light of the investment patterns *into* and *within* Europe. From the mid-1980s to the early 1990s, over 60 per cent of total direct investment into the EU was in services, illustrat-ing the globalisation of sectors such as retailing, wholesale distribution, banking, insurance, business and legal services. But the central regions of the EU have had a high share of this investment. This is partly because there is a greater presence of large cities in central regions supportive of high-level services. It is also due to the way central location remains an attractive site for head offices responsible for corporate strategic planning, and for distribution.[53]

One issue here for cities like Belfast, on 'the Atlantic Arc', is how far their improved transport networks into continental Europe and telecommunications infrastructure may help to reduce the signifi-cance of 'peripherality'. For instance, SMEs, which can play a pivotal role in modernising a city economy, can make useful cost savings by the application of efficient telecommunication. However, the use of new information networks varies among firms even within the same city region:[54]

> The firms most dependent on telecommunications are mainly large multi-branch enterprises in services, especially business services (consultancy and research) and those with large distribution networks or many sub-contractors. For example, in Northern Ireland, 80 per cent of firms and organisations with more than 500 employees use the British Telecom 'Kilostream' network while only 8 per cent of SMEs do so.

Good access to digital services which allow for high speed data transmission systems, alongside a financial sector responsive to industrial venture and innovation, and a research and technology development capacity are key goals of weaker city regions. But it is not essential, or indeed feasible, for such urban centres to pursue a major investment in advanced frontiering research. It is preferable that cities such as Belfast concentrate on building the capacity to absorb and creatively adapt new technologies through transfer.

In this respect, effective local development still demands the nurturing of *native* enterprise and know-how. The evidence rests in examples such as the Western Crescent around London, the Munich region, the south-west arc of Paris, and the San Francisco Bay Area – places which have fostered clusters of small-to-medium enterprises in growth sectors geared to *high-tech* knowledge-intensive industries such as biotechnology and telematics, or those places like the Third Italy geared to the *high-touch* sectors such as fashion and media, but which increasingly combine *high-touch* with *high-tech*, to avail of features such as computer-aided design.[55]

As far as possible networked together to provide mutual servicing, trading and sharing of ideas, such districts are seen to gain from the extra scale and scope which development corridors bring. And the whole approach puts a premium on *local human capital*, on underpinning regeneration effort with a culture of *learning* and *creativity*.

The US Experience 1950s–1990s

For three decades since 1945, urban policy in the USA focused on inner-city decay. Initiatives included the Urban Renewal Programs of the 1950s, the Model Cities Program of the 1960s,[56] and the 1974 Housing and Community Development Act. In the relative prosperity of the Eisenhower 1950s, frantic downtown renewal saw some 700 Central Business District plans published by 1957, attempting to reclaim retail and other activity, following the investment flight to the suburbs.[57]

A similarity of public and private sector interest saw alliances between corporate executives and leading politicians, often formally billed as growth coalitions. Certain private sector businesses – banks, law firms, newspapers – could not as easily join the rush to the suburbs. Beyond their economic attachment to downtown, they appreciated proximity to cultural and leisure facilities, and wished to amplify these as focal points to city life. While the property lobby's inducement towards this endeavour was evident, the pay-off for prominent politicians was equally seductive:[58]

promoting the downtown economy was just the latest expression of civic boosterism. Further, development plans for downtown fit into the time-honored tradition of using construction to generate political support ... still fresh in the memory from New Deal public works of the 1930s.

Highway developments and Urban Renewal encouraged the comprehensive reshaping of the US city with Federal funding at this time.[59] The 1960s urban unrest prompted Johnson's Great Society programme, which included the 1964 Economic Opportunity Act.[60] This channelled federal funds directly to local community action agencies, whose independent financial base facilitated their challenge to town hall development priorities, and helped to foster principles of equal opportunity and community participation. City government faced a dual crisis: simultaneous demands for improved services and for reduced taxes. Some viewed the scattered community insurgencies as:[61]

part of a larger dialectic between local government's attempt to solve a central city land value and revenue crisis, and its striving to manage the unanticipated, but nevertheless sharp, political consequences of the 'solution' chosen.

In other words, the tension between City Hall's promotion of political cohesion and its facilitation of central city development grew acute. Even as large-scale clearance abated, community demands for participation in planning mounted. Voices such as Jacobs characterised the renewal process as the 'sacking' rather than the 'rebuilding' of the city,[62] portraying it as destructive of the natural ambience galvanised by vibrant communities. The urban problem was being reconceptualised away from the plight of central business districts to that of deprived neighbourhoods.

In the 1970s, urban policy, still geared to relieving urban sprawl and congestion, offered subsidies for new suburban settlements as inducement for the partial dispersal of inner core populations. Ironically, this policy was soon compelled to face evidence that the growing problem was, in fact, the coincidence of urban economic and demographic decline. By the early 1970s, Nixon, keen to distance the presidency from these urban controversies, declared a New Federalism, involving greater decentralisation of Federal fund allocation to states and cities. Under the community development block grants, introduced in 1974, Federal money was reduced in total, and awarded on needs estimates, with the particular distributional decisions about that block left to the particular state/city.

Carter's administration witnessed new schemes, such as the Employment Initiative, which sought to co-ordinate Federal subsidies for local economic development. A new Urban Development Action Grant subsidised reclamation of decaying industrial and commercial spaces, and was designed to bridge project funding gaps where City Hall and private sector investment were jointly committed. A 1978 official report[63] outlined the President's approach:

> National urban policy must reflect a strong and effective partnership between the public and private sector. ... Federal, state and local funds, no matter how plentiful, will not be enough to solve our urban problems. The private sector must help. Only it can provide the capital needed for rebuilding and growing; only it can carry out the large-scale development programs necessary to provide healthy local economies.

These sentiments were attuned to the rising profile of public–private partnerships in urban renaissance.[64] In reality, they were merely acknowledging the endurable alliance among large corporations, real estate developers, building contractors, City Hall technocrats and politicians. As expressed by Mollenkopf:[65] 'Those with the largest stakes in land use have reciprocally found local government ... a bountiful vineyard in which to labor.' Despite its comprehensive ambition, Carter's urban strategy performed modestly,[66] confronting as it did a growing anti-tax movement; a declining political constituency in favour of large cities in general, and of resource targeting to the most distressed communities in particular; and inadequate state government involvement.[67] Many proposed new programmes never materialised,[68] for instance, the National Development Bank, designed to subsidise credit for distressed urban areas.

The Reagan years witnessed a reversal of the Carter faith in Federal intervention. Restoring responsibility and tax resources to states and localities assumed priority,[69] supported by accusations that previous programmes had not 'been effective in creating new jobs or capital investment'.[70] Under Reagan, effective urban policy was to be founded on a successful national economy.[71]

In place of Federal intervention, which corralled labour and capital in high-cost locations, efficiency-oriented markets would distribute gains to those cities embracing the challenge of deregulation, privatisation and decentralisation.[72] The main architect behind the new urban policy was explicit about this 'trickle down' agenda, even while conceding its limitations:[73]

although not all cities will benefit equally, and some may not benefit at all. Improving the economy is the single most important program the Federal government can take to help urban America.

The key elements of the new approach were clear from the President's National Urban Policy Report in 1982, which emphasised the need for localities to generate leadership, and to look to the private sector. As argued previously, macro socio-economic policies in the 1980s – in particular tax benefit changes and defence spending – had the most negative impact on urban centres in the Northern regions. Glickman, in a review of the spatial impact,[74] concluded that 'cuts in social programs and increases in military spending reveal a consistent pattern in which states and cities most in need (as measured by unemployment, fiscal stress, or bad housing) were hurt the most'. In short, revenue-deficient urban areas, already beleaguered by loss of their suburban tax bases, bore a disproportionate share of costs associated with these changes. This contention that Reaganomics, particularly its tax programme, provided further incentives for corporate investment shifts to growing regions finds detailed endorsement from Bluestone and Harrison.[75]

As the Fainsteins note:

had attainment of its budget goals not been blunted substantially by Congress, the administration would have gone far in destroying the capacity of the central government to subsidize business or to conduct even the weak regional planning efforts that characterize the US system.[76]

Legitimised under the rubric of Reagan's New Federalism, this transfer of Federal obligations to the states,[77] was designed to reduce Federal spending in general, and social spending in particular.[78] Between 1978 and 1986, as a share of local governments' own money, Federal aid plummeted from 26 per cent to 12 per cent for cities and from 19 per cent to 7 per cent for counties.[79] Curtis noted that between 1978, the high point of Federal support to cities, and 1988, when Bush assumed the Presidency, 'direct aid to cities decreased by nearly one-third'.[80] Acute repercussions for city/state budgets followed, including increased state dependence on regressive sales taxes, which in turn exposed their vulnerability in the depressed consumer conditions of the 1990–91 recession, when state funding support to distressed cities was further retrenched.

Faced with such fiscal hardship, urban government was expected to become more entrepreneurial and proactive in striking development deals with the private sector.[81] Promoting this option, the Presidential task force approved 'the shift from urban renewal bulldozer and anti-poverty campaigns of the '60s to limited, tightly negotiated urban development agreements between the public and private sectors in the early 1980s'.[82] Savas noted that under such policy pressure, urban mayors 'discovered *new localism*, that is, building coalitions with the private sector, aggressively seeking foreign investments, promoting technological advances, and otherwise enhancing their cities' competitive advantages'.[83]

In this regard, Eisinger identified the range of local development inducements in the USA.[84] On the supply-side, there are labour subsidies; tax abatements, increment financing and enterprise allowances; debt financing; industrial revenue bonds; site acquisition and preparation; infrastructural investment; favourable application of regulatory policy; and publicly funded boosterism. The demand-side package includes venture capital financing; provision of business incubators; and assistance in research and development. The supply-side logic is that cities seeking competitive edge in attraction of mobile firms have to trim production costs in the context of minimalist local government. But Eisinger observed a shift towards a demand-side emphasis, whereby city government is more proactive, and strategically plans its development on the basis of market and sectoral analysis.

Among the factors nudging this redirection are a recognition of the zero-sum game involved in all distressed cities auctioning their revenue base for incentives, which may only operate at the margin of locational decisions; the poor experience of North and Midwest cities, which tied their wagon to that star to compensate for the investment and jobs drain to the 'sunbelt' regions of South and West; the new focus on the capacity of indigenous firms to expand by targeting global markets; and the move from manufacturing to services, which has prompted attempts to amplify comparative advantages in promising sectoral niches.

But, whatever its rational appeal, this underrepresents political constraints on any particular city being first in the queue to bow out of the orthodox contest. So much kudos has been attached to those cities sending sympathetic business signals, that many are reluctant to dispose of the symbolic significance of supply-side efforts.[85]

Similarities Between UK and US Urban Policy

In the 1980s, there were many similarities in UK and US urban policy. One example was the use of Urban Development Grant (UDG), introduced in the UK in 1981 as a virtual replica of the US Urban Development Action Grant (UDAG).[86] Ironically, payments in the UK version are made under the Local Government Grants (Social Need) Act, 1969, even though they are explicitly designed to minimise commercial risk for developers. Herein lies the immediate question of 'substitution', that is whether public funds are donated to projects capable of generating them on the private market.

Given the speculative nature of many project appraisals – predicting volatility of land and building costs, availability of capital finance, rents, yields, letting periods, and such like – flawed assessment of grant qualifications can take easy refuge in data deficiencies. The paradox here is that such grant aid risks the subsidisation of inefficiency. Nor can this be avoided by reliance on leverage ratios since 'it is surely realistic to assume that the higher a project's leverage ratio, the more likely that public sector funds were not needed in the first place'![87]

In the USA, the Urban Development Action Grant was launched early in the Carter period, and was designed to foster mixed land uses – industrial, commercial and neighbourhood – which would strengthen the tax and employment base of distressed urban areas. The grant remained at the heart of US urban economic development for nearly a decade. But in 1981, the stipulation about balanced development was eased, and over the Reagan years, allocation of UDAGs shifted from Federally-defined needy areas in favour of criteria prioritising urban economic growth amidst enhanced inter-urban competition. This municipal agenda, which facilitated construction of downtown shopping malls, leisure and entertainment amenities, hotels and convention centres, faced muted political contest:[88]

downtowns have been targeted for revitalisation at the expense of inner city neighborhoods. At issue is a geographical dilemma: cores have been restructured for more affluent consumption to the neglect of low-income neighborhoods. ... Voicing low-income concerns in this milieu proved politically detrimental. It could erode community support in the form of newspaper endorsements, campaign contributions and voter allegiance.

By late 1988, at the end of the Reagan presidency, an official evaluation of UDAG was positive about its outcome: 2,976 projects in 1,202 communities involving total expenditure of $38.5 billion, representing a private–public leverage of 7 to 1, a much superior ratio than previous programmes such as urban renewal.[89] These projects were predicted to create over half a million jobs, 57 per cent of which were to be directed at low and moderate income persons. Less successful was the tax generated, only 57 per cent of what was anticipated.[90]

But an altogether less glowing programme appraisal challenged the figures, suggesting that some of the full-time jobs claimed were actually part-time; some of the jobs 'created' were actually jobs 'retained'; that there was imprecision in the targeting of lower-income groups; and that no distinction was attempted between jobs attributable to the subsidy and those which would have come without it.[91] In any case, the Reagan administration had reduced the programme's budget authority by two-thirds, from $675 million in 1980 to $216 million by 1988, in July of which year it was abolished. A series of factors conspired to this end: general inhibitions about Federal subsidies; a mounting Federal deficit; a belief that the revived downtowns of major cities rendered the grant redundant; and a scepticism on the part of Democrats that the programme was actually improving the lot of deprived populations.[92]

In the UK, the Thatcher administration deemed early efforts to prod Labour local authorities into applying UDGs as too hesitant and grudging, and in 1986 introduced the Urban Regeneration Grant, for which private developers could negotiate directly with central government. In 1988, the process of bypassing local administrations was extended further through the initiation of City Grants, which replaced both its predecessors.[93] In the same year a review of UDG was produced, showing that by 1986 approval had been given for 177 projects, involving £78 million of grant aid, and achieving a leverage ratio of 1:4.5. The balance of development was: commercial – £35 million; industrial – £26 million; and housing – £17.5 million. Of the 30,000 jobs associated with UDG projects, a third were additional jobs to those areas, and three-quarters of these were new to the whole economy.[94]

A comprehensive review in 1993,[95] taking Urban Development Grant, Urban Regeneration Grant and City Grant together, emphasised the demand-led nature of such support to the private sector, and related defects in targeting. Thus, the grant system did not seek to

Figure 7.1 Total Expenditure in Urban Programmes

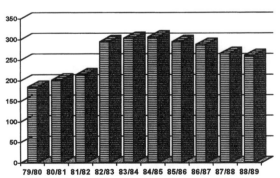

Source: National Audit Office (1990), 'Regenerating the Inner Cities', London.

influence developers regarding the type of development; source of employment; or particular location. This produced a very uneven spread of investment, with subsidy directed to sites offering optimal development gain rather than to those in greatest need, and with larger projects preferenced over smaller more imaginative ones. As Figure 7.1 illustrates, total expenditure on urban programmes decreased from the mid-1980s. At the same time, development grants and development corporations took a higher share of total spending.

In both the USA and the UK in the 1980s:

- national government funding to urban areas was reduced;
- planning was meant to be more accommodating to the priorities of investors and developers;
- property development sometimes became confused with economic development;
- the benefits of land use change in inner areas tended not to be primarily targeted to the residents;
- inter-urban and inter-regional competition for mobile capital was fostered, as part of signalling to each locale that self-reliance and promotion were paramount;
- manufacturing-dependent urban areas faltered further, while service-based ones relatively prospered;
- despite the anti-interventionist policy tone, certain schemes like enterprise zones in fact involved substantial market interference;
- and amidst the imperative to embrace entrepreneurial virtues, cities came under pressure to demote concerns about accountability and social redistribution.

In the 1990s, the US urban experience emphasised the following guidelines to a better policy:

- Choose programmes as social investments with clear rates of return – large-scale social programmes for the young have a good social payback.
- Define a consistent social contract between society and the recipients of government programmes – consistent, clear and realistic behaviour incentives should be attached to housing, welfare, job and community service programmes, incentives which are motivating rather than penal.
- Confront spatial segmentation – as long as cities are places of deep segregation by class, ethnic identity or income, they will be sites of social tension. This means encouraging mobility, making it easier for lower income people to move out to suburbs, while inducing the middle class to move back to the city.

- Recognise that all levels of the community and government have a contribution to make – some of the best programmes are those which begin with local neighbourhoods defining their priorities, and then collaborating with public authority to tailor provision to their own initiative.
- Human investment is critical – educational and cultural expectations for the deprived should be the same as for the advantaged.

US Urban Policy Now

The US Department of Housing and Urban Development (HUD) has set four principles to underpin policy: economic opportunity – extending enterprise and employment; sustainable community development – creating socially mixed neighbourhoods with balanced development in terms of affordable housing, cultural expression, safe streets, etc.; partnership – plans must come from a partnership process and be delivered by partnership structures; and a vision for change – being strategic, holistic, long term in perspective.

One key emphasis is that of education and skills enhancement as the means to improve productivity and competitive position. The choice is increasingly seen in terms of 'high skills or low wages'. Skills here are defined not merely in a narrow technical sense. Rather, there is recognition that in the new urban economy, social and communication skills, and capacity in problem solving and self-initiative are all critical.[96]

Urban Policy: What Way Forward?

Over the last 20 years, a number of features of British urban policy stand out:[97] the way local policy has been increasingly determined at central level; the failure to integrate such local initiatives into the full range of policy that bears on urban economies; the superimposition of a series of programmes on an existing set of statutory institutions, muddling rather than clarifying lines of responsibility; the policy priority changes, which militate against medium-term planning at local government level; the disproportionate administrative resources commanded by ad hoc and ultimately peripheral programmes; and the switch to a capital expenditure and economic emphasis to the relative marginalisation of revenue and social spending.

The Audit Commission is very clear that 'many of the regeneration success stories of the 1980s derived from, and were dependent upon, a buoyant property market which provided the stimulus and impetus for physical redevelopment.'[98] In this respect, once the property market waned, the main strands of urban policy also faltered. The UDCs had relied on generating sufficient income from land sales and property development leases\purchases to circulate for continuous rounds of redevelopment. City Grant, and its immediate predecessors, were also framed within assumptions about property yields. By the late 1980s, such reliance exposed these ventures to greater vulnerability. It was to be expected, then, that the DoE's 1990 document on regeneration, 'People in Cities',[99] demoted the role of physically reshaping the built environment, and promoted a focus on people and partnerships.

The most comprehensive evaluation of urban policy in England draws the following conclusions:[100]

- Economic gaps between the 57 Urban Priority Areas (UPAs) and non-UPAs narrowed in the 'boom' of the late 1980s. This relative improvement is significantly attributable to targeted urban spending.
- However, core localities in large conurbations have deteriorated both absolutely and relatively. Indeed, their predicament has extended across the heart of the largest cities. The improvement has come to smaller and peripheral districts, a pattern suggesting a more acute concentration of unemployment in the inner cores.
- While the attraction of private investment is seen as crucial, scepticism reigns about its long-term viability. Induced by incentives in property-focused projects, the private sector is not expected to continue its participation beyond the projects' life span. The long-term commitment of the private sector to the inner city remains in doubt.
- Public–private coalitions are key to regeneration. But their cementing is not assisted by macro-policy oscillation. Local authorities and communities need to be accorded a more pivotal role in securing partnerships. This implies more resources for city hall, and for community capacity-building, which taps the loyalty many deprived residents feel to place.
- Residents in areas that receive publicly-funded projects hold a more favourable prognosis for their communities compared to those in less assisted areas. Nevertheless, pessimism in distressed areas remains profound.
- Sustainable revitalisation demands policy coherence, which in turn depends upon a more strategic approach, that moves away from short-termism.
- *People* rather than *place* targeting is essential. But urban spending implies net positive discrimination. Evidence from some conurbations shows that the cuts in housing investment and rate support 'dwarfed' the gains from targeted urban funds.

- Linking development projects to the targeting of need has not been evident, a problem reinforced by a double bind: urban programme money has grown less as a share of total public spending, and within the urban programme, capital projects have been privileged over revenue ones.

In general, the authors note 'that infrastructural schemes may have had an impact on areas, especially those with commercial potential such as waterfront areas or areas close to the Central Business District, but that the residents themselves see little direct or indirect economic benefit from most of them'.[101] Some go further and argue that for much of the 1980s, urban policy focused on areas of economic potential to the comparative neglect of the poorest localities.[102] Promoted on the basis that private sector projects needed greater deregulation of planning, it neglected the fact that:[103]

where the stakes are particularly high ... the development lobby is advocating more, rather than less, government guidance to local planning authorities and the development control process, in order to minimise development risk.

Notes

1. Molle, W. (1996), 'Regional Development and Changing Location Factors', in European Commission, *Development Perspectives for the Wider European Territory*, Brussels.
2. DoE (1988), 'Action for Cities', HMSO, London. A 1989 Audit Commission report broadly endorsed claims by local government that its economic development role was being undervalued. In the same year, the DoE document 'Progress on Cities' did show some appreciation of this role, and the 1989 Local Government and Housing Act facilitated city council local economic development.
3. Nevin, B. and Shiner P. (November 1995), 'The Left, Urban Policy and Community Empowerment: The First Steps Towards a New Framework for Urban Regeneration', *Local Economy*, Vol. 10, No. 3, p. 207.
4. Department of the Environment (DoE) (1992), 'City Challenge Bidding Guidance 1993–94', HMSO, London.
5. De Groot, L. (1992), 'City Challenge: Competing in the Urban Regeneration Game', *Local Economy*, Vol. 7, pp. 196–209.
6. For this chapter, several City Challenge submissions have been reviewed. While they may lack innovative capacity, their attempt to establish baseline data, targeting and stage-posting is

impressive, e.g. Dearne Valley Partnership (31 January 1992), 'Strategy into Action: A City Challenge Action Plan for the Dearne Valley'; and Nottingham City (1992), 'City Challenge Action Plan', prepared with support from Cooper Simms Associates.

7. Atkinson, R. and Moon, G. (1994), *Urban Policy in Britain: The City, the State and the Market*, Macmillan, London, p. 125.
8. Oatley, N. and Lambert, C. (1995), 'Evaluating Competitive Urban Policy: The City Challenge Initiative', in Hambleton, R. and Thomas, H. (eds), *Urban Policy Evaluation: Challenge and Change*, Paul Chapman, London, p. 155.
9. Bentley, G. (1992), 'The Real City Challenge', *Local Work*, No. 34, pp. 1–5, 7, quoted in Atkinson, R.and Moon, G. (1994), *Urban Policy in Britain*.
10. Oatley, N. and Lambert, C. (1995), 'Evaluating Competitive Urban Policy: The City Challenge Initiative'.
11. Department of the Environment (1991), 'City Challenge Government Guidance: A New Approach for the Inner Cities', HMSO, London, p. 9.
12. Stoker, G. and Young, S. (1993), *Cities in the 1990s*, Longman, Harlow, p. 173.
13. The Community Development Foundation (1992), *Mind the Gap: The Community in City Challenge, An Analysis of City Challenge Bids 1992*, CDF, London.
14. Liverpool City Challenge (1995), 'City Centre East: The Transformation Continues', *Action Plan 1995/96*, Liverpool.
15. Hambleton, R. and Thomas, H. (eds) (1995), *Urban Policy Evaluation: Challenge and Change*, Paul Chapman, London.
16. *Employment Gazette* (December 1993), Employment Department, p. 535.
17. Government Offices for the Regions (1994), 'Bidding Guidance: A Guide to Funding from the Single Regeneration Budget', HMSO, London, p. 4.
18. Department of the Environment (January 1994), 'Bidding Guidance: A Guide to Funding under the Single Regeneration Budget', DoE, London.
19. Sir George Young, quoted in Economic Policy Team of National Council for Voluntary Organisations (1994), 'The Single Regeneration Budget: Handbook for the Community/Voluntary Sectors: the Urban Forum', p. 14.
20. Nevin, B. and Shiner, P. (January 1995), 'The Single Regeneration Budget: Urban Funding and the Future for Distressed Communities', *Local Work*, No. 58, p. 7; the authors emphasise how 'targeting expenditure on distressed metropolitan and urban areas is being reduced progressively at the same

time as all authorities are affected by other large reductions in mainstream programmes which underpin urban regeneration initiatives'.

21. House of Commons Environment Committee (November 1995), 'Single Regeneration Budget' Vols I and II, Paper 26, HMSO, London.

22. BURA, 'Gummer Announces 170 Winners of SRB Round 2', *Cities Management: The Urban Development Journal*, February–March 1996.

23. Stewart, M. (1995), 'Public Expenditure Management in Urban Regeneration', in Hambleton, R. and Thomas, H. (eds), *Urban Policy Evaluation: Challenge and Change*, Paul Chapman Publishing, London.

24. Thake, S. and Staubach, R. (November 1993), *Investing in People: Rescuing Communities from the Margin*, Joseph Rowntree Foundation, York; their proposal is a UK-wide network of 200 Community Enterprise Zones (CEZs), designed to support and link locally-managed Community Enterprise Agencies, co-ordinated at government level by a Community Enterprise Corporation, responsible for recommending CEZ status, registering CEAs and assessing their capital and revenue bids.

25. Gaffikin, F. (March 1994), 'Truth Trickles Up: Inner-City Regeneration', *Fortnight*, pp. 26–7.

26. Commission for Social Justice (1994), *Social Justice: Strategies for National Renewal*, Vintage, London.

27. Centre for Local Economic Strategies (1992), *Social Regeneration: Directions of Urban Policy in the 1990s*, CLES, Manchester; and Centre for Local Economic Strategies (1994), *Rethinking Urban Policy: City Strategies for the Global Economy*, CLES, Manchester.

28. Association of Metropolitan Authorities (1994), *Urban Policy: The Challenge and the Opportunity*, AMA, London.

29. Labour Planning and Environment Group (June 1994), *Empowering Urban Communities: The Argument for Urban Regeneration that Starts with the People Most Affected by Urban Change*, London, p. 1.

30. City 2020 (1994) *Cities for the Future: A New Urban Policy*, City 2020, London, p. 13.

31. The Scottish Office (1988), 'New Life for Urban Scotland', Edinburgh; the orthodox assumption that 'economic development comes from profitable businesses which provide jobs'; and the 'passive' request from government to business: 'the government look to the private sector to continue to regenerate urban areas by pursuing opportunities for profitable investment, and hope it will examine carefully the scope for investment in areas currently neglected' (p. 11).

32. Ibid. Among many references to partnership, it also says: 'most importantly, plans for the regeneration of problem areas must have the full understanding, involvement and commitment of the local community' (p. 8).

33. Ibid.; 'the main goal of the Partnerships and other similar initiatives will have been achieved when people themselves begin to regard the areas as good places in which to live and bring up their families' (p. 7).

34. Ibid. For instance, in relation to the Castlemilk area, it avows: 'On the economic front, the Partnership target is to reduce unemployment and increase incomes, so that levels of economic prosperity in Castlemilk correspond to at least the Glasgow average' (p. 9).

35. Correspondence between the authors and the Urban Renewal Unit, Industry Department, the Scottish Office, Edinburgh, on 19 January 1994.

36. Scottish Office (1990), 'Urban Scotland into the 90s: New Life – Two Years On', Edinburgh; 'an important recent initiative enables representatives of the community to participate directly with the Scottish Office and the local authorities in final decisions about the allocation of Urban Programme finance to projects within defined areas, on the basis of dedicated budgets' (p. 5).

37. Scottish Office, 'Urban Scotland into the 90s: New Life – Two Years On', p. 7.

38. Tsoukalis, L. (1993) *The New European Economy: The Politics and Economics of Integration*, Oxford University Press, Oxford.

39. CEC (1994), 'Community Initiatives Concerning Urban Areas (URBAN)', COM (94) 61/Final/2, CEC, Brussels.

40. European Commission (1996), 'The Structural Funds in 1994: Sixth Annual Report', EC, Brussels, p. 119.

41. Chapman, M. (1995), 'Urban Policy and Urban Evaluation : The Impact of the European Union', in Hambleton, R. and Thomas, H. (eds), *Urban Policy Evaluation: Challenge and Change*, Paul Chapman, London, p. 79.

42. European Commission (1996), 'The Structural Funds in 1994: Sixth Annual Report', Brussels, p. 1.

43. European Commission (1994), 'Europe 2000+ Co-operation for European Territorial Development', Luxembourg, p. 97.

44. European Commission (1994), 'Competitiveness and Cohesion: Trends in the Regions', Brussels.

45. Brunt, B. (1990), *Western Europe: A Social and Economic Geography*, Gill and Macmillan, Dublin; 'These axes of urban development are closely associated with the principal trade routes of Europe (the Rhine Valley, Alpine passes and the east–west lowland route called the Hellweg) ... Advantages for urban

growth have been so great around the intersection of the two axes that *polycentred* urban regions have emerged' (p. 262).

46. Parkinson, M. (1995), 'The European Urban System: Trends and Developments', in Council of Europe/European Commission, (1992), 'Urbanisation and the Functions of Cities in the European Community', Centre for Urban Studies, Liverpool John Moores University.

47. European Commission (1994), 'Competitiveness and Cohesion: Trends in the Regions', Brussels.

48. Ibid., p. 43.

49. Audit Commission (February 1991), 'Urban Regeneration and Economic Development: the European Community Dimension', HMSO, London.

50. European Commission (1992), 'Towards a Europe of Solidarity: Intensifying the Fight Against Social Exclusion, Fostering Integration', Brussels.

51. European Commission Directorate-General for Regional Policies (1995), 'Regional Planning for the Year 2000', 14.04. 1995 EN.

52. European Commission (1994), 'Europe 2000+ Co-operation for European Territorial Development', Luxembourg.

53. Ibid.

54. Ibid., p. 59.

55. Hall, P. (1995), 'Toward a General Urban Theory', in Brothchie, J. et al. (eds), *Cities in Competition: Productive and Sustainable Cities for the 21st century*, Longman, Melbourne.

56. Higgins, J. (1978), *The Poverty Business*, Blackwell, Oxford; and Marris, P. and Rein, M. (1973), *Dilemmas of Social Reform: Poverty and Action in the United States*, Aldine, Chicago.

57. Frieden, B. and Sagalyn, L. (1989), *Downtown Inc.: How America Rebuilds Cities*, MIT Press, Cambridge, Massachusetts. Fearing a massive drain on their treasuries, city halls fought back with comprehensive redevelopment proposals. Local administrations in the late 1950s generated over two-thirds of their own revenue, with property taxes alone constituting half the total. The biggest contributor was the central business district, typically accounting for a quarter or more of city hall funds.

58. Ibid., p. 19.

59. US National Commission on Urban Problems, (1968), 'Building the American City: Report to the Congress and the President of the United States', Government Printing Office, Washington, DC, p. 154; it allowed urban authorities to demolish poor housing with no automatic responsibility to re-house the poor. Together with the highway programme, it provided an opportunity to displace lower income communities, substitute

offices and retailing, thereby extending the central business district. By the late 1960s, approximately two-thirds of urban renewal funds had gone to projects in or near downtown. Ironically, though small enterprise would later be projected as the engine of urban regeneration, many small businesses fell victim to bulldozers in this process. Of course, in such comprehensive clearance policies, superficial cost–benefit analysis can represent the dislocation of poor areas as the most economical solution.

60. Piven, F. and Cloward, R. (1972), *Regulating the Poor*, Pantheon, New York.
61. Mollenkopf, J.H. (1975), 'The Post-War Politics of Urban Development', *Politics and Society*, Vol. 5, p. 249.
62. Jacobs, J. (1961), *The Death and Life of Great American Cities*, Random House, New York.
63. Department of Housing and Urban Development (1978), 'National Urban Policy: Report to the President', HUD, Washington, DC, p. 121.
64. Schaefer, W.D. (1979), 'Public–Private Partnership: Views and its Future', in National League of Cities, *City Economic Development*, Washington, DC.
65. Mollenkopf, J.H., (1975), 'The Post-War Politics of Urban Development' p. 255.
66. James, F. (1990), 'President Carter's Comprehensive National Urban Policy: Achievements and Lessons Learned', *Environment and Planning C: Government and Policy*, 8, pp. 29–40.
67. US Housing and Urban Development (HUD) (1982), 'The States and Distressed Communities: The 1982 Report', US Government Printing Office, Washington, DC.
68. US Housing and Urban Development (HUD) (1980), 'The President's National Urban Policy Report', US Government Printing Office, Washington, DC.
69. US Housing and Urban Development (HUD), (1982), 'The President's National Urban Policy Report: 1982', US Government Printing Office, Washington, DC.
70. United States Office of Management and Budget (OMB) (1981), 'Program for a New Economic Recovery', US Government Printing Office, Washington, DC.
71. US Housing and Urban Development (HUD) (1982), 'The President's National Urban Policy Report: 1982'.
72. Levine, M. (1983), 'The Reagan Urban Policy: Efficient National Economic Growth and Public Sector Minimisation', *Journal of Urban Affairs*, Vol. 5, pp. 17–28.
73. Savas, E.S. (1983), 'A Positive Urban Policy for the Future', *Urban Affairs Quarterly*, Vol. 18, p. 447.

74. Glickman, N. (1984), 'Economic Policy and the Cities: In Search of Reagan's Real Urban Policy', *American Planning Association Journal*, Autumn, p. 473.

75. Bluestone, B. and Harrison, B. (1982), *The Deindustrialisation of America: Plant Closings, Community Abandonment, and the Dismantling of Basic Industry*, Basic Books, New York.

76. Fainstein, S. and Fainstein, N. (1989), 'The Ambivalent State: Economic Development Policy in the US Federal System Under the Reagan Administration', *Urban Affairs Quarterly*, Vol. 25, pp. 41–62, p. 50.

77. Peterson, G.E. (1984), 'Federalism and the States: An Experiment in Decentralization', in Palmer, J.L. and Sawhill, I. (eds), *The Reagan Record: An Assessment of America's Changing Priorities*, Ballinger, Cambridge.

78. Clark, C. and Clark, J. (1992), 'Federal Aid to Local Government in the West: An Irony of the Reagan Revolution', *Policy Studies Review*, Spring, II, 1.

79. Advisory Committee on Intergovernmental Relations (1989), 'Significant Features of Fiscal Federalism', 1989 edition, US Government Printing Office, Washington, DC.

80. Curtis, L. (1995), *The State of Families: Family, Employment and Reconstruction, Policy Based on What Works*, Families International Inc. in association with Family Service America, Inc., Wisconsin, p. 21.

81. Leitner, H. (April 1990), 'Cities in Pursuit of Economic Growth: The Local State as Entrepreneur', *Political Geography Quarterly*, Vol. 9, No. 2, pp. 146–70; Leitner, speaking of the US context, remarks that 'the local state has moved beyond its traditional activities of land-use control and planning and the provision of public services to become a major player in urban land development ... [involving] a tendency to mobilise resources locally rather than relying on state and federal resources; a significant intervention by the local state into the capital market, in particular through the extensive issuance of industrial revenue bonds; the frequent use of quasi-public development agencies rather than city agencies to administer development projects; increased reliance on public–private partnerships and joint public–private ventures; and an assumption by the local state of a higher degree of risk as a part of its involvement in local property development' (pp. 147, 148, 149).

82. US President, Task Force on Private Initiatives (1983), 'Investing in America', US Government Printing Office, Washington, DC, p. 7.

83. Savas, E.S. (1986), 'Commentary on Urban Policy', in Clark, T.N. (ed.), *Research in Urban Policy: A Research Annual, Managing Cities*, Vol. 2, 1986, Part B, p. 140.

84. Eisinger, P.K. (1988), *The Rise of the Entrepreneurial State*, University of Wisconsin Press, Madison.

85. Wolman, H. (1988), 'Local Economic Development Policy: What Explains the Divergence Between Policy Analysis and Political Behavior?', *Journal of Urban Affairs*, Vol. 10, pp. 19–28.

86. Parkinson, M. (1989), 'The Thatcher Government's Urban Policy, 1979–1989', *Town Planning Review*, Vol. 60, pp. 421–40.

87. Alderton, R. (December 1984), 'Urban Development Grants: Lessons from America', *The Planner*, p. 20.

88. Wilson, D. (1989), 'Community Development Block Grants, Politics and Local Development', *The East Lakes Geographer*, Vol. 24, p. 141; see also by the same author (1989), 'Towards a Revised Urban Managerialism: Local Managers and Community Development Block Grants', *Urban Affairs Quarterly*, Vol. 8, pp. 21–41.

89. US Department of Housing and Urban Development (HUD), Office of Program Analysis and Evaluation (1988), 'Consolidated Annual Report to Congress on Community Development Programs' (CDBG, UDAG, Rental Rehabilitation, Section 312, Urban Homesteading), GPO, Washington, DC.

90. US Department of Housing and Urban Development (HUD), Office of Program Analysis and Evaluation (1989), '1989 Annual Report to Congress on Community Development Programs', HUD, Washington, DC.

91. Center for Community Change (1988), 'Bright Promises, Questionable Results: An Examination of How Well Three Government Subsidy Programs Created Jobs', Washington, DC, referenced in Barnekov, T. and Hart, D. (1993), 'The Changing Nature of US Urban Policy Evaluation: The Case of the Urban Development Action Grant', *Urban Studies*, Vol. 30, No. 9, pp. 1469–83.

92. Barnekov, T. and Hart, D. (1993), 'The Changing Nature of US Urban Policy Evaluation: The Case of the Urban Development Action Grant'.

93. Parkinson, M. (1989), 'The Thatcher Government's Urban Policy, 1979–1989'.

94. Department of the Environment (1988), 'An Evaluation of the Urban Development Grant System', Inner Cities Directorate, HMSO, London.

95. Price Waterhouse (1993), 'Evaluation of Urban Development Grant, Urban Regeneration Grant, and City Grant', Inner City

Research Programme, Department of the Environment, HMSO, London.

96. National Center on Education and the Economy (1995), *America's Choice: High Skills or Low Wages*, NCEE, New York.

97. Parkinson, M.H. and Wilks, S.R. (February 1985), 'Testing Partnership to Destruction in Liverpool', *Regional Studies*, Vol. 19, No. 1, p. 66.

98. Audit Commission (October 1991), 'The Urban Regeneration Experience – Observations from Local Value for Money Audits', Occasional Papers, HMSO, London, p. 14.

99. Department of the Environment (DoE) (1990), 'People in Cities', HMSO, London.

100. Robson, B. et al. (1994), 'Assessing the Impact of Urban Policy', Department of the Environment, HMSO, London. They arrived at their conclusions 'through an exhaustive process of collecting and analysing data on financial outputs and socio-economic outcomes across a large sample of authorities, of discussing issues with experts who have influenced or determined policy and with those residents and employers affected by it' (p. 55).

101. Ibid., p. 54.

102. Moore, C. and Booth, S. (1986), 'Urban Policy Contradictions: The Market Versus Redistributive Approaches', *Policy and Politics*, Vol. 14, No. 3, pp. 361–87.

103. Morley, S., Marsh, C., McIntosh, A. and Martinos, H. (1989), *Industrial and Business Space Development: Implementation and Urban Renewal*, E&FN Spon, London.

8 The Role of Culture in Remaking Cities

Charles Landry

The 'Comedia view' on cities is derived from a particular perspective. This is less focused on hard infrastructure like roads and sewers, important as they are. Rather, the concern is with soft infrastructure:

- what makes people tick and motivated to change?
- what processes create change?
- what organisational mechanisms match such processes?

Especially we highlight the cultural dimension, broadly defined (anthropologically) as the way of life of a city. This approach is not just a narrow focus on the arts, although they are one important expression of a city's culture.[1]

> Historically, creativity has been the lifeblood of the city. Cities have always needed creativity to work as markets, trading and production centres with their critical mass of entrepreneurs, artists, intellectuals, students, administrators, and power-brokers ... they have been the places which allow people to live out their ideas, needs, aspirations, dreams, projects, conflicts, memories, anxieties, loves, passions, obsessions and fears.

It is often forgotten that culture may hold things together or tear it apart. Understanding its subtleties better may teach us where we come from, who we are and where we might be going to as cities. It shapes our identity, our sense of place, which is why it is so important to control. Culture provides the texture, the sinews and the nervous system of a city. It is in the cultural arena – although economics and social issues are important – that the battles of the future will be fought. It explains so many urban trends and counter-trends.

In a world of media images, cities are combinations of realities – lived experiences – making the cultural perspective especially relevant. Cities even have collective psychologies, and when they work well, one

151

might say the city has a good 'soul'. Indeed, one notices looking at cities in this way that some seem to say 'yes'. They feel approachable, accessible and open, while other cities seem to say 'no' – see Doncaster or even New Orleans. They are frightening, daunting and restrictive. This may sound simplistic, yet it is possible to read cities in this way. Thus, a cultural perspective needs to move centre stage in the planning of our cities. Interestingly the more mobility there is, the greater the discourse about culture and place, because of the threat of losing out to standardised, mid-Atlantic mono-culture.

Comedia has worked in large and small cities, rich and poor, in the UK and abroad, East and West, Northern hemisphere and Southern, all of which are restructuring. We have worked with traditional decision makers and those at the receiving end of those decisions. We have focused on the idea of the creative city and how one establishes a creative innovative milieu, so cities can reinvent themselves. We have concluded that this should be the key focus for the future. We also focused on public institutions and how they can contribute to overcoming urban problems. These are 'the anchors of the civic', who in a world where the relation between the public and private is wrongly skewed, have usually been marginalised. For example, we have assessed the role of the public library in *Borrowed Time – The Future of Public Libraries*, crucially important in a society where access to knowledge is a pre-condition for the informed and competent citizen. Or the role of parks in *Parklife – Urban Parks and Social Renewal* or *The Other Invisible Hand – Remaking Charity for the 21st Century*, even on the role of cemeteries.

These are all institutions that can bring people together in a neutral space. The city is an amalgam of such public organisations and the people who work in them as well as, of course, private organisations. The conclusion of this work is that planning needs to be rethought in twenty-first-century terms.

The Interlocking Crises of Cities

Importantly, cities suffer from a set of interlocking crises. These concern:

- Politics, especially when the anchors of the civic are under threat and when the idea of the town hall, governance and democracy has not yet been reinvented to address the needs of the various stakeholders that want a share in decision-making. Indeed, there are many social innovations which may make the city more bearable, yet the idea of social innovation has not yet been given the same status as technological innovations.
- Cash – there is a declining tax base to fund urban infrastructures – all over the world tax rates are going down rather than up. This

is why the notion of partnership and strategic alliances for public sector institutions are so important.

- Commitment – when the private sector is no longer committed to place in its constant search for new markets and cheaper production facilities globally and where little is put back to generate what used to be called civic pride.
- The problem of sameness and homogeneity and monopolisation, especially in the high street. I once counted the shops in Oxford's high street, a city whose image is different, unique and diverse. The result – 87 shops; 78 of which were well known multiples – McDonald's, Benetton, etc.
- The crisis of dispersal when shopping, leisure and even education continually moves to the edge of the city. Thus the heart of our cities can be anywhere rather than as traditionally the city centre.
- In turn, this creates a crisis of community when the sources of community – immobility, social homogeneity and close networks – are no longer there.
- Instead we have ghettoisation and the increasing impacts of a divided city, where the idea of the fortress city is re-emerging as in the Middle Ages as a jointly owned public realm declines.
- This creates also a problem of social cohesion and social fragmentation, which makes it difficult to see what we share rather than what divides us.
- Most importantly, the capacity of the city to compete economically in the international arena is substantially eroded.

And of course there are other problems like the bedrock of unemployment, which is proving difficult to ameliorate. There remains a contradiction between the continual shift to the global and the fact that many of the solutions need to be local. Strategies need to be locally derived yet internationally oriented. This, in turn, creates a problem of place when everywhere seems like nowhere. It also creates a problem of the public sphere, when every move one makes has to be paid for. You can't, for example, just sit in a shopping mall and have your own sandwich, you need to buy one from the food hall. Thus we are losing free spaces where incidental encounters may occur. This is why libraries and other kinds of public institutions to which people can have access and within which they can casually interact are increasingly important.

All such developments generate a crisis of planning. The key dilemma is how to combine public purpose and the private interest, and how to frame order within chaos and chaos within order.

But there are also other trends that affect urban dwellers, with which institutions, structures and processes have not kept up. These include:

- the shift from formality to informality, which can be seen in many spheres from leisure, education to work. Indeed the University of the Third Age is one of the fastest growing organisations in the UK and it is a form of informal education;
- the shift from hierarchy to flatter structures in business, the voluntary and public sectors;
- the move towards self-reliance and independence, which can be seen in the desire for people to do for themselves rather than it being done for them. This can be witnessed in everything from self-help groups in health and related areas to tenants' control and is obviously a challenge to the professionals, particularly in the public sector;
- the fact that in Western countries we increasingly live and work in a 'knowledge economy' where what we know is as important in creating value-added as, in former times, what we produced. This means turning data, information into knowledge, wisdom and judgement;
- this in turn highlights the need to think of ourselves as living in a lifelong learning society, where we have to relearn what we know quite frequently.

Cities Cannot Think in Nineteenth-Century Forms about Twenty-first-Century Contexts

We cannot think and act in boxes, as all problems are interrelated. What are the implications of focusing simply on box-like thinking? The major one is that it becomes difficult to grasp the essentials, to see the all-pervading contradictions that govern our lives or even to ask the right questions or to harness our potential by seeing the synergies. And let us not forget that if we cast our minds back 200 years that what we now call the separate disciplines of the arts, economics, science and the social disciplines were seen more as one.

However, the separation of knowledge has moved apace so that we can't even talk to each other as there is no common language. And when the capacity to communicate goes and when words lose their meaning, we know something is wrong. This is why partnerships, essentially getting different types of people into the same room, are so important.

Accordingly, it is possible to sketch out some tentative conclusions about urban development. First, successful cities have a strategic focus and have a common, widespread understanding of the dynamics of urban change, where cities are going and where they realistically fit in. This determines their margins of manoeuvre. Second, they develop an overarching picture of where they want to go – their vision.

They imagine forwards and plan backwards, they do not simply extrapolate trends. Urban history shows there are paradigm shifts and if one treats the trend as a friend, one may become irrelevant. Remember cities, like people, die too, albeit slowly. By planning backwards, one is forced to focus on obstacles. That becomes the focus of urban planning. Third, there is as much creativity in having ideas as implementing them. Fourth, a vision implies ultimately joint agenda setting. City planners have:[2]

> paid new attention to expanding economic sectors like leisure, tourism, the media and other cultural industries including fashion and design, in an attempt to compensate for jobs lost in traditional industrial sectors. A lively, cosmopolitan cultural life was increasingly seen as a crucial ingredient of city marketing and internationalisation strategies designed to attract mobile international capital and specialised personnel, particularly in high-tech industrial and advanced services sectors.

Note the differences between these processes and co-option where representatives are chosen, but have no real input or power and where tasks are assigned, with incentives, but outsiders decide the agenda and direct the process. This is related to a form of consultation where local opinions are asked for, outsiders analyse and decide on a course of action or collaboration where local people work with outsiders to determine priorities; responsibility, however, remains with outsiders for directing the process.

To make visions happen, cities need to move up the scale to co-learning and collective action. Co-learning occurs where local people and outsiders share their knowledge to create a new understanding and work together to form action plans, with outside facilitation. With collective action local people set their own agenda and mobilise to carry it out, using outsiders not as initiators/facilitators but as required by local people.

The Sources of Visioning

As so many of the innovative techniques used by business and government, visioning has come from the alternative movement, often initially marginalized. A key figure was Kurt Lewin, a social psychologist who directly and indirectly inspired nearly everyone concerned with organisational change. He believed both in the innate capacity of individuals to offer something to the world and that their capacity to do so was affected by how they operated in groups. He set up the

National Training Laboratories and, by the 1950s, T-Groups operating widely with companies and successfully on organisational change.

Then Ron Lippitz developed 'therapy for normals' and trainers began collaborating on a wide range of exercises, games and workshop formats – encounter groups, truth sessions, etc. When consulting with YMCA in Michigan, Lippitz developed the idea of a preferred vision. He asked groups to brainstorm a list of problems they faced. As the list became longer, the vigour in the room deflated, people blamed each other and grew despondent. So he started asking people to imagine a picture of the future they preferred: 'Let's say in twenty years from now, and you're flying over this region in a helicopter. What do you see down there?'

The more detailed and sincere people were in envisioning a desired future, the more energised and excited they felt. Suddenly, they began coming up with mutual solutions to problems that had seemed insoluble before. All of the corporate and city 'vision' and 'mission setting' consulting of the 1980s descended from this practice. Many people in T-Groups had been teachers, academics, social workers and church group members.

Scenario planning (a second key plank) started seriously via Shell. Ted Newlands knew that the future would change, but could never convince the top bosses to adopt appropriate policies. He knew he would have to find a way of making the future seem visible. Having searched around, he found Hermann Kahn of the Hudson Group who specialised in future stories. Kahn had begun to 'think the unthinkable' in the 1940s working for RAND, which was set up to employ physicists, mathematicians and policy analysts to research new forms of weapons technology. Essentially, they engaged in war games. The basic principle was to cloister people up for a week and let them come up with a scenario. The concept of the 'Word' was suggested by Leo Rosten of 'The Education of Hyman Kaplan' fame who walked into a meeting of physicists wanting to find an alternative description of how satellites might work. The point of the exercise was not rigorous forecasting, but to come up with mythic story that drove the point home.

By the mid-1960s Kahn had left RAND, bored with military scenarios and wanted to look at the economy and culture. He got an assignment from the Academy of Arts and Sciences to look at year 2000. Indeed, he predicted that communism would collapse in 20 years. He called his exercise the 'surprise free' future – at least no surprise to him. Kahn himself was a mythic figure, 300 pounds of relentless energy, striding through airports with two plastic bags full of books, harried assistants trying to keep up. Striding around stages, cracking jokes, sweating; charming audiences who could feel their place in grand history and cosmic time frames. Loose with facts, but photographic memory.

Shell began to take this up, predicting in one scenario the consequences arising out of the oil shocks, and have continued and refined the process ever since. This has become part of the strategic planning repertoire in public and private sector, as has the Europe + 30 project in the early 1970s for the EC – although perhaps the only true prediction was for the necessity of lifelong learning.

Good examples of visioning come from three different types of city:

- Potentially successful ones, for example, Barcelona or Frankfurt. These are opportunity takers, often focused on cultural vision. What are the underlying drivers for their success? Primarily it was economic opportunity, e.g. available finance capital in Europe; the economic impact of the Olympics and, significantly, the cultural independence of Catalonia – a real unifier providing the confidence to make the transition. The long-term objective is to stay ahead of the game;
- Crisis-ridden cities like Baltimore, Pittsburgh, Cleveland and even Detroit, where a key component is the racial divide, where essentially a moral argument about human equality has had some force. In these, part of the restructuring process has been to shift from manufacturing to services;
- New opportunity cities such as emerging gateways like Helsinki with the core idea of ending the tyranny of distance through new technology uses or Vienna as a gateway, making itself part of the East.

Five Models of Visioning

The comments on visioning have benefited greatly from the work of Bob McNulty from Partners for Liveable Communities in Washington.

The first is the 'charismatic leader led' model where a key political figure mobilises the population in creating the future. A good example is Montpellier, although it should be recognised that this model has good and bad features. It succeeds in creating a dynamic for change, but one that is essentially top-down rather than bottom-up.

The second is the 'strategic local authority' led model. This has been typical of Glasgow leveraging money from the Scottish Development Agency and the Glasgow Development Agency. The central objective has been to establish a 'creative milieu' capable of driving innovation and development.

The business model is essentially about 'boosterism' (upgrading the city's image) or creating coalitions for growth. Pittsburgh was characterised by this approach from the 1940s onwards. The Allegheny Conference was concerned initially with air and water. Then, the

Urban Renewal Authority rebuilt the 'golden triangle' going through a number of stages and is now into social renewal; in the 1950s, Baltimore launched the Charles River Center office development, then the inner harbour development. Later, there was considerable focus on the arts. Baltimore presented itself as a partnership.

Fourth, there is the community-led model as evidenced in Stroud or Greater Rochester. This occurs where disparate community organisations come together to generate a composite vision for their areas and neighbourhoods.

Finally, there is the partnership-led model as can be seen in Adelaide or Denver or Chattanooga. In these instances, partnership can be seen as a new form of democracy with real joint agenda setting. A variety of techniques are employed, but whatever the means, it has to be jointly owned if partnership is to be fully functional.

Do any of these models apply to Belfast? The following are 'outsider' comments. They are not based on detailed, insider knowledge and are thus largely in the form of questions. Belfast is a crisis-ridden city, the primary location of a 30-year conflict and divided by religion, class and politics. Nevertheless, it can grasp the emerging opportunities of peace and the capacity to seize a niche in the new 'global village' economy. The fact that the organisational structure of Northern Ireland is in flux provides an opportunity to reinvent democracy. Equally, there is a font of goodwill waiting to be unleashed and, in relative terms, far more public sector resources per head than in other UK cities.

However, the central challenge will be to bridge the political/religious divide. What type of argument, opportunity, threat, challenge or crisis can be engendered to lift debate and implementation on to a new plane? Examples of doing so in the United States have been triggered ultimately by a moral argument about racial disadvantage. The religious divide in Northern Ireland appears to operate on a different dimension where there is no moral consensus about the causes and consequences of disadvantage. What are the comparative examples? – Beirut, Jerusalem or Sarajevo. All of these have been based on an ethnic/religious divide. The latter two are also like Northern Ireland in that one group of the protagonists sees the creation of a separate state as the only resolution of the conflict. Can they teach any lessons? First, Belfast needs a visceral and deep-seated belief that these should not be the role models. Perhaps Belfast needs a Millennium project on rethinking religion, or a world centre for comparative religion. Belfast could be the centre of a new network where divided cities meet.

The divided population of Belfast has to ask itself this question – Can one ever like (not necessarily love) the other side? How can one conciliate, let alone reconciliate, if the parties have never liked each other? Liking is a precondition for listening and listening a precondition for trust. The key point in city visioning is that it can never be sectional.

It has to be remembered that cities die as well as succeed. The factors that cushioned cities that failed to seize new opportunities for change like long-term public subsidy are decreasingly available. Belfast has to be aware of the elements that inhibit a successful transition. Primarily, this is a lack of strategic focus and a failure to understand the underlying dynamics of urban development. History can be a trigger for creativity and reinvention or cities can be locked in history. A failure of access and communication among all the city's inhabitants denies the opportunity for networking that is essential in generating a collective vision. Can one organise efficiently and effectively across a sectarian divide and so create the organisational capacity for development? There needs to be a general recognition that there is a crisis or challenge to be solved – how bad does the situation in Belfast need to get before this emerges? Fostering the change dynamic requires approval and recognition of its value. As a first step, Belfast needs creative spaces and neutral territories, which is why the city centre is so important. Thus, planning has to be anticipatory, reflective and flexible – a metaphor for the 'learning institution'.

How to Vision?

Visioning is essentially about imagining forwards and planning backwards – it is a joint quest. It needs one-year, three-year and ten-year planning. It should provide staging posts and markers of progress. All actions need to be defined through core principles to address the most difficult – in the case of Belfast, breaching the religious divide. Visioning and leadership are inextricably interwoven. Combined, these can create a culture of collaboration by:

- depersonalising leadership;
- institutionalising leadership;
- creating a climate for leadership.

How do we start this process? First, we have to recognise that boundaries are blurred – not everyone has the answer – partners are thus essential. Second, we have to create a culture for leadership to salute those who have done extraordinary things and bid them farewell when they step down as the norm. This is a precondition to preserve long-term commitment to a vision, a goal and a strategic plan. A community that creates that kind of leadership builds civic capacity, creates an infrastructure as essential as roads and sewers. Civic capacity buttresses community in time of stress and allows it to take bold new actions. This needs a sense of trusteeship. In every community non-elected men and women function as trustees of community.

The next step is to treat leadership as a renewable, developable resource. Leaders are found by looking for them in new places. Depersonalising leadership ensures that good ideas – strategic oppor-tunities – are part of a common agenda rather than an extension of one person. This allows good ideas to have many parents – for adoption without difficulty.

Institutionalising leadership ensures leadership endures and involves planning for leader fatigue, retirement or death. There are obvious dif-ficulties in this process. It should flow directly from the broad group, tacking on to a trustee group. Moreover, this implies a process for training new leaders – there must be leadership opportunities for young people to develop new skills, to welcome and usher out new leaders. Leaders should be honoured for their contribution and let move on. The community can then move ahead with new leadership. Leaders are often found among business, civic and cultural organisations and the professions. Typically, they play collective roles in the community as in their jobs.

They are, in effect, the community's inner circle, and become official trustees of the community when they realise they cannot focus solely on a single issue or agenda, but must see and deal with the broader interrelatedness of the issues to their community. In many cases, they come from old traditional power structures. They might represent the current and the past, but do not represent the true diversity of today's and tomorrow's community.

The first step is to get current and future trustees together. Initial meetings require a non-confrontational setting, in which people who should be working together but have not yet found occasion to do so, can get to know each other. The role of a key civic individual 'whose invitation to dinner cannot be turned down' is indispensable.

A good example of leadership development was the 'Seeds of Richmond Renaissance'. First biracial leadership groups were planted by a prominent social leader (Leslie Cheek). He invited the city's black and white leadership together. Their initial reaction was 'We cannot work together for our future'. However, what they needed to do was to undertake a project so visible and so public, that if they stopped working together their failure would be humiliating. We all need a Leslie Cheek.

Leadership must represent the basic parts of community together with local government officials, and local politicians. These are the cheerleaders, boosters, healers, collaborators and brokers of community.

Local businesses, especially those locally owned, need to be partners for joint ventures. Out-of-town ownership makes it important to find ways that executives on the move see themselves and their futures tied to successful participation in local civic affairs. Volunteers remain the workhorse and mainstay of leadership, but volunteers like any other resource need to be used wisely. Non-profit organisations, formerly advocates, angry and unempowered, are increasingly in community development and, today, these are entrepreneurial in approach. The media have enormous power to gather, to suggest, to encourage and, equally, to oppose. Few can achieve much without the media on their side.

The philanthropic community–foundations, etc., must all remember to move away from minimal investments to the maximum number of recipients to bring their skills gathering, convening, packaging promoting and investing to bear on bold issues or major needs for their communities. Regional interests – problems of health care, education, etc. – do not respect political boundaries. A city is not an island and thus other jurisdictional collaborators (township, counties and other states) have to be seen and must act as contributors, partners and shared stakeholders in the future. Leadership must include those closest to problems and most affected by changes.

How does one weld such a diverse group into a process of action? As a representative group, a partnership must find pleasure in their association and profit in learning together. One way is shared experience – retreats, study trips, seminars that build first-name familiarity and personal bonds that foster collaboration. For Belfast, a relevant question might be – how many new Catholic/Protestant friends are you going to make over the next month? It is important to depoliticise issues too important for political division. But, in the process of learning about their city and its possibilities, they learnt about one another. Partners find unlikely partners elsewhere leading to pleasure and trust and association.

Second, provide useful work. Nothing can disillusion more than the feeling that their work amounts to nothing. Civic capacity building is a perfect opportunity for putting visioning and goal setting to work to set the agenda. This is often politically motivated because someone thought having '2000 vision' sounds good. But even in goal setting, visioning and futuring, action speaks louder than planning.

Create a change agent. The resources and players used for strategic planning, public participation and goal setting may not be appropriate ones for the next step – they are tired, compromised or still so excited about the process, they cannot concentrate on getting something tomorrow. What is needed is a change agent – a non-profit organisa-tion whose sole function is to show that something is happening and to lay the foundation for a long-term agenda for change. This can be an amalgamation of existing organisations, but, ideally, since it is a symbol of new opportunity, it should be a new entity. Such an agent can take on first-year management and promotion. Frequent successes that can be celebrated show people that change can occur.

Another useful asset is an animation authority, a group whose sole purpose is to establish staging posts and set achievable targets. Usually these are put together by arts councils and chambers of commerce and funded in the USA through a business surtax or creation of a special assessment district.

A difficulty of visioning is that it takes so long to implement. By its very essence, it must look far ahead and it is difficult to sustain a vision when administrations change every few years – when gypsies of city government come and go, when recession and inflation are felt within a decade, when the typical corporate executive is rotated in and out of a community every three years, as increasingly fewer banks or insurance agencies are locally owned.

How then to sustain vision and steady on course? Institutionalising local leadership is the key. The trustees of the community must be organised as a permanent association. Call it a conference, a venture, a renaissance or alliance, but diverse stakeholders have to be institutionalised as an ongoing public–private force that will be around far longer than politicians and corporate CEOs. It is the public/private synergy that keeps the vision before the public and renews it as times and opportunities change.

It is interesting that the 'grandfather' Allegheny conference focused on the air and water quality of Pittsburgh. It evolved as a leadership forum to look at job diversification and unemployment caused by the decline of the steel industry. Today, the agenda is even broader as it takes on community self-determination and regional economic issues in Western Pennsylvania and inner-city Pittsburgh.

Recruit, Recognise and Renew Leadership

Civic leadership is hard work, people get tired, grow old and the capacity to give and support diminishes. Thus, there must be a constant process of recruiting younger people to renew the civic leadership resource. Most leadership programmes give little more than a briefing after which participants wait perhaps years to be called on. Developing leadership requires a process, not an event. It involves the identification of new people, either assigned by corporations temporarily to the community or people representing new and important constituencies for an area's future and diversity, and incorporation into the group of power players.

At the same time those who have given need to be honoured, so others are encouraged to give. The celebratory aspect of honouring people should be undertaken regularly if a community wants to encourage and perpetuate true civic capacity. Thus, more and more people were once leaders.

Best practice shows that urban problems are only solved through interdependent civic partnership. Each partner has different skills, for example, local business understands the economics of its city. Many municipal authorities still see themselves in traditional roles – maintaining facilities, providing services and protecting the public – but some are imbued with a new civics mentality, taking an entrepreneurial posture – initiating, cajoling and bargaining instead of reacting. They see planning moving from *planning to control* to *planning for growth*. Non-profit organisations through a new civics can be brought into financial partnerships with other actors. Foundations that traditionally gave money now need to invest money to develop social entrepreneurship.

Citizens too often exclude themselves, mostly those who become active only in last-minute opposition to something. A new civics would involve citizens from start to finish. State and regional government should provide enabling structures along the lines that everything is allowed unless forbidden, instead of competing with them. National government needs to provide flexible tools that can be shaped by local leaders searching for local solutions.

The key point again is that leadership may come from government, business or community, but it has to be there – leadership that understands the benefits of mutual collaboration. It is necessary to invent a culture of collaboration within an enabling creative milieu.

In all of this there are three key issues:

- In managing public participation, do not raise false expectations with or without outsiders.
- Generate a flagship idea which cannot be allowed to fail – a building or regenerated area, say a mixed religious one. There must always be a result.
- Establish benchmarks for progress – one-, three- and ten-year plans with staging posts.

Notes

1. Landry C. and Bianchini, F. (1995), *The Creative City*, Demos in association with Comedia, Paper No. 12, London, p. 5.
2. Bianchini, F. (1993), 'Remaking European Cities: The Role of Cultural Policies', in Bianchini, F. and Parkinson, M. (eds), *Cultural Policy and Urban Regeneration*, Manchester University Press, Manchester, p. 2.

9 The Role of Culture in the Regeneration of a Divided City: The Case of Belfast

Frank Gaffikin and Mike Morrissey

This chapter examines the economic, social and political role of culture in a divided city like Belfast seeking regeneration from its industrial decline. It notes the emphasis accorded the city centre as an assumed neutral space capable of accommodating new growth in the service sector, and the relationship between this revitalisation and the prospects of the city's most deprived communities. At this point, the chapter considers the potential of the cultural industries in the city as a whole, and in particular in those communities most scarred by economic restructuring and political violence. It questions the capacity of Belfast to achieve full regeneration without at the same time redressing the deep social and sectarian division. Outlining the difference between ethnic, neutral, transcendent and shared cultural space, it examines the possibility of a city whose international appeal could rest with a more multi-cultural future, where diversity is prized as a social and economic asset.

Creating the Post-Industrial Belfast?

Within a general shift to the service sector in the city, the main focus has been on resuscitating the central business district with retailing and office expansion, and extending its catchment by opening the city to the river by means of the waterfront Laganside scheme. The general rationale has been that 'improvements to the central area and the Lagan will play a major role in the regeneration and attraction of investment to the urban area as a whole'. This reasoning is not without merit:

- In each recent decade, regional investment has been mainly generated from one clear source. Up to the 1950s, it was still from indigenous industry; in the 1960s, it was from multinational capital, while in the 1970s, it was from boosted public spending.

The 1980s saw an upsurge in private consumer spending,[1] and it was natural that planners should seek to accommodate this apparently buoyant sector.

- Manufacturing collapse in the 1970s led some observers to proclaim the inevitability of post-industrialism. Accordingly, a development package based on services seemed opportune.

- Emphasis on such service sector activities in turn is held to offer urban centres a new purpose, since many of these services remain labour intensive and, unlike new manufacturing, they still require to be located in large settlements of population.

- Focusing much of the regeneration effort in the concentrated space of the urban core lends it a high visibility. Arguably, similar investment spread more widely across the city would have a diluted impact on citizen morale and business confidence.

- Downtown Belfast suffered the ravages of the 1970s intensive bombing campaign, which destroyed property, and deterred custom and investment. Its rehabilitation in the 1980s could be considered proper recompense.

- The new employment generated in these downtown developments could be said to offer labour market opportunities in a neutral and safe location to some of the unemployed deterred by the 'chill factor' from seeking jobs elsewhere in the city. The former Minister, responsible for the Belfast Plan, Mr Needham, emphasised this point. In justification of public investment in a mega shopping mall, known as Castle Court, and in Laganside, he noted:[2] 'it will actually be spent so people currently in the ghettos can find jobs in the city centre and enjoy a quality of life and an opportunity of choice which they don't have now'.

- By the 1980s, there was a trend to out-of-town shopping complexes. Without intervention to revitalise the urban core, there could have arisen a 'doughnut' effect, with further suburbanisation of people and activity and greater urban desolation.

- Belfast is a compact city. Thus, its downtown is more accessible to many of its neighbourhoods than its counterpart in many similarly sized cities.

- Since the new Urban Plan anticipated that 'most of the future growth in employment will take place in the service sector',[3] Belfast city centre, accounting for approximately a quarter of the urban economy's employment, was thought to be well placed to enhance its role as a regional centre.

Social and Sectarian Division

To repeat some of what was said in an earlier chapter, presently, Belfast is a city of just under 300,000. Between 1971 and 1991, it lost

a third of its population. During this period, its population share of
the wider Urban Area (BUA) fell from 70 to 59 per cent. But, the big
decline happened in the inner city, where residence decreased by over
half (55 per cent). Much of this pattern is familiar in industrial cities
in Britain like Liverpool and Glasgow. What is distinctive about Belfast
is the way this change has been also tracked by deepening segregation
during a period of massive public housing redevelopment and intensive
violent conflict.

It has become a more 'Catholic' city – thus, whereas Catholics
made up a third of the city population in the early 1970s, they are now
just over two-fifths. Meanwhile, there has been increasing residential
segregation, based on both religion and class. This can be seen starkly
in the division of the city between two sides of its main river – the Lagan.
Whereas the core city to the west of the Lagan is 55 per cent Catholic,
to the east it is only 12 per cent. (In the late 1960s, six in ten of public
sector households in the Urban Area lived in streets that were
segregated. A decade later, it was nine in ten households.) The city
faces a challenge to ensure that these dividing lines do not become
battlelines, convincing the already embattled that neighbourhoods
working against the odds cannot afford to be at odds with each other.

In the 1980s, Belfast's share of the region's population fell by just
over 3 per cent. Its share of regional employment fell by nearly 4 per
cent. The city centre was experiencing a revival. The city was also
reopened to its river by a prestigious waterfront development. But the
job gains of these major investments have so far mostly benefited
commuters over city residents.[4]

Economic and social malaise remains rooted in the North and West
of the city, which for most of this decade have accounted for nearly
eight in ten of total inner-city unemployment. If anything, this under-
estimates the problem because substantial numbers of men in these
areas have dropped out of the labour market altogether. Of the 50 most
deprived wards in Northern Ireland, six are in North Belfast and eight
are in West Belfast.

Urban deprivation involves spatial concentration of poverty as part
of a markedly uneven distribution of poverty across the city – a feature
described by Byrne as 'socio-spatial segregation'.[5] In this sense, the
urban poor are often not merely socially excluded but also spatially
contained in enclosures, which inhibit physical as well as economic
access to wider city opportunities. In these areas people not only suffer
from particular problems such as poor health, low income and
educational underachievement. Rather, they are caught in a dynamic
of the reproduction of poverty, whereby the interplay of these factors
creates a social exclusion, marked by its severity and durability.

Moreover, they have borne the brunt of the violence. Large barriers
of brick and metal, which form 'peace walls' to protect each side of
the community from the other, scar the landscape and bear grim

witness to the bitter sectarian animosities. Yet, despite, or maybe because of, these relentless assaults on the decencies of life, people in these areas have shown remarkable resilience and resourcefulness. And their ingenuity finds no better expression than in the vitality of their culture.

A Tale of Two Cities: Downtown versus Neighbourhoods?

The 1980s saw a prevalent trend for declining cities in the UK to adopt US models of urban regeneration, which focus pre-eminently on downtown. Reservations have arisen about several features of such models:[6] unequal public–private partnerships;[7] the largely physical development emphasis;[8] the tendency to produce highly segmented cities, most acutely between the gleaming towers of glass downtown and the dereliction faced by 'the urban underclass'; the significance accorded image investment – place-marketing, geared to conveying the city's conformity to cosmopolitan traits, while simultaneously identifying its distinctiveness for tourists and investors; and the sidelining of contentious urban issues.[9] Upbeat proclamations that Belfast's 'got the buzz' or that Glasgow is 'miles better', meant to mobilise citizenry in common identity, may underplay the extent to which cities are sites of contest as well as of consensus.

Government relocation of jobs to new city centre offices has helped reinforce demand for core retail activity. The expanded presence of UK multiples in Belfast city centre, attracted by reduced security risk, relatively low occupancy costs, and sound trading figures, has in turn been linked to significant rental growth, which itself has encouraged property developers to boost investment and construction. The rush of prestigious developments, following Castle Court, suggests a speculative element to this boom. Building has begun on malls before anchor tenants have been committed. Such speculative schemes can help increase competition for land, and thus inflate land costs for other much needed social consumption such as housing, play and open space or health facilities. Once built, they may require that key tenants are given incentives to come and stay. But, from another viewpoint, such prestigious developments signal not just an economic revival but also a political recovery of a city subjected to years of deliberate destruction. As one Northern Ireland Minister expressed this 'normalisation':[10]

You cannot be anything but impressed by the new skyline of Belfast city centre as shops and offices rise to herald a new era of prosperity. On the cultural and entertainment side, too, there is an encouraging spirit of enterprise.

This is echoed by leading local planners in their promotion of the 're-birth' of Belfast in professional journals: '... the physical evidence of achievement in Belfast stares you in the face. Witness the commercial confidence and new prosperity in the city centre. ... The city is being re-built. For citizen and businessman what this signifies is a new spirit of hope and confidence in the future.'[11] This pride demonstrates the distinctive symbolic importance attached to development in Belfast's centre. There, in physical form in the region's lead city, is evidence from one perspective of ultimate government triumph over a sustained paramilitary campaign, designed to deny the normality and reformability of the region as a political entity. But Belfast has become aware of the danger facing all cities keen to remake themselves – that development can come to be equated with building, and all development can then come to be seen as virtuous. In this way, building can occur with primary concern for rental yield and image enhancement, with only secondary concern for its impact on social need, open space, aesthetics and ecology.

Consumption Over Investment?

Arguably, the revitalisation of many city centres in the 1980s was over-reliant on a few areas of growth like retailing. There are at least two problems with this. First, it underplays the cultural and natural attributes of cities that can enliven and enrich urban living. Second, the retailing boom has been dependent on an expansion of consumerism, which itself may be very vulnerable in the long term. Factors behind the late 1980s consumption-led reflation in the UK included the abandonment of monetarism, the deregulation of the financial sector which facilitated a credit-led expansion, a significant decline in the savings ratio, fiscal relaxation, a rise in real earnings and a fall in interest and exchange rates. In other words, a somewhat unique combination of events stimulated a rapid consumer boom that appeared to augur well for further growth. Optimistic predictions about future retail growth, made at the height of the consumer boom in the late 1980s, proved rash. The big retail corporations expected high spending to help offset their investment and borrowing, which saw property values, rents and rates spiral.[12]

But this credit-based boom sucked in imports and stoked inflation to an extent that government was compelled to cool the 'overheating' and its attendant trading imbalance. In the early 1990s, consumer spending in the UK faltered in the context of recession, penally high interest rates, and consumer confidence impaired by tax rises and fear about unemployment. Though the Belfast service sector has avoided the worst effects, it remains confronted with an economic policy shift, geared more to investment and export-led growth.

Meanwhile, Belfast's neediest communities did not attain a proportionate share of the benefits from the physical-led regeneration in terms of jobs and income. Government recognition that this 'regeneration gap' demanded more focused intervention led to specific compensatory urban programmes, targeted at the most deprived communities, particularly in North and West Belfast. At the same time, in both the depressed local communities and the city as a whole, a new awareness emerged about the potential of sectors such as tourism and the arts to draw in outside investment. Throughout the city, but particularly in West Belfast, local cultural societies have been flourishing. Increasingly, they are seeking to translate this energy into an economic dividend that can provide local jobs and income. At the same time, the city as a whole is recognising that its need for a diversified economic base could include a cultural sector.

The Role of Arts and Culture in Belfast's Regeneration

Against a formidable background of decline and division, government and local communities are exploring the way the *Cultural Industry* could contribute to the restoration of the city, and in particular to the prospects of its most battered communities. A recent study[13] has assessed the economic significance of the Arts for the region as a whole. Among the good news, it noted that:

- the sector accounts for 8,330–9,000 jobs, both direct and indirect (somewhere around 1.5 per cent of total regional employment);
- there has been a notable recent boost to artistic talent (evidenced by such honours as the Nobel Prize for Literature bestowed on Seamus Heaney);
- the voluntary sector component to the Arts is strong relative to Britain;
- the market has increased in the last five years, pointing to more positive developments in N. Ireland compared to those in Britain;
- there is good scope for expansion of local demand, which peace and stability will further promote;
- and that recent moves by the local Arts Council and different strands of government to think more strategically about the sector represents an improvement, which can be developed further into a proper policy co-ordination (particularly between the departments of economic development and of education).

However, it also recorded that:

- the sector is smaller relative to other metro regions in Britain such as Greater Glasgow;
- a much lower share of the adult public attend arts events than in Britain;
- problems within the sector which impede its progress include: a *narrow production base*; *skills deficits*; *low market volume*; *poor marketing* and *promotion capacity*; lower *public sector resourcing* than the UK average; and a limited *venue infrastructure* – even allowing for a new Waterfront Concert Hall in Belfast.

It also found that relative to Britain, the patrons of museums, concerts and theatre come disproportionately from the wealthier social classes. Thus, it involves a form of *regressive* taxation policy: 'arts funding involves a redistribution of income from poorer to richer persons' (p. xviii). The Northern Ireland Arts Council is recognising this, and suggesting ways for improvement, such as: stronger links being formed between the arts and deprived communities; greater awareness and wider promotion of the arts in the media; encouraging the provision and use of a broader range of venues; and expanding the provision, promotion and awareness of the arts in education.

This under-use of the traditional arts by the most deprived populations contrasts with the vibrant condition of local community arts in the worst-off areas of Belfast. A recent review showed:

- the city's Community Arts was very *vibrant relative to other UK regions*;
- its *range* and *quality* are impressive;
- but that its very diversity – within the current funding regime and limited budgets – promoted *internal competition*;
- that this rivalry was not conducive to *collaboration* and *co-ordination*;
- and that while community-based arts in the most disadvantaged areas *impact significantly* on the *quality of life*, *social cohesion*, and *training and job opportunities*, they suffer from weak management;
- not helped by the fact that funders themselves do not operate a coherent strategic approach to the sector

Currently being examined are the policy and institutional implications of the report's suggestions for developing a sector that provides:

- *diversity*
- good channels for public *participation*

- *clarity* of objectives, which allow for *flexible response* to demand and opportunity
- sustainable *viability*
- *voluntary* under-pinning to help protect *community ownership*, and
- proper accountability in terms of *efficiency* and *effectiveness*

To take one example of how this agenda might be pursued, the concept of a *cultural corridor* has been advocated, linking the most deprived segment of the city, North and West Belfast, to the relatively vibrant city centre. Recent successes in the operation of community radio and the organisation of comprehensive community festivals in North and West Belfast bear testimony to significant cultural talent and interest in these localities. There has been a renaissance of the Irish language and Gaelic culture in part of this area over the past two decades, typified by the creation of primary and a secondary school where teaching is through the medium of the Irish language. Scope for broadening the cultural ambit to include music, film and video production also exists.

There would be clear gains to developing a Community Arts/Cultural Corridor in North and West Belfast:

- It would tap creativity in the area, helping to bond civic culture, and promote cultural pluralism, which are key to a tolerant politics, and thus greater social stability. If Belfast is to become a pluralist city, its citizens must be prepared to engage with and embrace more than one culture. The ghettoisation of particular cultural forms will not contribute to overall city regeneration. Without a greater sense of common ownership and stakeholding in the city by the two sides of the community, there will not be the civic pride necessary to market the city to its full potential for tourism and investment. There is little point in trying to re-image downtown as a normal cosmopolitan space, if this is a contrivance in terms of the reality in surrounding neighbourhoods.
- It would contribute to the city's 'liveability' – important for the quality of life of *existing citizens*; and could be a factor in attracting *inward investors* concerned about lifestyle opportunities for their imported management.
- It would provide *direct and indirect jobs* – in technical and artistic contracts, and the purchasing of goods and services.
- It would attract visitors and tourists, and particularly function as a *magnet for 'business tourism'*.
- It would *stimulate land values* and thus the rates base for the area.
- It would enhance *morale and confidence* in the many communities in North and West Belfast, battered by a quarter of a century of violence and hardship.

Such a cultural quarter has to embody the right mix and critical mass to ensure an animated ambience and distinctive character attractive to a range of interests and ages. Following experience elsewhere[14] – for example, in Dublin's Temple Bar – this includes a network of galleries; artist studios; fashion and furniture design outlets; alternative book shops; literature and language facilities; specialist retailing; music warehouses; theatres; craft and jewellery stalls; print and photography facilities; diverse ethnic restaurants, etc. But beyond the particular composition, certain features seem critical to success:

- Capacity for exchange of services and ideas: for instance, the availability of expertise and provision in multi-media and film technology could support artists and designers; the centralisation of props, costumes, script/video archives could be useful for different users.
- Major flagships, which act as magnets for the whole area: for instance, an attraction like an interactive Children's Museum brings parents, children, schools, etc.
- Flexible use of amenity and space: for instance, a quality public square could also offer opportunities for open-air performances; studios could operate as exhibition space, and small conference facilities; rooms above shops and lofts in warehouses could offer attractive accommodation for a socially mixed resident population.
- An environment with visual and security appeal: for instance, one that is pedestrian-friendly; offering access for elderly and disabled; with good street furniture and public art; and surrounded by a 'greening' of trees, plants and flowers.
- Respect for historical roots: for instance, identifying landmark sites, artefacts and buildings which capture the distinctive and memorable in past social life in the area.
- A business support service: for instance, a set of advice and help services, which recognise the need for regular information bulletins within the area; promotion and marketing of the area; legal and accountancy advice; and customised training for 'cultural entrepreneurs'.
- A partnership management board for the entire complex: comprising representation from funders, users, owners and local community.
- A broad financial base of funding subsidy: for instance, there is a need to engage and commit many different agencies of government, private sponsorship, international trusts, EU money, and so on (e.g. Northern Ireland Tourist Board; City Council; Arts Council; the main urban social programme, known as Making Belfast Work; the Community Relations Council; the

International Fund for Ireland; European Investment Bank; European Peace and Reconciliation Fund; the Northern Ireland Film Council; and such like), together with consideration of any helpful tax, rental and rates concessions.

In all of this, hard choices loom. For instance, would there be a flagship multi-purpose Performing Arts Centre, as an anchor to the whole scheme? Should such an expensive resource be located in the city centre as an assumed neutral location to give expression to a diverse and pluralist cultural form? Or should it not be located in the heart of the areas of greatest need? After all, such areas at present suffer badly from not having a quality civic building, which draws people from other parts of the city.

If the ambitious model of a *cultural corridor* is pursued, major investment is required. Designed to achieve a critical mass in terms of art galleries, restaurants, cinema, theatre, and musical outlets, etc., it would need to be linked into the incubation of a whole set of local industries around multi-media, film/video production and editing. These, in turn, could be linked to the Media Studies and Art and Design departments of the local university. But, in such a grand scheme, some doubt that a high level of community ownership can be maintained.

An alternative model suggests the priority to spread finance around many small groups to help them leverage other funding to ensure their viability, and thus help to foster the organic vitality on the ground, which is the bedrock of a creative arts capacity. But how could such widespread distribution of funding ensure that the result is more than a series of separate and isolated developments? Tackling fragmentation would require a complicated funding mechanism, which would be graduated to reward most those projects prepared to collaborate most with others.

Another dilemma that has been identified concerns the conversion of cultural talent into commercial opportunity, requiring systematic forms of enterprise learning through appropriate channels for business training. Moreover, can such commercialisation of culture be achieved without collapsing into a philistine approach?

Such issues throw up the wider question of the role of arts and culture in renewing industrial cities. As smoke stacks surrender to the gleaming towers of modern offices in revamped city centres and riversides, where does this sector fit into the scenario of urban economies built more upon services? The first obstacle to clear thinking on this is the *problematic definition* of the sector. If the culture industry is to move beyond its esoteric image as 'frills and thrills' to a more centre-stage position in the overall economy, we have to be able to designate its range. Clearly, it embodies the visual and performing arts – from music to dance to theatre, to film and photography, to literature, painting and sculpture, and so on. And, we know that these can be found as much in festivals as in museums. But what else may be included? Increasingly, some are throwing in libraries, parks, zoos and botanical gardens, and also 'supplier' areas like publishing. Beyond all this, the interface between the cultural industries and the leisure industries, and between both and the general 'hospitality' sector remain ill-defined and poorly measured.

The underlying factor that drives the increasing economic significance of the arts and culture is the relationship between economic development and the changing composition of demand. As societies become wealthier, the satisfaction of material need is supposed to leave ever greater scope for the satisfaction of aesthetic and cultural pursuits. In a world determined largely by the concrete and practical, people are thought to welcome that which graces and decorates the otherwise grey routines of life. Moreover, as those in work operate under greater stress, the premium on quality relaxation and cultural enrichment is said to increase. But all this raises further critical questions. Can you *consume* culture just as you consume a car? What about the *equity* dimension, in relation to those whose material well-being is not adequately met? Would they welcome public resources being devoted to an abstract piece of public art over that money being spent to enhance medical care?

In grappling with these difficult questions, there are *six* distinct dimensions of this relationship between art and the economy that may reward further detailed consideration:

First, the *implication of the global market:* we are told that we are now all subject to the process of globalisation – a single market world increasingly subject to the standardised and homogenised, in which the emblem of a McDonald's signals development and sophistication, and in which culture is neutered to a point where all human drama can be depicted through the bland lens of American or Australian soap opera. Clearly, this is not the case. Multi-culturalism thrives. And, even if we fail to engage with it for its intrinsic value of human enrichment, we have to learn to appreciate and respect diverse cultures as the key to doing business worldwide. In this sense, it has been said that 'the greatest distance between peoples is not space, but culture'.

We can see this on the European doorstep where people who share space in Kosovo divide to the point of death over culture and identity. So, even as we are told that the new global economy order erodes national sovereignty and diminishes cultural distinctiveness, we are seeing the re-emergence of exclusive cultural expression. The challenge we face here – and we know this only too well in Belfast – is to elevate the civic over the ethnic, but in a way which affirms difference in language and cultural form.

Second, even if we don't buy into all the analysis of post-modernism, we know that old-style economic and urban planning no longer offers the path to utopia. We don't live in a world subject to certitude and ready prediction. It is a much more messy and chaotic place than that. Thus, nobody has a ready-made blueprint for how to remake cities enduring industrial decline. There is even legitimate argument over whether we should set our sights on moving to the Advanced Industrial City or the Post-Industrial City. For instance, some say that we need still to produce tradeable goods, but that this can be done at comparative advantage to the developing world if we concentrate on a high-value niche based on cutting-edge technologies. They insist that if we in cities throw all our economic eggs into the one basket of services, that we will become a basket-case economy.

But, what is really needed is the Creative City, in which networks of innovation and fresh thinking are nurtured through multi-agency and cross-sectoral partnerships Out of this will derive a distinctive agenda for regeneration appropriate to the particular histories and current needs of particular places. And in this process, arts and culture has a special role, because its whole 'ethos' is built around creative imagination. In a way, a vibrant cultural base to a city can act as a leaven that generates many other kinds of productive activity.

Third, in an information age based on micro-chip and digital technologies, there is the likelihood of a proliferation of audio and visual output. The prospect of multi-channel television alone promises an *overload* of material and images to digest. Several risks loom. For instance, it offers heaven for the couch-potato resigned to passivity. But, it stands to turn culture into *spectacle* rather than *activity*. Furthermore, insofar as it may lead to a 'more equals less' phenomenon, an increased diet of pap may corrode the critical faculty to discern and discriminate. In such a scenario, the *technical* world of machines and gadgets will dull the *creative* world of social interaction.

Such reservations should not reduce us to a new Luddism. With appropriate adaptability, multi-media – which brings together the capacities of text, broadcasting, computers and other forms of telecommunication – could be a servant to local arts in terms of community video, community cable channels, computer graphics, animation, and so on. And surely, the world of arts and culture that can accommodate the *surreal*, can readily accommodate the new worlds of *virtual reality*. So, the challenge here is to adapt the high-tech products of the new economy for an interactive and creative expression. These can be used at community level in ways which promote confidence, celebrate cultural pluralism, and which in turn can produce marketable outputs with their own economic dividend.

Fourth, we speak much these days of *sustainable development*, forms of development which are particularly sensitive in their use of non-renewable resources. Well, certain aspects of culture are like that. They are non-renewable. For instance, if we package our heritage into an endless round of theme parks, we may start to deform the meaning of architecture and place. Selling history and past culture purely as commodity risks debasing and destroying the very asset you wish to exploit – the distinctive tapestry of former ways of living which makes particular places unique. Some cynics characterise industrial England as a 'vast floating museum' of quaint tourist attractions, designed to depict in aspic bygone days of industrial community life.

And indeed, if we venture down to some of the riverside developments around our cities, we can see a sanitised version of the real textured maritime tradition – a version that leaves little signature of the hardship and struggle of those who devoted their working lives to building its former wealth. We need here to safeguard standards of conservation so that the cultural rendition we get from rehabilitated industrial architecture speaks to us in a more rounded historical narrative.

Fifth, in the field of urban regeneration, we strive hard these days to see planning in an integrated way, to connect the social with the economic, and both with the built environment. Again, arts and culture can help bring vision and shape to these links. For instance, many environmental improvement schemes are meant to improve residents' quality of life while enhancing business investment confidence. Such schemes could benefit from a greater role being given to aesthetics and design. This includes the more imaginative use of public art – gateways, sculpture, murals, banners, street furniture, etc. But it has to offer quality in conception, material, and production, and participation by the community being 'served'.

Too often, what pass for community murals for example, are ill-conceived, tatty, carried out with materials that are not resistant to the vagaries of our climate, and which can end up in truth as scars on the community landscape, which depress rather than exalt. That is not to insist that we stick with a grand notion of art as that which is capable of universal and durable appreciation by the well-initiated. Rather, it is to draw the simple lesson that good community art, *like all good art*, does not come cheap. And, this leads to the sixth point:

Much in art and culture can benefit from *public subsidy*. But, it is also true that public subsidy carries with it a public accountability. This is not simply down to the current robust economic climate, in which perhaps we have learned 'the price of everything and the value of nothing'. It is simply that when social spending as a whole is subject to rigorous prioritisation, funding for arts is going to come under greater scrutiny. Yet, an appropriate accountancy is not easy to specify.

Do we justify subsidy in terms of *size* or *type* of audience? Can we ensure that subsidy does not infringe *artistic freedom*? Do we fund most that which seems likely to *bind* best various civic interests? If so, will this not demote an important role of cultural expression – to challenge through the *contentious* and *controversial*?

Of course, good art both soothes and stirs the human spirit. It offers no simple calculus for any of this. In that sense, we have to go *beyond the economic* dimension. We have to look more at the 'social wealth' created. To put it crudely, if Man is *nature*, humankind is *nature plus culture*. It is culture that marks us as social beings. We used to speak of 'the *cultured* person', as an elitist reference. One index of how seriously we take the role of culture in social life is when that reference has a purchase on the popular imagination, when being *cultured* is considered a prized attribute by all.

Culture in a Divided City

While acknowledging the contribution that cultural activities can bring to the new urban economies and to the quality of urban living, the thorny issue of how diverse cultural expression operates in a conflict-ridden city needs to be addressed. In Belfast, the republican community was first off the mark in its recognition of the Gramscian links between culture and politics. The legitimation of an Irish space in what was professed to be a British city demanded visible signs and symbols of an Irish identity. Thus, the apparent cultural autonomy of places like West Belfast is linked to the aspiration of separatism from the British state.

As such, it is seen to challenge the loyalist identity in the city with its allegiance to the union with Britain. Loyalist communities now vie with their republican counterparts in expressions of their fidelities, through wall murals, flags and emblems and other cultural forms. The intensity of the conflict for the last three decades has seen the most troubled parts of the city carved into mutual antagonistic 'turfs', where those who do not share an affinity with the cultural/political orthodoxy in particular neighbourhoods can feel under severe pressure, if not intimidation. Such heightened senses of territoriality have, at times, inhibited efficient and equitable allocation of social resources such as housing. For instance, a particular community may suffer from poor or overcrowded housing, but it is difficult to infringe on the space of an adjoining community of the opposite persuasion, even where land and housing supply is more available, since such a move is seen as a threatening incursion. Thus, the growth of cultural activities on both sides of the Belfast community has been successful *within* each community in terms of offering a channel for creative expression and a common bond among local residents. But, by the same token, it has been a source of some division and tension *between* the two protagonist sides.

To offset the segregation of these 'ethnic spaces', government has tried to emphasise common accessibility to the 'neutral spaces' of the downtown and Waterfront. But, simplistic assumptions that the entire city centre is open to all are not borne out by research. For instance, a study of young people living at the interface between the two sides of the community suggests that some young Protestants regard the prestigious shopping mall, known as Castle Court, to be largely a preserve for young Catholics.

Of course, it is possible to designate certain areas and events that could be regarded as 'transcendent spaces', that operate above the conflict and draw audiences from the two traditions in the city. In particular, major stage shows in the new large concert hall and music festivals that attract big international entertainers like Garth Brooks or U2 win attendance from throughout the city. Indeed, in an apparent effort to erase the image of the local Parliament Building from being regarded as the site of a partisan government, a recent concert by Elton John was held there.

A different ambition would be to create alongside the 'ethnic', 'neutral' and 'transcendent' spaces, genuinely 'shared spaces' that express a common belonging to the city. At this stage, it remains a challenge to find cultural forms that can cover this ground. For instance, an attempt to create a St Patrick's Day Festival for the whole population, tapping into the talents of all the local cultural societies across the city, did not succeed. The Protestant community argued that St Patrick had been appropriated by the Catholic community as an Irish icon, in a way that did not respect their British identity. Similarly, there was an appeal in 1998 for Catholics to join Protestants in displaying the symbol of the poppy, deployed in the annual commemoration of those who died in the Second World War. But this appeared to be greeted by Catholics with the view that the symbol was associated with the British Legion, and therefore alien to their Irish affiliation. Meanwhile, Sinn Fein as the political wing of the IRA, now functions as the second largest party in the City Council. It maintains that the ambience and appearance of the City Hall is mostly loyalist, and that such a prominent civic building should evoke a common belonging by all citizens. Such disputes mark the persistence of the basic fault line in the city between Catholic nationalists and Protestant unionists.

Yet, there is a minority third tradition in Belfast, which has never been animated by these kind of ancestral and tribal contests. Much of this 'third' section is liberal and labour in politics, but has lowered its voice amid the polarisation in the city in the past 30 years. Another section of it is a population, mostly young and disaffected with all politics and into alternative lifestyles and music. Besides this 'third' group, there is a small population of ethnic origin, mostly Chinese and Asian. More positive recognition of such differentiation, and related cultural nuances, could see in time the creation of a more multi-cultural city, wherein 'shared space' represented the coming together of these separate idioms for a rich diversity appreciated by all in the city.

Notes

1. Coopers & Lybrand Deloitte (January 1990), *The Northern Ireland Economy: Review and Prospects*, Belfast.
2. Wilson, R. (13 May 1988), 'Putting the Gloss on Belfast', *New Society*.
3. Ibid., p. 17.
4. Based on data supplied by DoE (NI) Statistics Branch and analysis for DoE (NI) by Andreas Cebulla, NIERC.
5. Byrne, D. (1989), *Beyond the Inner City*, Open Univesity Press, Milton Keynes.
6. Frieden, B. and Sagalyn, L. (1989), *Downtown Inc. How America Rebuilds Cities*, MIT Press, Cambridge, Massachusetts.
7. Squires, G. (ed.) (1989), 'Unequal Partnerships: the Political Economy of Urban Redevelopment', in *Post-War America*, Rutgers University Press, New Brunswick
8. Barnekov, T., Boyle, R. and Rich, D. (1989), *Privatism and Urban Policy in Britain and the United States*, Oxford University Press, New York.
9. Davies, M. (1990), *City of Quartz: Excavating the Future in Los Angeles*, Vintage, London.
10. Quoted in Wilson, R. (13 May, 1988), 'Putting the Gloss on Belfast', *New Society*.
11. Morrison, B. (December 1990), 'Making Belfast Work', *The Planner*, p. 32.
12. Northern Ireland Economic Council (1993), 'The Recession in Northern Ireland and Britain 1989–92', NIEC, Belfast.
13. Myerscough, J. (1996), *The Arts and the Northern Ireland Economy*, NIEC, Belfast
14. For instance, the concept of Temple Bar in Dublin as elaborated in Temple Bar Properties (1992), *Development Programme for Temple Bar*, Dublin; and Temple Bar Properties (undated) *Temple Bar Shopping*, and *Temple Bar Living*, Dublin.

IMPLEMENTING POLICY

10 The Future Governance of Cities

Patsy Healey

The Broad Context

The quality of city governance is increasingly important for urban economies, societies and environments in the contemporary European context. Thus, we need to develop new ways of thinking about and doing governance. Why is this so?

At national and international level, there is much general policy discussion and action on the widely shared policy objectives of economic competitiveness, environmental sustainability and social cohesion. The first is connected to the obvious competition between places for business investment, tourist attraction and government and EU subsidy. The second aims to reduce environmental damage, work within environmental limits and develop environmental assets over the long term. The third seeks to limit social tensions and polarisation, and to spread access to opportunity. But the real challenge is to work out how they link together. Making such links involves developing a capacity for integrating policy across the different sectors of traditional policy delivery, and making it relevant and user-friendly from the point of view of people as residents and citizens, and for firms.

This challenge is leading to increasing concern with a strategic and integrated approach to developing the qualities of places, of urban regions, cities and neighbourhoods. The aim is to replace the old vertical and hierarchical forms of government organisation, with an emphasis on horizontal linkages, a form of territorial integration. This was of course emphasised in the 1960s. But then we could imagine that the relationships of places and the organisation of city activities were inherently well integrated with each other. Now it is clear that cities are very open systems, transected by multiple relations which do not always interconnect.

Nevertheless, the quality of urban places, and the capacity to limit the conflicts and tensions between the various transecting relationships, is important for both the quality of life for residents and the quality of the business environment.

To respond to this new context requires a new focus on place-making and territorial integration in urban policy. The need for change is reinforced by the widespread demand to take steps to overcome the 'democratic deficit' in the relations between government and citizens. Widely recognised throughout Europe, this is particularly acute throughout the United Kingdom, with its high degree of government centralisation. The distance between citizens and government, and between much of business and government, leads to distrust – of politicians, officials, civil servants, professionals and experts. There has been much experimentation in the present period in new governance forms, new agency structures, new partnerships and new consultative processes. This seeks to move forward from government as a 'provider', working *for* people, to government as an 'enabler', working *with* people, firms and agencies. But what kind of urban governance does this involve? What kind of 'institutional capacity' should we try to develop? And how can partnership initiatives make a difference?

Rethinking Urban Governance: Three Models

These experiments in new governance forms are paralleled by more general discussion on how urban governance should change.[1] The themes permeating this discussion are summarised in Figure 10.1.

These tendencies are not in a single direction, however, and they have different implications for the emphasis on the quality of urban places. One way to describe these different directions is in terms of three models, one representing the 'past', and the others, two alternative directions for future urban governance. The traditional model (see Figure 10.2) emphasises bureaucratic organisation, in which the parts of government are hierarchically linked to the political and executive authority at the top of the organisation. Paper flows upward and downward to get authorisation for action. Individuals in an organisation are anonymised representatives of the organisational entity. The sections of the organisation are divided functionally, in relation to the legal and political authority which allows government to perform particular tasks. Education, social welfare, health services, economic development, housing provision and management, transport delivery, planning development and regulation are set up as distinct sections with their own staff and ways of working. The staff of the organisation are professionally trained, as guardians of knowledge about the issues and procedures for addressing them. Accountability is achieved by the hierarchical checking of actions against policies and principles

Figure 10.1 Tendencies in Urban Governance

Providing to Enabling

Delivering to Developing

Representing to Empowering

Producer-driven to Consumer-driven

Hierarchical to Fragmented

Technical knowledge to Local knowledge

Functional separation to Integrated collaboration

developed by politicians and translated by senior officers into principles for executive action.

In this model, as noted above, people and firms are not seen by the agency 'in the round', but in terms of the focus of each functional service. The result for people and for firms is a 'split-up' everyday life.[2] Places too are 'split up' in this focus, with services from different functional programmes arriving in, or landing on, an area with often little consideration for the way they link together. This model also leads to a domination by professionals and administrators of the definition and delivery of governance products. However well trained and well intentioned these staff are, the result is that people and business feel distanced from government. This distance in its turn leads to distrust. The traditional merit of the model was that it limited corruption, through the checks and balances of the formal bureaucratic organisation. But the distance and distrust which it engenders, combined with the general distrust of politicians and officials these days, makes people

Figure 10.2 Model 1: Delivering Services

Bureaucracy

Functional divisions

Clear administrative process

Hierarchical responsibility

Professional staff

imagine corruption even where little exists. And the enclosed and centralised nature of the organisation allows corruption which subverts the central apex of the organisation to permeate the whole, with little check.

Figure 10.3 Model 2: Multiple Initiatives

Contracting out

New agencies

Management trusts

Partnership arrangements

Multiple voices

The second model, vigorously promoted in the 1980s in the UK, seeks to break out of the bureaucratic straitjacket. The objective was to foster innovation, encourage new initiatives and perspectives, and to promote greater efficiency and value for money, as the hierarchical structure of accountability was seen to generate complex 'paper-trails' inside organisations which inhibited flexible responses to rapidly changing situations. The second model encourages multiple initiatives (see Figure 10.3). Much of the work formerly done by government may be contracted out to private firms which compete on price and quality to deliver a service. New agencies are created with their own remit and accountability structures. Management trusts and boards replace political accountability and partnership arrangements draw in new players to shape the actions of governance. This allows new and often diverse voices to have a role in shaping the agendas of urban governance and often to play a key part in implementing programmes.

This model has certainly been the carrier of innovative energy across the landscape of UK urban governance in the past 15 years, and much of it looks here to stay. New networks, particularly those of the business sector, have been drawn into governance, displacing or at least coexisting with local political networks. But there are considerable problems with the model which are increasingly recognised. The traditional complaint was the lack of accountability. Many feel that accountability to appointed boards is no substitute for accountability to local politicians. But there are other problems too. The model increases the segmentation of governance activity. Functional divisions are complemented with agencies focused on particular groups of people or particular areas. These help to focus on these groups and areas 'in the round', but they give little attention to how one group and area relates to another.

The 'split-up' phenomenon becomes fragmented governance. As a result, the groups and areas may find themselves in an unpredictable competitive situation for subsidy and opportunity with other initiatives. The model, left to its own devices, creates a confused 'market' of governance initiatives. Like all markets, some initiatives succeed and some fail. This leads to considerable waste of energy and resources. Business now talks of 'partnership fatigue' and the community sector of a 'crisis of volunteering'. 'Downsizing' the state and 'offloading' to business and the community seems to have limits. Without an alert media and citizenry, and very careful monitoring, it is also wide open to corruption.

It is in the context of this experience that the third model is developing. This accepts that the old model needs to change, but recognises that there remains a key role for formal urban government. While encouraging all kinds of initiatives in governance forms, for projects and for programmes, and seeking to turn government 'inside out', to be more open and sensitive to citizens and consumers, the model emphasises the importance of a strategic framework within which experimentation can occur (see Figure 10.4). This strategic framework benefits from being rooted in representative urban government, to give it a base of legitimacy, but it needs also to be embedded in a rich network of key stakeholders concerned with the future of the locality. It emphasises the way shared ideas about future trajectories are developed, and the importance of these in establishing stable frameworks within which citizens and firms can become involved in governance activity. It acknowledges that, while technical knowledge is important, so is the 'local knowledge' of companies, households and families, community groups, local shopkeepers, sports and cultural clubs and societies, and such like.

It also emphasises that the key to developing the urban governance capacity to readjust flexibly to changing circumstances is to encourage a continuous and broadly-spread learning capacity in the locality. Knowledge acquired in one place, perhaps about new markets, new techniques or new ways of accessing funds, needs to be shared around, to foster local synergy and make the capability of the whole much more than that of the individual parts. This kind of strategic governance requires efforts to build up the quality of the relationships within a locality, in terms of knowledge resources and the capacity to learn and in terms of the ability to develop sufficient trust and understanding to work together to build more internal cohesion and to link to external sources of power to capture funds and interest, as well as the capacity to mobilise to act when new initiatives need to be undertaken. A strategic view of the quality of the relationships within a locality is thus, in this model, a key complement to a shared strategic framework and 'vision' of possible trajectories for a place.[3]

Figure 10.4 Model 3: Strategic Capacity-Building

Strategic collaboration

Involving many stakeholders

Developing shared visions

The vision as a shared 'frame of reference'

Encouraging many initiatives

Combining technical and local knowledge

Encouraging innovative learning

Building relationships

This is not an easy model to develop, especially in the UK context, with its history of centralised government and functional organisation. People in government are used to working in separate segments and take time to learn how people in other segments work. Citizens and firms are impatient and distrustful of government. Some localities are deeply divided, citizen against citizen, 'community' against 'capital', pro-roads groups against pro-public transport groups, and so on. There is much in our govenance history which has created these divisions. This does not mean that model 3 is impossible to develop in the UK context. In fact, there are some cities in where there are strong signs of its emergence, and there is much experience in the more decentralised contexts of other European countries where such an approach is evolving relatively easily.[4] But it takes time to develop, and to build the trust and understanding which will provide a foundation for the next steps. It is not a quick fix. However, neglecting to build up such trust and understanding reinforces divisions and tensions, strengthening the criticism of model 1 and the dissatisfaction with model 2. Learning to 'do governance' in model 3 ways is perhaps the key challenge for urban governance as we go into the next millennium.

Three Examples from North East England

To illustrate the challenge involved in the increasing diffusion of model 2 in UK urban governance and the potential for model 3, three examples from my own region are informative. The North East, by many indicators, has had major economic problems for most of the present century. The old industries of mining, engineering and ship-building have lurched from attempts at resuscitation to almost wipe-out. Unemployment rates are high and the social costs to individuals and families of the loss of the employment basis of an old working-class culture have been very high. There have been vigorous efforts at establishing a new industrial base centred in inward investment, exploiting the region's position in relation to the European mainland. Capturing central government subsidy has been the name of the game for many years. The region has benefited from every urban and regional development initiative in England. It remains dominated by old Labour politics, though with a pragmatic eye to how to capture funding. It is well organised in terms of the promotion of economic development initiatives, with a long history of partnership between the public and private sectors to support the Northern Development Agency, a key arm in the organisational capacity to attract inward investment. But it has been much more problematic to link economic development with environmental sustainability and social development objectives.

The first example is the Cruddas Park Development Trust on Tyneside, set up in the late 1980s and still running. It was in effect a forerunner of the City Challenge initiative. It was a top-down project hatched by senior civil servants in the region and taken on by the business sector in the newly formed Newcastle Initiative. It involved multiple stakeholders in the private, public and community sectors in a community development effort aimed to expand what would have been a housing estate regeneration project into a wider community development agenda. The estate concerned was highly fragmented and factionalised within itself, and violence, on the streets and in homes, was a powerful language of communication and social control. Citizens distrusted government in general, including the local council, and saw business as having a narrow and self-interested agenda. Council politicians and officials distrusted business, and felt the initiative was invading their 'patch', and business had little grasp of how either government or local communities worked.

Nevertheless, in this unpromising ground, over the years, a slow process of building new relationships across these old divides has evolved, in which many in the community have been able to access new resources and learn new skills, of benefit to themselves and the area. In particular, the building of sufficient mutual understanding and appreciation has led to a degree of trust which has helped to open routes from the community, one of the most disadvantaged in the region, to sources of external resources and power. There are still tensions within the estate and between the estate and the local council, but there is now a history of positive relationships to draw on as people keep on trying to do things differently.[5]

The second example is from the City Challenge experience itself. It serves to emphasise the importance of the fine-grain of social interaction in building up relations of trust and opening up possibilities for real collaboration. Once again, these City Challenge partnerships were 'top-down' initiatives. Local authorities were asked to bid for national funds, but they had to compete for funding on the basis of the quality of the bid and the funding that lay behind it. A requirement was the establishment of a three-way partnership between local government, business and the community. In most cases, this was consolidated into a partnership board of some kind. But there were many ways in which these boards could work. How they actually worked provides a revealing window on the quality of the governance relationships in the early days. This can be illustrated by two cases from Tyneside at the start of the projects.

In one, the board was run along familiar local authority lines. The City Council managed the agendas, which were long and backed by rather impenetrable papers. The board had equal representation from the council, business and the community. Meetings were held in public, and provided with sandwiches. The council group came to the meeting having already discussed the agenda and developed a strategy for each point. The business group were not familiar with 'caucus' politics, and very uneasy in a public arena. They wanted to discuss issues openly but found themselves in a position where they had to assert and defend their 'position', which they had barely articulated as a group. The community were equally put off by the organisation of the arena, and found it hard to articulate a position. They had sufficient links with councillors to demand help, and soon had acquired a facilitator to help them understand the agenda and put forward their views. The business group eventually developed similar practices, having learned the rules of the game. But the game remained one of 'caucuses and sandwiches'.

In contrast, in a second example, the local authority, in setting up the board, sought to emulate the way a business board worked. The board was chaired by a businessman, and managed by a chief executive from the council. Its members consisted of representatives of other businesses and funding agencies, a few other council officials and some community representatives. These latter stood out because of their clothes (colourful in a sea of dark suits) and their gender (women). The discussion in the board meetings, held in private, were open and friendly, with lots of constructive ideas coming forward. But no one noticed that some people did not speak at all. The community representatives had never encountered such an arena before and it activated deep-seated feelings of their own inadequacy and insignificance. This then was a business game of 'suits and silences', imagining an openness and democracy which in reality was closed and oppressive. Gradually, in both cases, the various parties learned to communicate, appreciate and understand each other a bit more, but it took time to recover from these early experiences. This emphasises the importance of the quality of the first steps in the process of building new relationships.[6]

The third example comes from a district in Durham, an area of scattered former mining communities and a new town in an agricultural landscape, made famous as the current Prime Minister's constituency. Over the past 15 years, the local authority had worked hard to provide and manage good quality housing, and it had a track record for innovative economic development initiatives. Organised into functional sectors, the two agendas were largely separate. But by the 1990s, other issues, notably to do with environmental quality and health, were beginning to attract the attention of officers and councillors. Funding opportunities also stressed the links between estate regeneration and community development. A few partnership schemes attracted funding, but they were uneven in quality and some of the partner agencies were complaining of an overload of demands for their involvement. In this context, the councillors asked their officers to commission a study to develop an overview of their area. They wanted to know what their district was like these days, how they should understand it and what role they should play. In effect, they were seeking help to reposition themselves to continue to capture funding effectively and to work out how to shift strategically from a 'provider' authority to an 'enabler'.

The study set out to look at the work of the council from the 'outside', from the point of view of business and of residents. Despite the efforts of the council in working with business and community groups over the years, the message which came back was that both felt isolated from the council. Many smaller businesses and most residents also felt isolated generally, from access to information, to opportunities, to chances to influence what happened in their communities. It could be said that many were suffering 'relational deprivation', which compounded problems of low incomes and low levels of qualification among residents, and lack of contact with new markets and technologies for some smaller firms. Several recommendations emerged from the study, but an important one was that every initiative taken by the council, and every programme or project, should not only consider how it linked with other programmes affecting an area, a resident or a firm, but also how, through the specific action, it could be possible to enhance the quality of the knowledge and relationships of all those involved in it, to help increase their 'relational resources', or 'social capital',[7] as it is sometimes called.[8]

Building Urban Institutional Capacity

In line with the ideas in model 3, there is now increasing interest in the role of urban governance in enriching the knowledge and relational qualities of localities. It is hoped in this way to generate a local social environment which provides rich resources for residents and firms, and a store of understanding and trust within which actual and potential conflicts can be understood, addressed and possibly even reduced in scale. Moreover, it needs to be an environment which can provide a capability for mobilising local energy and capability to 'make a difference' to the qualities of places in a way which is more than the sum of the parts.[9] In these days when public finance resources are limited and have huge demands placed upon them, and when localities are thrust into a tough competition with each other, releasing such local capability has to be a key task for urban governance.

But, as emphasised above, this cannot be a quick fix approach. It requires time to develop such capabilities, though potential for them may be found in unexpected and surprising places. Nor is there a template solution. Each place is different, and has its own trajectory and potentials. There is no predetermined pathway to building effective institutional capacity. People create it as they go along. Building a rich institutional capacity to maximise the chances of a place, its firms and its people in the years ahead thus needs to harness and respect the capabilities which can be found in a place into a collective 'place-making' project. This is what model 3 is all about, and why it holds so much hope at the present time. Those places able to develop it effectively are likely to be seen as the 'successful cities' of the early part of the next century. It is in such places that integrated policy agendas and programmes, relevant and user-friendly in development and delivery, are likely to be most evident, and where real reductions in the 'democratic deficit' are likely to ocurr.

Notes

1.   Stoker, G and Young, S. (1993), *Cities in the 1990s*, Longman, London; Wilson, D. et al. (1994), *Local Government in the UK*, Macmillan, London.
2.   Nord (1991), *The New Everyday Life*, Nordic Council, Stockholm.

3. These ideas are developed further in Healey, P. (1997), *Collaborative Planning: Shaping Places in Fragmented Societies* Macmillan, London.

4. See Healey, P., Khakee, A., Motte, A. and Needham, B. (1997), *Making Strategic Spatial Plans: Innovation in Europe*, UCL Press, London.

5. See Healey, P. (1997), 'City Fathers, Mandarins and Neighbours', in Kalltorp, O. and Elander, I. (eds), *Cities in Transformation: Transformation in Cities*, Avebury, Aldershot; and Wood, J., Gilroy, R., Healey, P. and Speak, S. (1995), 'Changing the Way We Do Things Here: The Cruddas Park Initiative', Department of Town and Country Planning, University of Newcastle, Newcastle.

6. Davoudi, S. and Healey, P. (1995), 'City Challenge: Sustainable Process of Temporary Gesture', *Environment and Planning C: Government and Policy*, Vol. 13, pp. 79–95.

7. Putnam, R. (1993), *Making Democracy Work: Civil Traditions in Modern Italy*, Princeton University Press, New Jersey.

8. See Healey, P. and Norwood, T. (1997), 'The State of the Borough: Main Report', Report for Sedgefield Borough Council, Department of Town and Country Planning, University of Newcastle, Newcastle.

9. See Healey, P. (1998), 'Building Institutional Capacity through Collaborative Approaches to Urban Planning', *Environment and Planning A*, Vol. 30, pp. 1531–46.

11 Belfast: A Partnership Approach to Local Governance

Brian Hanna

In September 1995, *The Economist* carried a chilling account of 'ethnic cleansing' in the former Yugoslavia. Under the title 'Blood and Earth', the first sentence of the article evoked both distaste and apprehension: 'If peace comes to Bosnia it will be tempting to conclude that ethnic cleansing – the creation of homogeneous populations by way of mass exile – has, in its murderous way, worked.'

For those of us who have lived and worked in Northern Ireland over the past quarter of a century those words are both a warning and a challenge. For, make no mistake about it, a failure to resolve – or at least accommodate – the problems of diversity within both countries and cities inevitably leads to disaster. Within cities throughout the world there are complex issues which can only be dealt with in a co-operative manner. Professor John Stewart of the Institute of Local Government Studies (INLOGOV) has described these as 'wicked issues'. Examples are:

- problems of law and order and the aspiration to community safety;
- environmental issues and the aspiration to sustainable development;
- racial discrimination and the aspiration to an equitable society;
- poverty and unemployment and the aspiration of people to lead meaningful lives.

To these, we in Northern Ireland could add sectarianism and opposing political aspirations. Stewart rightly argues that these issues are difficult to resolve and demand joint working and co-operation between the many different agencies and organisations operating within society.

They are, in fact, beyond the capacity of any single organisation to fully understand, never mind to resolve. Co-operation is therefore demanded. Partnership is not an option; it is an essential prerequisite to tackling the multi-faceted problems facing cities. Roisin McDonough[1] has described partnership as follows:

A process by which several partners of a different nature agree upon a means of achieving some specified objective, the results of which represent more than the sum of their respective parts. It implies sharing both the risks and the benefits with each other in a mutual fashion.

This helpful definition immediately focuses our attention on the sharing of objectives and the agreeing of actions which might lead to achieving them. This chapter is an attempt to look at the developing partnership approach in Belfast from a local government perspective. To do that, some background on both Northern Ireland and Belfast is essential.

Northern Ireland and Belfast: The Government Context

Up until 1921, the Parliament and government of the United Kingdom ruled Ireland from London. Irish members sat with their English, Scottish and Welsh counterparts in the House of Commons at Westminster, and representative Irish peers sat in the House of Lords. Executive authority was vested in the Lord Lieutenant, who represented the Crown in Ireland, and in a Chief Secretary who was a member of the British Cabinet answerable to Parliament and who directly supervised the Irish departments of government. The Parliament of Northern Ireland was established in 1921 and a government was formed with responsibility for a wide range of regional or domestic services.

Westminster, however, retained supreme authority over the Parliament of Northern Ireland and continued to deal with matters affecting the United Kingdom at large, including defence, foreign affairs and national fiscal policy. In recognition of this, 13 members were elected from Northern Ireland to sit in the United Kingdom Parliament, a number subsequently reduced to 12 when university representation at Westminster was abolished in the 1950s. This dual system of government lasted just over 50 years. (Northern Ireland currently elects 18 members of the Westminster Parliament and 3 MEPs to the European Parliament.)

In 1972, however, the Westminster Parliament, in exercise of its sovereign powers, suspended and subsequently abolished the Parliament of Northern Ireland in response to insistent demands for political reform. Subsequently, attempts to find an acceptable basis for restoring some measure of regional self-government have proved unsuccessful, and the system of government has accordingly reverted to something like the pre-1921 model. The country is ruled directly from London through a Secretary of State who is a member of the

British Cabinet answerable to the Westminster Parliament. Assisting him/her are several junior ministers who supervise, on his/her behalf, several departments.

On 15 November 1985, the United Kingdom and Irish governments signed the Anglo-Irish Agreement. This set up an Intergovernmental Conference to provide a framework for regular meetings between the two governments at Ministerial and official levels. Under the agreement, both governments explicitly recognise that any change in the status of Northern Ireland can only come about with the consent of the majority of the people there. Separately from the Agreement, a British–Irish Inter-Parliamentary Body was established in February 1990 to consider a wide range of political, security and European Community, economic and social issues.

Since the election on 1 May 1997 of a new Labour government, a second IRA ceasefire led to such talks beginning, and on Good Friday 1998, an Agreement was reached, supported substantially in a subsequent referendum in both parts of Ireland. Thus, there is now the basis for a regional Assembly in Northern Ireland, complemented by a series of cross-border co-operations on matters of mutual concern to the two jurisdictions on the island.

As far as local government is concerned, since 1973 there have been 26 elected district councils, each of which discharges various local functions. The major public sector social services, however, including housing, health, social welfare and education, are administered by statutory boards whose members are appointed by Ministers after consultation with the appropriate interests, including the district councils. The courts and the legal system are modelled closely on the system in England, although there are some differences from English law and practice in respect of a restricted range of matters enacted in temporary legislation, connected with terrorism.

Belfast has been the capital of Northern Ireland since 1921. It is a city which is more often known of, rather than known about. Though internationally images prevail of sectarian conflict and terrorism, this chapter seeks to explain why the city is what it is and attempts to outline some of the things that we, as a community, are trying to do to bring about peace, reconciliation and regeneration.

In a recent book on Belfast, Boal describes the city as 'clinging to the sea and hugging the land'.[2] He goes on to explain that the city developed at a point 'where the river Lagan completed its wandering lower course by slowly discharging into Belfast Lough'. There are hills to both the north-west (the Antrim Plateau) and the south-east (the Castlereagh and Holywood Hills).

The site of Belfast was occupied during both the Stone and Bronze Ages but its modern history really began in 1613 when the town received a Charter of Incorporation from King James I. The ruling family, the Chichesters, effectively controlled the fate of the town for the next 200 years, during which time it developed in wealth and importance as a market town and port. It was during this time that Belfast became the market centre of the Ulster linen industry developed by French Huguenot refugees under the patronage of King William III at the end of the seventeenth century. It was, however, during the nineteenth century that Belfast experienced rapid growth and development. Indeed, it can be said that Belfast is basically a creation of nineteenth-century industrialisation. The city grew from a population of some 50,000 in 1830 to 350,000 by 1900. Linen manufacture and shipbuilding were the backbone of this industrialisation, which drew large numbers of migrants from rural Ulster. These new arrivals were of both the Protestant and Catholic faiths. Thus was created that volatile mix of population which makes up the city today.

It is worth noting that an influx of Irish Catholic labour from rural to urban areas was a common feature of nineteenth-century industrialisation not only in Belfast but also in cities such as Glasgow, Liverpool and Manchester. Indeed, this rapid industrial development was more typical of Great Britain than Ireland, and Belfast had more in common with Glasgow and Liverpool than it had with Dublin. By 1900, Belfast was a larger city than Dublin and the city's economic fortunes were firmly tied in to mainland Britain. Thus, it has been suggested that Belfast in the nineteenth century was a British industrial city that just happened to be on the island of Ireland.

In 1888 the town officially became a city by Royal Charter granted by Queen Victoria. The status of Belfast was thus elevated by this Royal 'seal of approval' *and* this was further emphasised at the beginning of this century when the Belfast Corporation built its new City Hall on the site of the old White Linen Hall. By 1911 Belfast's population had reached 386,000 but conflict about Irish Home Rule cast a long shadow over the city. This was relieved by the economic boom of the First World War, which also resulted in the deaths of many of the city's young men on the battlefields of France and Belgium.

In the 1930s, Belfast was badly affected by the worldwide economic slump since its heavy industries were dependent upon exports and these declined drastically during this period. The Second World War gave a further boost to the city's industry – particularly aircraft, shipbuilding and engineering. A heavy price was exacted for this and in 1941 German bombers attacked Belfast on several occasions destroying 3,200 houses and damaging 53,000. Even worse 1,000 people were killed in these raids. Shipbuilding revived briefly after the war but then, along with linen manufacturing, suffered a serious decline. Both industries have not died, however, and they continue to provide jobs in the city, albeit in smaller numbers. Indeed, two of Belfast's great industrial landmarks are the shipyard cranes – known locally as Goliath and Samson.

While the 1950s and 1960s were decades of boom, and Belfast benefited from an influx of new industries, all that came to an end in 1969 when the so-called 'Troubles' began. The combination of civil disorder, political uncertainty, terrorism and economic recession left Belfast with an inheritance of: poor housing; economic degeneration; low business morale; unemployment at around 20 per cent for much of the period; an ageing population; emigration; a declining city centre; a neglected river and waterfront; deepening community division; loss of external confidence; and poor educational achievement in inner-city areas.

Belfast and its people were to be put to the most severe test over the next three decades. In 1977 the Department of the Environment for Northern Ireland issued a report entitled 'Northern Ireland: Regional Physical Development Strategy 1975–95'. In this report the Department stated that Belfast faced a combination of economic, social, commercial and physical development problems unparalleled in any major city in Europe. By the mid-1970s, the violent political conflict was at its height. Between 1969 and 1977 there were 1,050 deaths due to political violence in the Belfast Urban Area and 2,280 explosions were recorded. It is easy to imagine the consequences of this in human, economic and social terms in a relatively small community.

In the midst of this turmoil local government in Northern Ireland was reorganised (1973). Twenty-six new district councils were established – one of which was Belfast City Council – and these councils were given limited powers such as leisure services, parks, refuse collection and disposal, community services, building control and environmental health. Other services, which had previously been dealt with by local authorities, were either handed over to non-elected boards and agencies or retained within the Stormont Central Government Departments. These services included for example, housing, planning, education, health and social services, road and water/sewerage services.

In more recent times, government policy has gone even further by way of its 'Next Steps' approach and a plethora of agencies has now been created. All this is in a province of 1.6 million people – the size of Yorkshire. In Northern Ireland 'Quango land' reigns supreme. Thus since 1973 in Belfast the elected body, Belfast City Council, has played only a relatively small part in the running of the city's public services. However, with no regional elected body at Stormont, the council chamber became the major debating forum. Not surprisingly, given the turmoil occurring in the community, the City Council became a focal point for dispute and division.

This civic disruption was at its height in the 1980s, a decade which saw both the hunger strikes at the Maze Prison in 1981 and unionist protests following the signing of the Anglo-Irish Agreement in 1985. That so much progress has been made during this period (1975–95) is therefore almost a miracle. A visitor to Belfast today is struck immediately by the impact of its improved physical infrastructure:

- in housing where the Northern Ireland Housing Executive, which came into being in 1971, has presided over a considerable improvement in housing conditions (24 per cent unfitness in 1974 reduced to 7.3 per cent or 44,000 dwellings in 1996);[3]
- major infrastructure improvements in roads, railways, energy supplies and telecommunications;
- a major regeneration of the Belfast Port carried out by Belfast Harbour Commissioners;
- a major regeneration programme of the Lagan riverside directed by the Laganside Corporation including the construction by the city council of the new Belfast Waterfront Hall and currently the regeneration of the old gasworks site and St George's Market;
- the ongoing regeneration of Belfast city centre with many examples of new developments and rehabilitated buildings.

Unemployment has also improved dramatically in overall terms (currently 6.3 per cent in the Belfast travel-to-work area according to the Department of Economic Development) although it remains unacceptably high in some areas, and long-term unemployment continues to be a significant problem.

The Partnership Approach in Belfast

What has partnership to do with all of this? Particularly since the start of the 1990s, there was recognition that a means had to be found to build and develop a partnership approach to regeneration in particular, and social issues in general. This is accepted now by all sectors within the community and there is growing evidence of its implementation by the City Council, government, community, voluntary and private sectors.

The City Council has now embraced a system of proportionality for its committee places and the Department of the Environment is leading the way with its Belfast City Partnership Board initiative. In addition, various private sector initiatives are reaching out to both the public and community/voluntary sectors – e.g. the Growth Challenge initiative, involving leading business figures in a strategic appraisal of economic development opportunities into the next millennium, and the activities of the Business in the Community organisation, designed to bring greater private sector involvement in the most socially bereft communities.

Another feature of Belfast's emerging partnership strength has been the growth and development of the community and voluntary sectors. In a sense these sectors have strengthened over the last three decades to help overcome the democratic deficit and they have provided opportunities for men and women from both main traditions to work closely together for the common good. Their importance and value has been recognised by the European Union and the community/voluntary sectors are playing a vital role in the various emerging partnerships throughout the city.

This is evidenced in the recent European Union Special Support Programme for Peace and Reconciliation – the so-called 'Delors package'. A feature of this has been the setting up of district partnerships throughout the province. The Belfast European Partnership Board is one such body embracing City Council, community, voluntary, statutory body and private sector representatives.

Its work is helping to embed the partnership approach in Belfast by dealing with both economic development and social inclusion issues. That it is beginning to succeed as a method of working is evidenced by the following comment in the Northern Ireland Council for Voluntary Action (NICVA) Report (1997), 'Partnership – A View from Within':

> All sector representatives were enthusiastic about partnerships as a method of practising inclusion. There have been consistently positive comments on the value of the developing relationships, understanding and trust which have been built up between different sectors and individuals as a result of working together in this way, and a recognition of the importance of this method of working, even where there were practical difficulties. Of crucial importance in this has been the fact that it involves actual decision-making key issues including policy creation and allocation of finances.

Therein lies a crucial element of partnerships. It is not enough to meet to discuss problems and pontificate about them. The partnership must be constructed to allow for joint decision-making as well as consultation. Of course, the partnership approach which is developing in the Belfast European Partnership Board is not perfection and much hard work remains to be done to maximise its potential. If the approach does not add value within the community then it is doomed to failure. The signs, so far, are good.

The general movement towards a partnership approach in Belfast reflects the growing demand of people to be involved in decisions which affect them directly within their communities. Whether at city, area or local levels people want, and are entitled to, a say in the decision-making process. This is particularly obvious in the area of local economic development. Traditional methods of local economic development have often not been particularly successful. Over the last 15–20 years there has been a mixture of 'top-down' and 'bottom-up' initiatives, neither of which approaches appears to have engaged and enervated the public, private, voluntary and community sectors.

Of equal importance has been the realisation that the scale of the problems facing urban areas requires a new creative and inclusive approach to finding solutions. In Belfast the conclusion that has been reached is that if local action and local initiatives are to be taken and be successful, they must ensure the full engagement and ownership of those most directly affected by them. This has prompted the idea – as it has elsewhere – that within the city a partnership approach between all sections and sectors of society is likely to have the most potential for success.

Variety of Partnerships in Belfast

It is apparent in Belfast that there is a confusing array of partnerships. Most have developed independently, without any 'grand plan' and in a number of cases there is overlapping membership and objectives. In trying to make sense of the current scene it is helpful to identify a hierarchy of partnerships – strategic, area-based and singly-focused operational.

At the strategic level in Belfast, the Department of the Environment, in partnership with the City Council, has initiated a Belfast City Partnership Board. Composed of elected representatives from the council, and other representatives from the public, private, community and voluntary sectors, the aim of the board is to create a vision for the Belfast of the future, the Belfast which could exist in 25 years' time. It is intended that this vision should be shared and inclusive, recognising the diverse needs and aspirations of all sections of the community.

At area level a central government initiative called 'Making Belfast Work' has taken the lead to establish a number of area-based partnerships across the city. These area-based partnerships are intended to reflect local area needs within the context of the city as a whole. There is a strong presence of locally elected councillors on these partnerships. At local level, there are many groups operating in partnership mode. Most of these have a single focus. It would be helpful if their work could be more closely integrated with the area-based partnerships and more effort will need to be put into making this happen.

As has already been mentioned, Belfast and Northern Ireland have another significant partnership system, which has emerged from the European Union's Special Peace and Reconciliation Programme. This programme of special support, the 'Delors package' was created by the European Commission following the republican and loyalist ceasefires of 1994. A significant part of the funding which has been made available focuses on the creation of inclusive partnerships at district council level. Belfast has an independent 'European Partnership Board' which has about £14 million to spend over a three-year period. Similar boards have been set up in the other 25 Northern Ireland district council areas. The purpose of these boards is to encourage and embed peace and reconciliation within the Northern Ireland communities by directly assisting relevant projects. All boards are now up and running and the money is finding its way into the community to deliver the programme.

In the area of urban regeneration, Belfast City Council has established a successful partnership with the Laganside Corporation, a public Urban Development Corporation established to rejuvenate the city's riverside environment, to:

- build the city's new Belfast Waterfront Hall (a £32 million concert and conference centre);
- redevelop the city's derelict gasworks site as a business park (£9 million);
- rehabilitate the city's old Victorian St George's Market (£3 million); and
- liaise closely on the regeneration of the city's 'Northside' area.

The first three of the above projects have attracted both European and/or lottery funding. Finally, the city council has promoted several specific business partnerships itself. These include an Inward Investment Forum, an Information Technology Forum and the setting up of a First Stop Business Shop.

Common Features of Belfast Partnerships

While there is a complex maze of partnerships in Belfast, it can be said that there are common features which underlie each of them. Three key areas spring to mind. First, there is the inclusion and involvement of all sectors, with the recognition that each has an equal and valid part to play. Whether it is government, district council, other public bodies or private, voluntary or community sectors each has a place at the table. Secondly, the role of the district council is crucial and pivotal. The special democratic base of the elected members must be recognised as an enabling mechanism for the community as a whole. This position was clearly illustrated when the Belfast European Partnership Board was being established in 1996 with the city council acting as the facilitator to bring the various partners to the table. Once established, the council encouraged the board to take on its own independent life (albeit with one-third of its members being city councillors) with advice and support being provided by the council as and when required.

Thirdly, a common feature of partnerships is to develop a strategic focus over a period of time. The length of time will vary depending upon the nature of the partnership but the need to look forward is a key component of success. In the context of Northern Ireland, getting people to focus on the future has immeasurable benefits.

Most partnerships underpin their activities by producing detailed action plans with increasing emphasis on goals, accountability and performance indicators. This reflects the need to have sustainable partnerships with well-published achievements and the ability to correct failures when and where necessary. To ensure success, it is essential that the tangible benefits of the partnership approach are widely communicated and steps must be taken to build good communications into the process.

Problems with Belfast's Partnerships

In Belfast, bringing together individuals and groups from diverse backgrounds within a deeply divided community has brought a new and challenging dimension to the life and governance of the city. A situation now exists where all sections of the community and all sectors of society have an opportunity to put forward their views, be heard and, at times, be challenged. This process allows for the generation of new approaches, new ideas and the emergence of potential solutions to what have often been regarded as insurmountable problems. As with any new approach the move to establishing the partnership approach has not been without difficulties or setbacks.

One clear problem is the sheer number of partnerships and the difficulty of integrating what they are attempting to do with both existing statutory and non-statutory organisations within the community and also between themselves. The extent of the involvement of the private sector is also of some concern to many of those involved in partnerships. This is evident with respect to both the area-based partnerships and, to an extent, the Belfast European Partnership Board. A greater level of involvement and commitment by the private sector is essential to ensure the success of the city's various partnerships. People coming from the private sector have perceptions of the public, voluntary and community sectors and vice versa. The private sector members of partnerships often feel that things move too slowly and too much time is taken up on consultation. Their time frames and expectation of rapid results are often quite different from those from the other sectors.

The private sector has, however, a crucial place within this process and other sectors must come to terms with being more focused and business-like. In the context of Northern Ireland it is sometimes said that the process is almost as important as the outcome. While this sentiment can be appreciated, it is important not to lose sight of what needs to be achieved. The process must lead to positive results. Finally, one fundamental weakness, which hinders progress on partnerships is the absence of an agreed vision for the city. The solution to this, however, lies within one of the key partnerships – the Belfast City Partnership Board.

The creation of the city's 'Vision for the Future' will point all partnerships and organisations towards a common goal. Jointly chaired by the Department of the Environment and the City Council, the Belfast City Partnership Board is now firmly established. It has 22 members, 10 of whom come from the City Council with the remainder coming from the private, trade union, community and voluntary sectors. The board has made a major effort to consult the Belfast people on the Vision for the Future of their city. Undoubtedly, the future success of Belfast as a twenty-first-century progressive European city is tied into the need for all its various agencies and bodies to work together towards a common goal. An agreed Vision for Belfast has the potential to enable that to happen.

The Future of the Partnership Approach in Local Governance

If, as I believe, managing diversity is the key to Belfast's future success then a partnership approach to local government must be constructed. Strong local political leadership is essential but it must not be provided in an outdated municipalism. New models of local government must be found, based on co-operation and inclusion so that everyone in Belfast feels that they have a say in its future. The basis for this is already in place. Northern Ireland is the only part of the United Kingdom where proportional representation is used as the method of electing local councils. Belfast City Council now has a system of proportionality for places on its committees and there is evidence to support the view that the council is now much more co-operative than it was in the 1980s. Throughout the city, partnerships between the various strands of society are being constructed.

The new Labour government has indicated that centralism is no longer to be the main feature of the future government of the UK. Regional government is on the way in both Scotland and Wales and, is under way in Northern Ireland. Thus, agreement between the political parties in the province could lead the way to both rejuvenated regional and local government. This is happening just when a new approach to local government is now firmly on the agenda. Issues such as elected mayors, the use of referenda, citizen juries and other methods of consultation are all examples of new thinking in this area. None of these on its own will prove to be a panacea to the problems facing communities but taken together they indicate that there is a growing acceptance that a partnership approach to local government is essential. Tackling the problems facing communities must be the main focus of local government and in a partnership model local government can be more accurately described as local governance – citizens engaged with their elected representatives in the government of their communities not citizens receiving government from them.

The World Commission on Environment and Development Report (1987, 'The Brundtland Report') concluded that:

It is possible to join forces, to identify common goals and to agree on common action. In the final analysis this is what it amounts to furthering the common understanding and common spirit of responsibility so clearly needed in a divided world.

This chapter began with a grim quote from an article in *The Economist*. The article concerned, 'Blood and Earth', ended with a more positive statement and one with which many can find common cause:

The trick in a successful society is for minority citizens to be able to feel that they are more than one thing at once: to be able to feel American and Black, Scottish and British, an orthodox Christian and a Bosnian, a Muslim and an Indian. This is hard, and it is easy for anyone seeking a power base to make it harder still. Ethnicity raises so many difficulties precisely because it is easily appealed to and hard to question, especially from outside. But people will resist such appeals if it seems worthwhile to them. There are ideas that people value as they value blood and earth.

Nearer to home, Professor A.T.Q. Stewart, in his challenging book, *The Narrow Ground*, states:

The function of wise constitutions and just reforms is to help humanity to achieve a future that is better than the past, but if they are not to have the opposite effect they must take account of the grain, and not cut against it.

Recognising differences, respecting them and working in partnership with those of a different persuasion or from a different background to make progress seems to me to be simply 'taking account of the grain and not cutting against it'.

Notes

1. McDonough, R. (1996), 'A Partnership Approach to Regeneration', Making Belfast Work, Belfast.
2. Boal, F.W. (1995), 'Shaping a City: Belfast in the Late 20th Century', Institute of Irish Studies, Queen's University, Belfast.
3. Northern Ireland Housing Executive (1996), 'Housing Condition Survey'.

12   Conclusion: The Development of Cities and the Future of Belfast

Frank Gaffikin and Mike Morrissey

Changed Times: Changed Theory

The recent two decades have witnessed epochal change, comprising not just the rupture from Keynesian-Fordism to neo-liberal 'flexibilities', but also a greater circumspection about the diagnostic conceits of both positivist social science and Marxist scientific socialism. In other words, the change cannot be captured simply in terms of a *periodisation* of economic transformation. It also involves an *epistemological* shift in how social meaning itself is negotiated. The contention is that collisions of new, fragmented and 'hyper' realities confound totalising narratives, evoking more tentative and pluralistic interpretation.[1]

For some, the relativism and indeterminacies inherent in these post-modernist social adjudications induce conveniently apolitical introspection at the very time intensification of inequalities in polity and economy should be summoning commitment. However, it has been argued here that these new theoretical ambivalences bear significant implication for the whole field of urban planning.

The Fabian tradition of urban development was predicated on the rational and normative. Assumptions about consensus and homogeneity permitted planners to present themselves as professional arbiters of the public good. This approach always underrepresented cleavages of class and power in land-use determination. Even more so does it struggle to encompass the many publics in the more splintered and formless social perplexities of the contemporary period[2] – when divisions of class have been joined by those of gender, sexual politics, race, etc.; when each category has itself become more fragmented; and when the whole social arena has been both compressed and extended by, for instance, the twilight zones of the Internet's cyberspace, which permits affinities beyond territory.

All this suspends rules of time and space, upon which planning has been predicated. Diverse worlds cohabit the same spaces. Aspects of the social geographies of the Third World find echo in desolate inner cities of advanced capitalism. The most remote corners of the under-developed world can satellite into the soap operas of First World affluence. Yet, amid this topsy-turviness, certain durabilities like urban poverty beseech practical redress rather than tortuous angst about how the problem can be theorised in the 'New Times'. But, even if gems can be redeemed from the debris of myriad urban programmes, can they be sculpted into a figure of urban harmony, when the 'instructions' for such craft have been sundered? Is the linear quest for a better world to be discarded, not least because the value of 'better' cannot be arbitrated?

This book posits that within all the pessimism of intellect, the quest cannot be abandoned. But it has suggested four prerequisites: urban governance has to transcend compartmentalised intervention to embrace cross-sectoral and interdisciplinary collaboration; active citizenship has to interface with, rather than substitute for, active government; new pluralist mind-sets geared to inventive urban policy have to accommodate lateral thinking; and previously excluded voices, such as the disadvantaged, women, youth, the politically margin-alised, etc., have to be engaged.

The Urban Problem

For three decades, the working population of inner cities has declined, though not as fast as job opportunities there. Relocation of employment to suburbs and rural areas has been partly responsible for ex-urban migration, although suburban working populations expanded faster than available employment in such areas. Thus, suburban residents have increasingly commuted to city centres,[3] a trend complicated by inter-sectoral developments. The decline of manufacturing, once located in the inner city, deskilled many inner-city residents. Coinciding with that decline there has been an increase in central city employment in banking and insurance, finance and administration, mostly filled by suburban commuters.

While Belfast's development over the same period has confronted these general patterns, they have been refracted through the prism of its particular circumstance, as shown in Figure 12.1. In the 1960s, focus was on *regional* modernisation, with economic diversification pursued through the dispersal of population and investment from Belfast to new growth centres. This was accompanied by comprehensive redevelop-ment in the city itself, whose built environment was substantially changed by major housing and roads programmes, just at the moment

Figure 12.1 The Development Decades

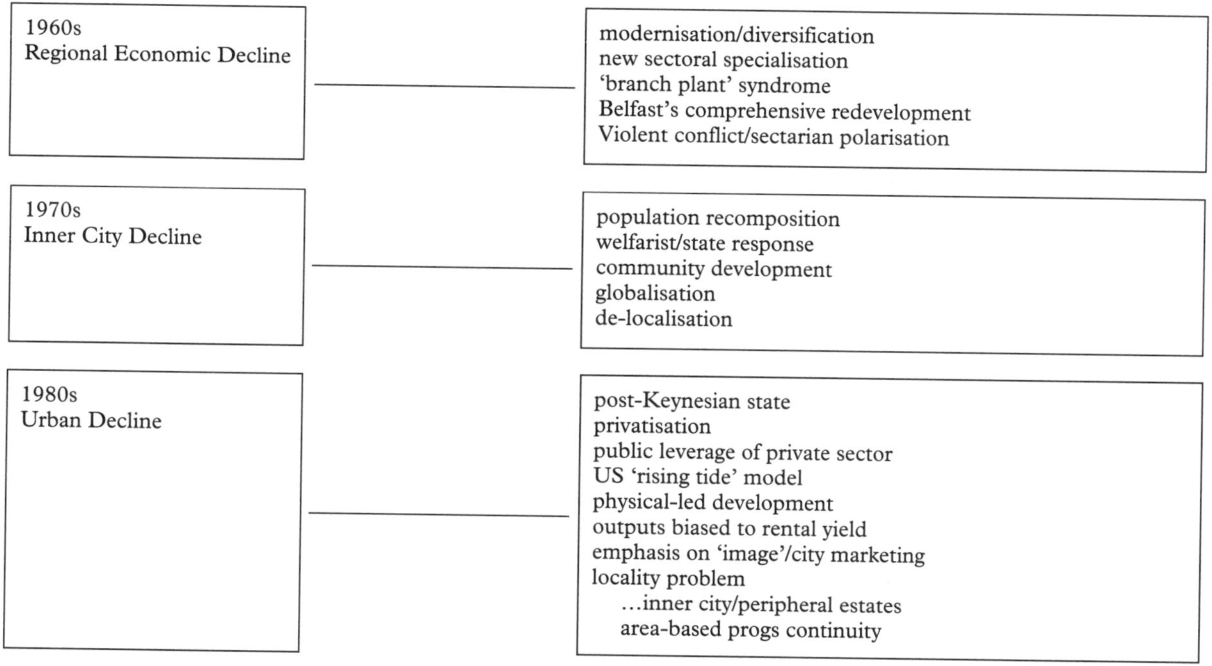

1960s Regional Economic Decline	modernisation/diversification new sectoral specialisation 'branch plant' syndrome Belfast's comprehensive redevelopment Violent conflict/sectarian polarisation
1970s Inner City Decline	population recomposition welfarist/state response community development globalisation de-localisation
1980s Urban Decline	post-Keynesian state privatisation public leverage of private sector US 'rising tide' model physical-led development outputs biased to rental yield emphasis on 'image'/city marketing locality problem ...inner city/peripheral estates area-based progs continuity

when violent conflict and sectarian polarisation were reinforcing social divisions. Partly due to the decanting of the more skilled and mobile, the 1970s witnessed the festering of an *inner-city* problem, whereby socially imbalanced communities endured the escalating impact of deindustrialisation. Statist welfare responses, including the Belfast Areas of Need Programme, intervened alongside mushrooming community development activity to achieve local amelioration, at a time when increasing globalisation of the economy made such effort appear disproportionate to the formidable pace of decline. By the 1980s, the problem was *urban*, rather than merely inner city in character and scale. Renewal was seen to come from a subsidised private sector, and was manifest most obviously by physical-led development. Though premised on 'trickle down' theory, its benefits largely bypassed residents from localities such as the city centre, inner city and the peripheral estates. Even the direct compensation programmes such as Making Belfast Work have, so far, struggled to impact significantly in these communities.

The urban edifice of the 1980s/90s is characterised as one of multiple division, unsteadied by the social erosion attendant on marketisation and globalisation. Crucially, it is no longer simply a crisis of manufacturing. Even high value-added producer services, seen as critical to urban renaissance, are themselves more subject to flexible location. Whole communities having endured economic dislocation, have become dependent on social receipts whose value has diminished relative to average earnings. In its starkest manifestation, these urban segmentations have created a 'drawbridge' society, whereby fenced communities fortify themselves against anti-social inclinations of the disaffected and impoverished.[4] As cities re-model their downtowns, based on virtual monopoly for services and consumerism, economic contradictions twin with social tensions around differential spending power. By the early 1990s:[5]

> not only were enormous numbers of people falling out of the labour market, but their loss of income was even more dramatic. With income support worth 7 percent less in relation to average earnings than during the previous recession in 1979–81, demand fell by some £4 billion or 0.66 percent of GDP more than it would have done had the old relationship between income support and average earnings held. ... Rising inequality had robbed the economy of at least £13 billion of spending from those sections of the community whose capacity to save is minimal ... in the recession years between 1990 and 1992, consumer spending actually fell by £7.6 billion – the sharpest drop since the war.

The underpinning of the 1980s boom by credit-boosted consumption failed to confront the tension between rising unemployment and poverty associated with marketised economic restructuring and the increasing reliance of many deindustrialising cities on services like retailing and leisure. Sustainable development could not be based on mortgaged spending leading to rising import penetration as domestic productive capacity declined. This profligacy has exacted consumer atonement, with the leisure and retail sectors now enduring the frugality that usually shadows indulgence. Raised taxes and interest rates, negative equity in a depressed housing market and greater job insecurity do not auger well for a 'feel good' factor. Besides, it will take more than faith to move the mountain of debt many households have already incurred.

This book has drawn sobering lessons from the USA, whose own speculative property bonanza came to grief.[6] So much of the US economy has been diverted into property that its value meltdown has been a drag on recovery and growth. The mortification of these grandiose schemes demonstrates the distinction to be drawn between the immediate gratifications of consumption and the deferred gratifications of investment into more competitive production capacities. It is useful to examine how such policy contradictions might be addressed in the regeneration of cities like Belfast.

Urban Regeneration: Contradictions and Dilemmas

A clear message in the book is that deprived communities consider redress of unemployment as fundamental to their regeneration. Two dilemmas arise here. First, the link between job creation and unemployment rates is not automatic. For instance, new jobs may lead to higher female participation rates, or may lead to recruitment of those already employed, whose current job may then disappear through 'natural wastage'.

Secondly, jobs and firms in depressed areas may receive public support to the comparative disadvantage of other regional firms. Indeed, this may merely subsidise inefficiencies, detrimental to the region's overall competitiveness. By the same token, as Eisenschitz and Gough note,[7] increasing competitiveness per se does not increase final demand. Thus job creation on this basis is likely to be at the expense of jobs in less competitive enterprises. All this suggests that local economic development is beset by a confusing overlay of goals, as represented in Figure 12.2. The outcome will be determined by whether certain aims, such as tackling poverty, are privileged over others, such as creating competitive enterprise. Thus, programmes whose primary constituency is the urban poor face an uncomfortable choice: to promote jobs in the local area where they are difficult to sustain or in the broader labour market where the disadvantaged frequently fail to get them. The solution may be to concentrate intervention in the wider labour market, while addressing issues like transportation access and discrimination whether against a religion, a stigmatised area or the long-term unemployed.

Figure 12.2 Diverse Aims of Local Economic Development

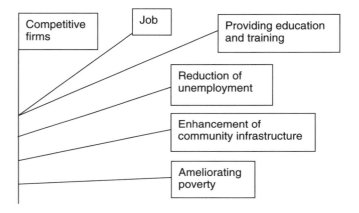

Source: Morrissey, M. and Gaffikin, F. (1994), 'Strategic Framework for Local Economic Development: A Review', commissioned by the Department of Economic Development (NI).

Different conceptions of local economic development pertain. One concentrates on small business formation with conventional commercial criteria (efficiency, profitability, etc.); the other proposes holistic neighbourhood development with participative structures and goals embracing both social and economic outcomes. The former benefits from focused remit, unencumbered by social development processes. Its failing lies in limited accountability and overdependence on multipliers to deprived localities. The latter gains from comprehensive strategy and democratic structure. However, it risks impact diffusion by attempting to accommodate a plurality of goals, some of which may 'crowd out' the imperative to establish efficient and competitive firms.

However, even if jobs in the wider labour market become more available to the disadvantaged, there remains the potential problem of skills 'mismatch'. One proactive approach at pre-recruitment stage, is to customise training to meet labour demands of existing or new employers, with whom compacts can be drawn to give trainees 'first-in-the-queue' status in job application. But the possibility of a non-work culture among long-term unemployed suggests that training has to transcend skills enhancement, to include post-recruitment support components.

Another issue is the degree of *linkage* of large projects that are underwritten by public subsidy. A local-labour clause in the negotiation about levels of public subvention could involve incentives for every local person employed above an anticipated norm. Conversely, financial penalties could be imposed for every job under the target and the funds raised allocated to a local community trust. But, apart from potential legal difficulties, there may be hindrances to such intervention in a weak regional economy, where it could be argued that greater regulation would reduce competitiveness.

While there is no glib solution here, there are opportunity costs in not attempting to find one – community instability, violence and associated social overheads. One approach would be to establish data bases on local contractors and the self-employed and to provide information on projected public works and to assist their tendering capacities. Local communities might also exercise leverage on employing institutions through, for example, their savings with local banks and building societies. Identifying their collective shares in such institutions, they could explore the potential pressure they could exert.

Much expectation of job generation programmes is vested in small businesses. These, however, tend to have short life spans and, in deprived areas, suffer from low demand; undercapitalisation; overdependency on grants; overburdened managers; poor training; and inadequate financial control.[8] These factors weigh even more heavily on community enterprise, which tries to balance commercial and social dividend.[9] Supporting small businesses can take the form of utilising economies of scale in necessary services – administration, marketing, accounts/cost control, exporting, etc.[10]

There is also the issue of job quality. Jobs that are easiest to create tend to be low-waged service jobs in retailing, distribution and leisure. Even if these make some impact on unemployment, they still pay poverty wages. This might be tackled by concentrating on quality training and higher order skills. But, even if skill levels are raised in deprived communities, social mobility is usually accompanied by spatial mobility – those with new jobs abandon these areas, increasing the poverty level among the residual population. Part of the solution here is to foster mixed housing tenure, thereby increasing housing choice. However, since public housing authorities are restricted to meeting need, this is most likely to involve subsidised private speculative building. As is evident in Belfast, this is likely to provoke hostility from deprived sections, who disfavour public money being targeted at private development at a time when public housing faces greater fiscal squeeze.

This issue is linked in turn to the difficulty of creating more socially-mixed communities without fostering gentrification that benefits land owners and middle-class entrants at cost to indigenous residents.

Area-based programmes 'are preferable to greater selectivism. Welfare provision is still seen as a matter of social rights. It reaches deprived individuals by virtue of their being resident in a priority area, not because they as individuals have been subject to means-testing.'[11] But there are difficulties with spatial targeting itself. It can infer that poverty is localised and limited. Moreover, benefits may leak to areas not considered deprived. The smaller the areas targeted, the greater tends to be benefit-leakage to other areas. Conversely, when larger areas are targeted, the process confronts the vagaries of 'trickle down' development. Benefit to one area may help to blight another and formal spatial boundaries (like wards) may not correspond with poverty distributions. However, spatial intervention can be made more flexible by sophisticated packages like Geographical Information Systems. Also, spatial targeting may be complemented by sectoral (identifying economic sectors that best renew deprived areas) and individual targeting (customised packages for individual needs). All this indicates the complication of intervention. In that sense, post-modernist perspectives do have some purchase on the messiness of a multivariate social world, which does not resonate with a regeneration debate polarised by the kinds of juxtaposition shown in Table 12.1. Of course, certain dichotomies remain helpful, for instance, targeting need rather than responding to demand. But, in general, an attempt to re-focus the debate has to locate a new agenda in alternative modelling of urban regeneration, beginning with principles.

Table 12.1 Neighbourhood and Downtown in the Regeneration Debate

	Neighbourhood	Downtown
Focus	Civic culture	Privatised lifestyles
	Citizen	Consumer
	Community	Individual
Instrument	Community infrastructure	Physical-led development
	State	Market
	Public	Private
	Planning	Deregulation
Outcomes	Manufacturing	Services
	Employment	Economic development
	Indigenous development	Gentrification
	Community projects	Flagship schemes

Alternative Principles

Remaking cities has to extend beyond land-use planning to set all regeneration effort in a strategic frame. In constructing a strategic vision, four dimensions can be suggested: the *conscious* city; the *sustainable* city; the *accessible* city; and the *liveable* city.

The first raises questions of identity and belonging. In Belfast, for instance, nurturing common pride is predicated on parity of esteem for both religious communities. Furthermore, while cities need to sell themselves to the outside world, they can be marketed in forms recognisable to their inhabitants rather than in ways that sanitise all contention and contest inherent in city life. Taking neighbourhood as the building block ensures that community development transcends the solidarities of parochial space, opening up to the development agenda for the city as a whole. The quest is for a long-term economic *renewal programme*, geared to new high value-added sectoral specialisations, alongside a short- to medium-term *rescue programme*, which lays the foundation for a *sustainable city*. This involves the integration of the physical with the social and economic.

In particular, it distinguishes the glamour of short-term property development from the haul of long-term economic development. It configures 'supportive city milieux',[12] which permit cross-fertilisation of creativities and innovations essential to the development of knowledge-based activities. Castells and Hall refer to this as essential to the development of technopoles, the concentrated centres of high-technology – the 'mines and foundries of the informational age':[13]

> The critical synergistic effects depend also on specific forms of social organisation and institutional support. Social networks, allowing for the informal exchange of technological information and for the interpersonal support of an entrepreneurial culture ... .

Clearly, city regions will be in competition to cluster such sophisticated production in agglomeration economies, and while such developments may trigger imitative counterparts in other industrial complexes within their region, they will also generate their own cumulative inter-regional disparities. If left mainly to market determination, the glass ceiling on such spatial polarisation is the negative externalities of overdevelopment. Preferably, new and more flexible forms of indicative planning can ensure a more even diffusion of such opportunities. But there remains a responsibility on individual city regions to position themselves as receptive to the dynamism of new ideas and techniques, and to avoid a narrow focus on tertiarisation, which pays little heed to synergies of inter-sectoral links.

The accessible city is one in which democratic partnerships widen opportunity, heedful of matters of mobility, equity and reciprocity of civic responsibility. Improvements in the hard infrastructure of road, rail and air are complemented by the soft infrastructure of mainframe, satellite, fibre-optic cable and modem. In otherwords, the accessible city is one keen to 'wire' its residents to the 'datasphere' destinations of the information superhighway. As the current multi-media tech- nologies blend, access will increasingly depend on the literacies that permit people to navigate the new 'World Wide Web', rather than cost:[14] 'As the power and reach of the communications infrastructure expands, the tools needed to harness that capability shrink. They will become smaller, cheaper, lighter, and more portable.'

Finally, the liveable city exemplifies hospitality, civility and security, built on an enfranchising civic culture. It facilitates the creation of a townscape, accommodating intensity and diversity. Its architecture is captivating rather than forbidding. Its habitats, consonant with human scale, are themselves humanising.[15] It recognises that city vibrancy is a matter of texture, fusions and ambience, idioms scripted by inventive living communities, not, for example, decorative versions of history reproduced by developers, keen to exploit markets in nostalgia. Genuine diversity and options are being forfeited in many of our cities. Behind the appearance of choice in the contemporary High Street lies the reality of increasing standardisation and monopoly. Concern about quality of life involves prioritising ecology and the 'greening of the city', and acknowledgement that downtown is not merely a location for office and shop, but can act as a theatre for civic celebration and expressive interaction in arts, culture and festival.

The contemporary urge to perceive development primarily in terms of building is linked to the imperative to commercialise land oppor- tunities. An alternative emphasis, designed to reclaim the civic and communal, would rediscover the *use* as distinct from *exchange* value of public space,[16] though unquestionably, in cities like Belfast, locating defensible public space is problematic in districts where territoriality is rampant.

But, in pursuit of these dimensions, the difficult challenge is to go beyond US 'trickle down' development models and devise explicit links between urban regeneration and its social redistribution. On this basis, impact assessment pays particular regard to the improvement of the most stricken neighbourhoods, according equity the same weighting as economy and efficiency. Within this goal, the relative configuration among the state, local communities and market can be negotiated on the basis of merit and argument as well as power. As Sayer argues,[17] there is no such thing as 'the market' operated by some invisible hand. There are markets, which are determined by various agents in diverse social contexts. Intervention short of socialised control remains feasible.

This whole approach implies discarding differentiated planning for a holistic system, so that new programmes are not simply grafted on to mainstream regeneration effort. But, because of the trenchant character of urban decay, planning has also to operate in a long time-frame with regard to outcomes. Performance measurement can include appropriate quality assurance mechanisms. Thus, the prominence accorded downtown flagship projects can be balanced with flagship schemes in the most disadvantaged areas. Quality renewal, in this respect, can be premised on the maxim that a city is only as strong as its weakest community. As Morrish and Brown note:[18] downtowns image cities, neighbourhoods define them.

Conceptualisation

From such principles, an alternative conceptualisation of urban development emerges. Improving the employment capacity and quality of life in the most deprived areas, programmes integrate with other socio-economic interventions, constituting a total regeneration package. Its central target could be to ensure that no particular urban area is more disadvantaged than the city mean. In reaching that goal, the mean itself will be improved. But, phasing is involved. The OECD has suggested[19] three key tasks of urban regeneration: moderating the pace of change; cushioning the impact of change; and diversifying the urban economy to respond to the contemporary economic environment. A new form of urban development has to locate itself within all three, as represented in Figure 12.3.

Cities face many disadvantages compared to greenfield sites when it comes to substantial inward investment. Besides, nowadays firms tend to develop *sectoral* rather than *local* connections.[20] They trade and supply within particular sectoral networks, rather than relate because they accidentally acquire a shared geography. In addition to other formidable handicaps, local economic development in the most bereft communities faces these general patterns. Across the industrial world, those areas which are succeeding most in overcoming this 'detachment from place' are nurturing 'corridors' – which cluster firms around limited sectoral themes, e.g. high value-added information and cultural industries.[21] Attributes key to such success are the *five Ms*: materials (land, plant, telecommunications, infrastructure), manpower (good skill supply), markets (marketing analysis and strategy), management, and money (proximity and access to venture finance).[22]

While these efforts take root, there are immediate economic dislocations to be addressed. It might be argued that the process of cushioning the impact of change should be undertaken by the private sector. Otherwise the public sector comes under strain, and fiscal

Figure 12.3 The Development Spectrum

Short- to Medium-Term Development Goals

Moderating the pace of change ------▶ Selective intervention for
job retention

Cushioning the impact of change------▶ Integrating and optimising
existing and new services
Developing the social economy

Longer-Term Development Goals

Diversification of the urban
economy ----------▶ Training   Education
Technological innovation and
diffusion
A new culture for work
A new sectoral specialisation

deficit imperils other social policies. The USA is frequently cited as the model where private sector activity in the form of low-tech job creation has cushioned the impact of displaced male, blue-collar jobs. However, as argued earlier, there the poverty of the unemployed is largely exchanged for the poverty of the low-waged. In addition, US cities are bearing the fall-out in terms of social fragmentation and violence. Unless intervention occurs, the social costs of change will fall somewhere. The choices are between the costs incurred by having to develop an increasingly coercive state and those associated with subsidising socially useful production. This involves a critical role for a *social economy* in the short to medium term since long-term development over a 25-year period may have to be oriented to investment in diversification to a competitive new sectoral specialisation, liberated from *job creation* as its immediate outcome.

As a key interface for both job generation and quality of urban life, the social economy consists of the production of use values (dealing with social need) rather than market values. It implies that there are jobs which generate community benefit, but which are uncommercial. Where profit is achievable in caring services, professional private companies quickly respond. Thus the social economy requires public subsidy and, though it may nurture small business in the longer term, the level of subsidy required to sustain it should be legitimated not on business principles but on the social and fiscal costs of mass, long-term unemployment. The EC White Paper on Employment proposed that three million jobs be created in the social economy.[23] Local research bodies have suggested that, with the intractable nature of the region's unemployment, social economy activities should be available to significant segments of the long-term unemployed.[24]

Based on the principle of matching local job opportunities to the meeting of local social need, it could include enhancing local firms' capacity to tender for contracted-out public services. In addition, an inventory of activities to redress need could be drawn (e.g. energy efficiency audits of local housing, play/sport facilities, community care, primary health work, etc.), as the basis for local employment creation. In this way, local social and economic strategies are harmonised. A list could be compiled, headed *local need, current provision gap* and *existing provider*. The purpose would be to examine how far 'provision gaps' could be met by local enterprise 'import substituting' for those services presently provided by outside agencies.

Such a strategy would involve restructuring the benefits system to accommodate flexible part-time community employment, complemented by training and education opportunity, which provide exits into conventional labour markets.[25] In this respect, education is critical to all development phases. Educational underattainment is severe in deprived areas. A 'holistic' approach requires revisiting some of the best lessons from earlier urban programmes, for instance Headstart in the USA, and the Educational Priority Area initiatives in Britain. This implies greater investment in early years education, supported by strong parental involvement. It also implies that the most disadvantaged schools have priority access to resources for multi-media and other advanced learning forms, geared to the flexible, knowledge-intensive work and leisure experiences of tomorrow. One approach involves compacts between disadvantaged schools and not only major city employers,[26] but also local universities, which could offer ongoing commitment of staff support, educational guidance, research assistance, etc.

In short, regeneration has to be a multiple strategy, comprising at least six main strands:

- retention and expansion of existing local business
- inward investment
- opening up the wider labour market
- community enterprise
- social economy.[27]

The important thing is that these are linked. The maximalist version of this phasing would comprise comprehensive integration of the social economy with the long-term drive for a new advanced industrialism. The minimalist version would make better connections among the present diverse interventions, ranging from welfare rights advice to small-scale community enterprise.

As part of this holistic development, it would be necessary for declining urban areas to move beyond demonstrating their indicators of deprivation to promote their *indicators of endowment*, including the following:[28] human resources;[29] locational;[30] infrastructural;[31] amenity;[32] financial;[33] and intangibles.[34]

Porter advances a model for rediscovering the comparative advantage of depressed communities.[35] While much of his agenda is familiar neo-liberalism – deregulate, demote the public sector to create more space for business leadership, avoid imposing social obligations on the private sector and elevate the economic, and the social will follow – there are some issues which merit attention from his ideological opponents. For instance, he rails against direct subsidies to business which retard efficiency imperatives, and advocates instead funds to be targeted at site assembly, extra security and environmental improvements, which can be undertaken by community-based enterprises.

He insists that the four key advantages available to the inner city are: *strategic location*, often near downtown; *local market demand*, which is often underestimated even when other markets are saturated, because attention is focused on the low average household income, rather than the significant aggregate income that can attend dense residential areas; *integration with regional clusters*, that is linking local business in systematic supply arrangements with the most vibrant sectors in the wider economic hinterland, geared to 'just-in-time delivery, superior customer service and close partnerships'; and, finally, *human resources*.

Regeneration of the most disadvantaged urban areas has to be concerned also to improve both the level of income/services and the circulation of these within localities and to delay the rate of outflow. This can be seen in Figure 12.4. At present, the problem is not just one of low levels of income and services, but a low rate of circulation

Figure 12.4 Income Flows within Communities

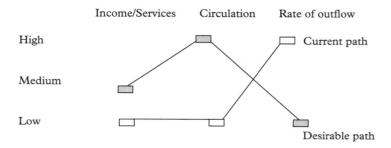

(and hence a low value for the locality multiplier) with a corresponding high rate of income outflow. The challenge is to raise incomes moderately in the first instance, and, importantly, increase the circulation rate. The social economy, in developing services to meet local needs, simultaneously increases income and circulation.

Process and Implementation

Agentisation of the public sector risks a fragmentation inamicable to this model of integrated development. This is not to hanker after a Fordist welfare state that delivered mass standardised services from a patrician bureaucracy. In the private sector:[36]

> Big companies are breaking up and becoming confederations of small, entrepreneurial companies in order to survive. ... At once, the global economy is growing while the size of its parts is shrinking. ... The almost perfect metaphor for the movement from bureaucracies of every kind to small, autonomous units is the shift from the mainframe to PCs, with PCs networked together.

Similarly, a flexibly specialised public service harbours potential for decentralising responsibility congruent with inclusive partnerships. Only such democratic and transparent procedures stand to mobilise citizenry around a shared urban vision in a way which engenders a genuine ownership of both its process and outcome. Operationally, this could adopt the Value-Adding Partnership (VAP) model,[37] whereby flexible inter-sectoral teams form to focus on particular issues and fold when appropriate. But, importantly, they function not simply as task-oriented groups, but rather as tactical teams within a strategic framework, benefiting from the cross-fertilisation of a multi-agency approach.

The challenge in the current period is for a regeneration agency like Making Belfast Work (MBW) to be integral to, and influential in, the mainstream regeneration drive in Belfast. But this process faces seven main problems. First, it seeks to target need rather than respond in an ad hoc manner to demand. Yet, identifying need in a sectarian environment is politically contentious. In a society devoid of credible democratic forums, where the culture of clientelism is rife, it is difficult to stray from the habits of 'doing deals' and 'buying peace' with various factions. In *realpolitik*, MBW likely will have to divert some resources to interests, whose denial could otherwise produce disproportionate disruption. However, because MBW has also set itself the goal of greater transparency and more rigorous evaluation, such deal-making will be easier to detect. While, the current peace process offers a more favourable climate for regeneration effort, bringing once excluded social forces, like Sinn Fein, in from the cold will also involve some favoured resource allocation. To balance any criticism from opponents of Republicanism, corresponding allocations will have to made to them, again reproducing distributive mechanisms based on political expediency rather than systematic need.

Second, MBW is caught in the dilemma between process and product. The programme was extended for three years on the prospect of better demonstrable performance against deprivation. Yet, it has set itself on a long-term process to develop partnerships, whose nurturing will absorb substantial resources and time, which could otherwise be devoted to more immediate if less participative poverty relief.

Third, it has set itself a goal of better targeting. A variety of models could be implemented in this pursuit. The orthodox model in area-based interventions is to select the most disadvantaged communities, to which services are delivered via resourced community development activities. Such programmes are generally demand-driven, responding to the most articulate community voices. Grant aid is front-loaded and success is judged on capacity to leverage independent funding sources that reduce dependency on the public sector.

Two other variations of this model are possible. The first, which can be labelled **individualist**, would focus on selected households in disadvantaged areas. They would be invited to establish a personal development contract with the programme whereby various outputs would be customised to their individual needs. This acknowledges that within households, individuals are affected differentially by segmented labour markets and experience different social and employment needs. It is designed to overcome a key failing of many area-based programmes – their inability to engage the inactive poor. The second variation, which can be designated **performance**, synthesises many of the elements of the previous two by an emphasis on a 'contractual obligation' with a community, to which public support is linked to performance. Hence, funding is not front-loaded but graduated. The more effort and success achieved by community effort, the more public funding rewards that attainment.

Finally, it is possible to conceive a model that is entirely **agency-based** whereby community participation operates at the level of programme benefit rather than implementation. The decentralisation of the public sector into quasi-autonomous agencies means that co-ordination of a multi-agency approach may be sufficiently taxing without the 'burden' of local partners. But what this approach gains at the level of professionalism and action, it forfeits at the level of democratic recipient involvement.

MBW clearly now leans to the performance model. Yet, if it rewards those areas achieving most, as explained earlier, this may in practice favour those with the most mature community infrastructure, rather than those in greatest need. The solution here has to be a complicated calculus of 'value-added', whereby resource distribution is proportionate to success relative to an area's starting point. This, in turn, infers considerable resources devoted to initial research to generate good baseline data, and subsequent intensive monitoring and evaluation. Yet, substantial sums spent on these activities detract from scarce resources to redress the need itself.

Fourth, MBW is intent on being a lead player in the main regeneration drama rather than a side-show. This must include striving to effect more 'bending' by mainstream statutory departments. In turn, this involves exacting from those departments, keen to lever MBW funds, an action plan in which the proposed project complies with MBW's overall strategic direction, and represents genuine additionality. In otherwords, they have to convince that the project goes beyond their normal statutory duty and their contribution to *Targeting Social Need* (TSN). Confusion can arise here because the latter targets differentials between the two religious communities, whereas MBW targets spatial disparities. In any case, this new MBW demand is a tall order, and public agencies are likely to be resistant to the imposition. Theoretically, MBW has the capacity to compel compliance since it can ultimately refuse funding support. But if it employs this sanction it is likely to underspend its budget, and thus undermine its case in future spending rounds. Thus, it is left with the option to cajole. Yet, mainstream agencies may feel confident that they can outlive the will of 'special' programmes.

Fifth, MBW is trapped between two conflicting government logics. On the one hand, there is a commitment to targeting social need, and thus socialised responses to urban deprivation. On the other hand, there remains the supposition that problems such as urban decline derive from market failure. Here, the purpose of public intervention is to readjust, not substitute for, market mechanisms. In the latter perspective, uneven development is inherent in capitalist economics. But, its function is to provide the seed for rejuvenation of divested areas, whose falling labour and land values supposedly provide the basis for new rounds of profitable investment. In areas of persistent decline, it is assumed that rigidities in property and labour markets have prevented this clearing process. Thus, MBW has been predicated on its capacity to restore the infrastructure of bereft areas to a point where private investment again becomes viable. Should business continue to fail as the main locomotive for development in such communities, it infers that the public sector has to breech the void on a long-standing basis. Yet, this violates a key tenet of government policy: that public spending imposes unsustainable fiscal burdens on the health of the economy.

This goes to the heart of the political fault line in Europe. In its Green Paper on Social Policy, the European Commission argues that the choices are between:

- a continuing process of US-style deregulation and 'freeing up' of markets to allow business the maximum flexibility to promote profit with the assumption that social benefit will result from social mobility and 'trickle down' effects;
- or, the operation of a proactive set of policies which integrate economic and social objectives and yet continue to promote international competitiveness.

Only the adoption of the latter can ensure that balanced and sustainable development will occur in Europe. Otherwise, as the Commission argues, there is the definite risk of:[38]

> a dual society in which wealth creation is in the hands of a highly qualified labour force, while income is transferred to a growing number of non-active people as a basis for a reasonable level of social justice. Such a society would not only become increasingly less cohesive, it would also run counter to the need for the maximum mobilisation of Europe's human resource wealth in order to remain competitive.

Here in the UK, New Right orthodoxy insisted that economic growth and related job creation are contingent on marketisation, deregulation of money markets, direct tax reduction, curbs on socially allocated capital, and privatisation. The limits of markets: information deficits faced by consumers, negative externalities, oligopolistic tendencies which undermine vibrant competition, and such like, are all underrepresented. At the same time, traditional Left orthodoxy that markets can be totally socially controlled has been discredited in the inglorious demise of command planning. Between market anarchism and state collectivist planning lies the imperative to reclaim indicative planning with a participative component. Such an infrastructure might be represented diagramatically as in Figure 12.5.

Optimally, markets provide flexible instruments to measure efficiency in terms of revenue surplus over costs – profit. Public intervention, targeted at social need, is best at measuring effect in terms of alleviating that need, but is less sensitive to issues of efficiency. What is required is a framework which directly targets need coupled with a set of more market-oriented intervention mechanisms. The integration of both produces *social cost effectiveness*, which elevates both dimensions equally. However, this process of regulating and supplementing markets cannot

Figure 12.5 Model of New Planning

Public intervention advantage

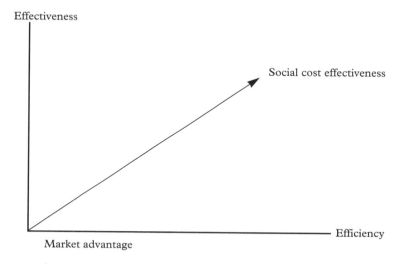

Source: Morrissey, M. and Gaffikin, F. (1994), *A Tale of One City*, Urban Institute, Belfast.

be residualised to disadvantaged areas. It must be part of a city-wide regeneration drive.

This leads to the sixth restraint. Urban strategy for Belfast confronts limits at the level of the macro-economy. It is most unlikely that the region will continue to enjoy relative insulation from public spending restraint. Over the 1980s, Northern Ireland enjoyed substantial subvention from the British Exchequer amounting to nearly two-fifths of the total bloc. Expenditure per head was equal to around 140 per cent of that in England. For a regional economy so public sector-dependent, any future curb on its growth bodes ill for jobs and spending power in the immediate period. Furthermore, there is the unpredictable impact of government's conversion to a growth strategy. The disciplines of possible membership of European Monetary Union (EMU) determine that combating inflation takes precedence over other social goals such as employment generation. This implies an unrelenting regime of fiscal probity, not a policy mix designed to make concessions to a weak regional economy. Moreover, the new policy demands stringent control over social spending in order to reassure the markets. While Northern Ireland cannot receive a great export boost from devaluation since so much of its trade is with Britain, it is particularly vulnerable to social spending restraint.

For instance, the professional dual career family here, currently bestowed with UK salary rates, will suffer from a changing fiscal regime which offers lower allowances for mortgages and married men, and may face regional pay bargaining in the public sector. Meanwhile, the unemployed are faced with benefit curtailment in the form of the Jobseekers' Allowance. In such circumstances, aggregate consumer disposable income may no longer demand the supply of office and retailing facility now in Belfast. An urban fabric already straining with the fault line of sectarian division is not well placed to withstand additional fragmentation related to increased social inequality.

For some time, the heavy public sector component in the regional economy has been portrayed as inducement to dependency and inhibitive of enterprise. Reduction and restructuring of the non-market sector has been regarded as a prerequisite for economic renewal in new strategies by the IDB (Industrial Development Board), the LEDU (Local Economic Development Unit) and the T&EA (Training and Employment Agency) following the DED's (Department of Economic Development) 'Competing in the 1990s'.[39] The privatisation programme in manufacturing and the creation of health trusts linked to competitive tendering have taken this agenda forward. But containment of social spending means that the targeting of social need could only be achieved by transferring resources from other areas. In practice, this implies that Belfast's deprived spaces can only substantially benefit at the cost of resource re-location from areas like affluent North Down. Given the concentrated residence there of the region's political and business elite, this again is a formidable proposition.

The seventh restraint is that regeneration policy now endorses the multi-dimensionality of urban decline. While conceptually correct, operationally this tends to promote scatter-gun effects, whereby endeavour to intervene across the range of need diffuses the impact of any single intervention. It may be preferable to adopt a strategy of *focused multi-dimensionality*, whereby the dominant determinations of decline are identified, and multi-dimensional instruments are summoned for redress. For instance, if long-term unemployment is taken as critical in particular cities, then multi-faceted assaults on this problem (via education, health and housing measures, etc.) can be adopted.

The European Context

This book has argued that regeneration in cities like Belfast has not only imitated many features of the US model, it has also copied the wrong things. For instance, it has only recently considered some of the best American practice in community empowerment. It has yet to adopt legislative intervention like the US Community Investment Act, which obliges lending institutions to ensure wide spatial and social spreads of their funding. The converse of this emphasis on the more deregulatory features of US cities, is the relative neglect of European experience. The increasingly amorphous form in US built environment, including the sprawl of megalopolis, whereby ad hoc development weaves a shapeless path out and beyond the suburbs, has led some to proclaim the death of cities. Such fatality is less evident in Europe. Seven EU countries have over three-quarters of their population in urban settlements. Western Europe comprises 22 cities with more than a million residents and 125 with over 250,000 inhabitants. Two main axes of urban formation operate: the primary one travels north-west to south-east (the Manchester–Milan belt), containing English Lowland cities through to those of the Rhine Valley to those of north-west Italy; the other axis extends from Paris to Hamburg. Though Europe has also experienced counter-urbanisation since the 1970s, the trend has been less severe, and there is evidence that it is weakening.[40]

Within Europe, the UK was once one of the weaker economies. Buffeted by two major recessions in the 1980s, it is characterised by uneven development and weak performance of its peripheral regions. Its recent Tory governments, as the most ardent supporters of deregulation and labour market flexibility, showed low commitment to social protection. Thus, places like West and North Belfast are weak areas in a weak region of what has been a relatively weak European economy.

The hegemony of 'Rhineland capitalism' in much of Europe, with its continued attachment to the social market, contrasts with 'Anglo-Saxon capitalism', which has involved the UK pursuing the US deregulatory and residual welfare model. The European social democratic culture contains the potential for a regeneration agenda based on concerted *reflation* (increasing demand levels) with *restructuring* (economic modernisation geared to advanced industrialism) and *redistribution* (greater equity in economic resource sharing). This includes greater emphasis on quality training coupled with policies to stimulate investment. In turn, these must be complemented by commitment to redistribution both among, and within, member states. Only these measures can simultaneously increase aggregate demand to foster growth and jobs while increasing competitiveness capable of minimising inflationary pressure.[41]

However, the EU arena is not just a source of certain macro policies and regional and cohesion funds. It is also a source of ideas. For instance, the term *economic convergence* is currently used to refer to the goal of harmonising the level of economic performance across all EU countries. Scaled down to the level of a particular city like Belfast, it could be employed as a target to bring certain economic indicators like unemployment and activity rates, income and earnings in the most deprived areas closer to the city average.

Similarly, the notion of *social cohesion* applies to EU efforts to dismantle patterns of uneven development and to move to greater standardisation of social well-being. Again, this concept could be usefully translated to the local dimension. Across a range of social indicators related to housing, health, education and social services, assessment could be made of how far areas of greatest need deviate from the city norm, and what form and amount of intervention would be required to close that gap. The benefit of these approaches would be that specific targets could be set, against which performance could be measured. Targets are a prerequisite to a strategic approach to urban planning.

Other concepts which carry increasing legitimacy within EU programmes merit adoption at local level. For instance, the Third EC Poverty Programme recognised the *multidimensional* aspect of the problem, which demands that measures to redress it operate through *integrated programmes*, linking the physical, social and economic dimensions to regeneration. It affirmed that structures for defining the needs, identifying solutions and delivering appropriate responses should involve contractual *partnerships* among the voluntary, statutory and private sectors. More recently, attention has been drawn to the principles of *subsidiarity*, which asserts that political decisions should be taken at the most decentralised level feasible, and *transparency*, which refers to the virtue of open government. Again, these ideas could be accorded distinctive meaning at the city dimension.

Of course, it could be said that little of this is new. Whereas, 30 years ago, reference was to multiple deprivation, today it is to multi-dimensionality; then we heard of participation, today it is partnership; then it was co-ordination, today it is integration, and so on. A cynic might charge that because intervention could not change the problem, it changed the vocabulary instead. However, these recent concepts do represent an advance in democratisation.

The central dilemma of applying macro concepts to micro situations is the contradictions at the macro level. For example, greater monetary stability and ultimate union within the European Monetary System are reliant on progress towards economic convergence. But such progress is itself undermined by present instabilities, which stem from the vulnerability of currencies like Sterling to speculative raids on the money markets. The process of European convergence thus confronts a series of economic problems. Yet, without convergence, both at the economic and social levels, it will remain difficult to regenerate the depressed city/region across Europe. It is something of a catch-22.

Final Comments

Belfast has been the location for a series of regeneration efforts stretching back almost 30 years. These have taken many forms – redevelopment, population relocation, major infrastructural investment in transportation and communication, compensatory social programmes, city centre and riverside development. There is, however, increasing recognition that such major investments have marginal redistributive impact – the most disadvantaged areas have not changed. Analysis of unemployment patterns between the 1971 and 1991 Censuses shows that the same areas continue to endure the highest unemployment rates. Acknowledgement of the limits of US-style 'trickle down' development models have prompted the re-launch of programmes like MBW. This book has examined these developments in the tradition of locality studies, acknowledging both the impact of general processes and the uniqueness of particular places.[42]

It has tried to extol a new discourse, emancipated from dichotomy and respectful of the subject's complexity. For instance, this discounts the local–global duality, whereby analysis of capital's commanding influence over local destinies promotes community paralysis against urban decline. Rather, it allows for contingencies of space, and ways 'in which local initiative can have some formative role'.[43] Clearly, *agency* has room for manoeuvre within *structure*, though not all 'options' are available. When open global capital markets severely curtail the autonomy of nation-states, it may seem absurd to pose the potential of local action. Moreover, the stability of place does increasingly contrast with the volatility of global finance, evidenced in the collapse of Barings. But at the same time, the demise of national Keynesian regulation amidst post-Fordist flexible accumulation has been accompanied by a 'glocalisation' process.[44] If the globe is becoming a village, so also is the village becoming globalised. Thereby, particular places, though circumscribed by transnational capitalism, can struggle to articulate their global niche, becoming cosmopolitan while cherishing the idiosyncrasy of the local. In this respect, city regions can operate in direct relation to each other, for instance across the EU, in networking and support formations independent of nation-state.[45] In this variable spatial geometry, urban areas need not be helpless passive recipients of global processes.

Similarly, conventional oppositions between *indigenous* and *market-driven* development are oversimplified. The former is represented as community based, with focus on inequality, aimed at employment creation, but balancing social with economic improvement and operating within deprived spaces to ensure minimal investment 'leakage'. The latter is seen as business oriented, pursuant of competitive-based growth, prioritising the economic and directed at the most commercial locations, from where benefits 'trickle down'. Effective development comprises a synthesis of these models, in ways which unravel customised mixes of *supply-side* components (addressing education, skill-mismatches, image, disincentives, mobility/access, etc.) and those on the *demand-side* (addressing inward investment, venture capital, urban programmes, macro-policy shifts, etc.). Thatcherism/Reaganomics were right to detect the underplay of supply-side dimensions in conventional Keynesianism. An alternative model which failed to acknowledge this would be operating with an ideological blindside.

Moreover, this model cannot be activated by posing the *enterprising individual* against the *dependency-ridden community*. But nor can *community* be automatically validated in its old collectivist incarnation. The 'communitarianism' evoked by Etzioni is being flattered into a philosophy by much recent hype,[46] ignoring its ideological ambiguities.[47] Claustrophobic and anti-libertarian traits of community[48] need to be surrendered for the flexible solidarities of a looser civic bonding. This suggests that 'civil society' may be a preferable construct. Dissolution of routine social deferences and wisdoms demands new *social reflexivity*, whereby the individual through self-determination and flair continuously negotiates through a less-ordered social life. Democratising a socially responsible framework for this 'de-massification' involves the creation of *dialogic spaces* capable of stimulating pluralist engagement.[49] Out of such discourse comes what we would call a *creative disturbance* – ideas which unsettle conventional canons and generate fresh agendas.

Also outmoded is the quarrel between *structural* and *cultural* explanations of urban deprivation. Both interact to form distinctive configurations of need and dependency in particular places. Their imprint can only be removed if unequal allocation of wealth and power on the one hand, and the social capacities and motivations of the deprived on the other, are both tackled. That implies that concepts of responsibility and incentive have to assume a higher priority in the lexicon of advocates of equity.

Likewise, the *public* versus *private* debate can be unilluminating. The state can be socially entrepreneurial and enabling without mutating into minimalist mode. Inter-sectoral partnerships may involve a blurring of boundary, whereby the more enlightened sections of business appreciate the commercial return from social cohesion, while the public sector appropriates virtues of managerialism and efficiency in more effective redress of social inequity. Nor is the edifice of the voluntary sector hermetically sealed. It can reinvent itself to avail of new opportunities for service delivery without forsaking its advocacy vocation. The quest is for an emancipatory urban politics, which accommodates self-expressions amid myriad solidarities, which indeed

sees the advance of the individual and the promotion of social con-
nectivities as mutually reinforcing.

But some cautionary notes merit registration. If attainment of
integrated planning was problematic in 'Old Times', it is an even
more formidable prospect in the less unitary arena of the contemporary city.

Moreover, while democracy is attested as integral to sustainable
development, the real world sometimes renders the imperative for
strategic alliances among 'prime movers' in ways which preclude comprehensive participation, never mind the mobilisation of the inactive
poor. Yet, rallying insurrection among the most subjugated in advanced
cities will hardly flutter, never mind clip, the wings of global economic
forces: needling the powerful will never in itself empower the needy.

There is no blueprint that gives the green light for equitable regeneration. Between 'girding loins and licking wounds', those social forces
intent on rediscovering the urban purpose are compelled to operate
with ad lib without collapsing into ad hoc, to indulge the intuitive
without the quixotic – to develop strategies which facilitate that
serendipity that springs from the impromptu amid structure. The
challenge is how to retain ambition and vision in social purpose, while
conscious of the modesty of outcome in many social interventions.

Does all this intimate retreat into the agnosticism of post-modernist
eclecticism, a glib pragmatism of pick-and-mix urban policy? Maybe.
The collapse of Marxism in both its theoretical and practical guise
certainly corrals the political and economic landscape in which
progressive strategies can unfold. For the foreseeable future, capitalism
is the only game in town. But that does not determine that every town
becomes a casino. Nor does it preclude some possibility of influencing
the rules and refereeing. Bidding farewell to reductionist Marxism for
a rendezvous with determinist capitalism is a bleak prospect for those
trapped in desolate urban enclosures, whose best hope must rest in
radical redefinition of social democracy.

Notes

1. Soja, E. (1995), 'Post-Modern Urbanisation: The Six
   Restructurings of Los Angeles', in Watson, S. and Gibson, K.
   (eds), *Post-Modern Cities and Spaces*, Blackwell, Oxford.
2. Watson, S. and Gibson, K. (1995), 'Post-Modern Politics and
   Planning: A Postscript', in Watson, S. and Gibson. (eds), *Post-
   Modern Cities and Spaces.*
3. Hasluck, C. (1987), *Urban Unemployment: Local Labour Markets
   and Employment Initiatives*, Longman, London.

4. Davis, M. (1992), 'Fortress Los Angeles: The Militarization of Urban Space', in Sorkin, M. (ed.), *Variations on a Theme Park: The New American City and the End of Public Space*, Hill and Wang, New York. Davis remarks on aspects of Los Angeles which were visible during the study tour undertaken by the author and MBW's Director in May 1995: 'Welcome to post-liberal Los Angeles, where the defense of luxury has given birth to an arsenal of security systems and an obsession with the policing of social boundaries through architecture. This militarization of city life is increasingly visible everywhere in the built environment of the 1990s' (p. 154).

5. Hutton, W. (1995), *The State We're In*, Jonathan Cape, London, pp. 179–80.

6. This is most visibly evident in scandals such as the Savings and Loan bail-out, and the demise of prominent developers such as Trump.

7. Eisenschitz, A. and Gough, J. (1993), *The Politics of Local Economic Policy*, Macmillan, London.

8. Storey, D., Deasey, K., Watson, R. and Wynaczyk, P. (1987), *The Performance of Small Firms*, Croom Helm, London; and Brown, P. (1991), *A Development Model for Community Enterprises*, Community Enterprise Training Initiative, Leicester.

9. Pearce, J. (1993), *At the Heart of the Community Economy: Community Enterprise in a Changing World*, Calouste Gulbenkian Foundation, London.

10. Some steps in this direction have already been undertaken by the local enterprise programme. Beyond this, it may be possible to establish consortia of trusts and financial institutions to make available venture capital and financial advice. MBW is set to explore this avenue.

11. Hudson, R. and Williams, A. (1995), *Divided Britain*, second edition, John Wiley, Chichester, p. 287.

12. Landry, C. and Bianchini, F. (1995), *The Creative City*, Demos in association with Comedia, London, p. 4.

13. Castells, M. and Hall, P. (1994), *Technopoles of the World: The Making of 21st Century Industrial Complexes*, Routledge, London, p. 233.

14. Naisbitt, J. (1995), *Global Paradox: The Bigger the World Economy, the More Powerful its Smallest Players*, Nicholas Brealey Publishing, London, p. 55.

15. Lynch, K. (1994 edition), *Good City Form*, MIT Press, Cambridge, Massachusetts.

16. Whyte, W. (1988), *City: Rediscovering the Center*, Anchor Books, New York. Whyte deplores the way street life in downtown US cities is being rendered obsolete. He reminds us that 'a sign of a

great place is triangulation. This is the process by which some external stimulus provides a linkage between people and prompts strangers to talk to each other as if they were not' (p. 154). And he extols the simple virtues of cityscape; 'A salute to grass. It is so adaptable; fine for sitting, napping, sunbathing, picnicking, and Frisbee playing' (p. 123).

17. Sayer, A. (1989), 'Ownership, Division of Labour and Economic Power', in Dunford, M. and Kafkalas, G. (eds), *Cities and Regions in the New Europe: the Global–Local Interplay and Spatial Development Strategies*, Belhaven Press, London.

18. Morrish, W. and Brown, C. (1994), *Planning to Stay: Learning to See the Physical Features in Your Neighborhood*, Milkweed Editions, Minnesota.

19. Organization for Economic Co-operation and Development (1987), *Revitalising Urban Economies*, OECD, Paris.

20. Geddes, M. (1992), 'The Sectoral Approach to Local Economic Policy', in Geddes, M. and Benington, J. (eds), *Restructuring the Local Economy*, Longman, Harlow.

21. Goodman, E., Bamford, J. and Saynor, P. (eds) (1989), *Small Firms and Industrial Districts in Italy*, Routledge, London.

22. Blakely, E. (1989), *Planning Local Economic Development: Theory and Practice*, Sage, London.

23. Commission of the European Communities (December 1993), 'Growth, Competitiveness, Employment: The Challenges and Ways Forward into the 21st Century', White Paper, Brussels.

24. Northern Ireland Economic Research Centre (June 1993), *Unemployment Forever? The Northern Ireland Economy in Recession and Beyond*, NIERC, Belfast.

25. Lipietz, A. (1992), *Towards a New Economic Order: Post-Fordism, Ecology and Democracy*, Polity Press, Cambridge.

26. Erskine, A. and Breitenbach, E. (August 1994), 'The Pilton Partnership: Bringing Together the Social and Economic to Combat Poverty', *Local Economy*, Vol. 9, No. 2, pp. 117–34.

27. Building a local 'social economy' into a local economic development strategy comprises the strategic integration of community business, credit unions, hospital trusts, etc.; recognition of the social wealth created by the local network of voluntary organisations; lobbying against public disinvestment, while at the same time maximising the local impact of public investment in terms of local services, jobs, and spending; improving the infrastructure, human capital, image and environment in the area, which makes it more receptive to inward investment; auditing the area in a way which accords due weight not only to the problems and indicators of deprivation, but also to the opportunities and indicators of success, and quality of life; achieving

development synergies through the integration of the social, economic and environmental elements; building and sustaining appropriate coalitions within and outside the area; tapping into the relevant sources of funding support in the public, private and voluntary sectors in a way which genuinely facilitates progress, rather than distracting from it, or creating new dependencies; exposing young people to opportunities of enterprise learning and collaborative problem solving, as an important social and economic investment for the future.

28. Coombes, M., Raybould, S. and Wong, C. (1992), *Developing Indicators to Assess the Potential for Urban Regeneration*, Department of Environment, Inner Cities Directorate, HMSO, London.

29. This includes skills supply, enterprise, social voluntarism, community cohesions, partnership potentials, community leadership.

30. This includes physical accessibility to markets, telecommunications networks.

31. This includes rail and road network efficiencies, housing market choices, industrial plant and land, and R&D capacities.

32. This includes environment, leisure, culture (inclusive rather than exclusive), health and education.

33. This includes the degree of local control of, or linkages to, key institutions like building societies, investment return, consumer demand, access to venture capital funds, and other sources; e.g. credit unions.

34. This includes quality of life, place image, socio-spatial polarisation, crime risk, insurance costs.

35. Porter, M. (May–June 1995), 'The Competitive Advantage of the Inner City', *Harvard Business Review*, reprint No. 95310.

36. Naisbitt, J. (1995), *Global Paradox: The Bigger the World Economy, the More Powerful its Smallest Players*, p. 50.

37. Johnston, R. and Lawrence, P. (1991), 'Beyond Vertical Integration: The Rise of the Value-Adding Partnership', in Thompson, G., Frances, J., Levacic, R. and Mitchell, J. (eds), *Markets, Hierarchies and Networks: The Coordination of Social Life*, Sage Publications in association with the Open University, London.

38. Commission of the European Communities (November 1993), 'European Social Policy: Options for the Union', Brussels.

39. Department of Economic Development (1989), 'Competing in the 1990s', Belfast.

40. Brunt, B. (1990), *Western Europe: A Social and Economic Geography*, Gill and Macmillan, Dublin.

41. Wolf, M. (1994), 'The Economics of Unemployment', *Demos Quarterly*, Special Employment Issue, No. 2. Again, this is not

to assert a symmetry between economic growth and job creation. In general, growth in the 1980s/90s has been associated with lower job creation than in the 1960s/70s; secondly, within developed countries, the ratio of growth to job creation has been variable – the US experience has been more jobs created per increment of GDP than in Europe, although the quality and remuneration of US jobs has been less; thirdly, in some late developing economies, like Spain, economic growth has been associated with net job loss.

42. Cooke, P. (ed.) (1989), *Localities*, Unwin Hyman, London.
43. Geddes, M. and Erskine, A. (August 1994), 'Poverty, the Local Economy and the Scope for Local Initiative', *Local Economy*, Vol. 9, No. 2, p. 200.
44. Swyngedouw, E. (1989), 'The Mammon Quest: "Globalisation", Interspatial Competition and the Monetary Order: The Construction of New Scales', in Dunford, M. and Kafkalas, G., (eds), *Cities and Regions in the New Europe: The Global–Local Interplay and Spatial Development Strategies*.
45. Benington, J., Geddes, M. and Mair, A. (1992), 'Europe: The New Arena for Local Economic Policy?', in Geddes, M. and Benington, J. (eds), *Restructuring the Local Economy*.
46. See for example, Paddy Ashdown quoted as saying: 'In trying to establish a new settlement between citizens and government, all three parties are now reaching towards community', in Baxter, S. (19 March 1995), 'I Am the Way and I Am the Truth': an interview with Amitai Etzioni, *Sunday Times*; the 'New' Labour Party has taken up some of Etzioni's concerns, such as 'the parenting deficit', and has professed its faith in *community*. This demonstrates the seductive allure of a political vocabulary, which positions the Party in convenient ambivalence between market individualism and state collectivism.
47. Walker, S. (Summer 1993), 'The Communitarian Cop-Out', *National Civic Review*, Vol. 82, No. 3, pp. 246–55; this is a special edition of the journal devoted to a wide-ranging discourse on communitarianism.
48. Sudjic, D. (1989), *The 100 Mile City*, Andre Deutsch, London.
49. Giddens, A. (1994), *Beyond Right and Left: The Future of Radical Politics*, Stanford University Press, Stanford.

Notes on Contributors

Peter Hall is Professor of Planning at the Bartlett School of Architecture and Planning, University College, London. He is author and editor of nearly thirty books on urban and regional planning and related topics. He has received the Founder's Medal of the Royal Geographical Society for distinction in research, and is and Honorary Member of the Royal Town Planning Institute. He is a Fellow of the British Academy and holds honorary degrees from the Universities of Birmingham, Newcastle-upon-Tyne, Sheffield and Lund; he is an Honorary Fellow at St Catherine's College, Cambridge.

Brian Hanna is Chief Executive of Belfast City Council. He is a member of the Belfast City Partnership. He is a person who is keenly promoting the institution of partnerships throughout the city.

Patsy Healey is Professor and Director of the Centre for Research in European Urban Environments, Department of Town and Country Planning, University of Newcastle upon Tyne. She is a specialist in planning systems, property development processes, urban change and planning and planning theory. Amongst her recent books are *Managing Cities* (with Cameron, Davoudi, Graham and Madani-Pour, eds), John Wiley, 1995; and *Negotiating Development* (with Purdue and Ennis), E&FN Spon, 1995.

Charles Landry founded Comedia, now Britain's leading cultural planning consultancy, in 1978. During that time Comedia has undertaken several hundred projects concerned with revitalising public and social life through cultural activity, quality of life studies and city strategies. He has been responsible for over 170 assignments for national and local authorities and funding agencies both in the UK and abroad.

Professor **Michael Parkinson** is Director of the European Institute for Urban Affairs, an urban research and consultancy group within Liverpool John Moores University. He publishes extensively, lectures nationally and internationally and is a regular contributor to the media about urban regeneration. He acts as adviser on urban affairs to the European Commission and the British government. For the Commission he led the research on cities for Europe 2000 and Europe 2000+ documents. He is the national evaluator of City Challenge for the Department of the Environment and is a Specialist Adviser to the House of Commons Select Committee on the Environment.

Joseph Persky is Professor of Economics at the University of Illinois, Chicago.

Professor **Wim Wievel** is Dean of the College of Urban Planning and Public Affairs at the University of Illinois, Chicago, where he is head of the Great Cities Programme. He has extensive experience in urban regeneration and local economic development and has written widely in these areas. He brings an international perspective to this field and has been instrumental in highlighting the catalytic role of universities in urban renewal.

Index

Note: Bold page numbers refer to Tables and Figures.

accessible city, concept of, 216
accountability, in traditional
    governance model, 184–5
Action for Cities (DoE) (1988),
    104, 118
active citizenship, 208
Adelaide, 158
agency, 229
  in development models, 221,
    222
  in partnerships, 118
agglomeration, advantages of,
    80, 81–2
Allegheny Conference
    (Pittsburgh), 157–8, 162
Alpine-Mediterranean area,
    urban growth, 129–30
Amsterdam, 70, 107, 128
Anglo-Irish Agreement (1985),
    196, 199
animation authority, role of, 162
Antwerp, 70, 128
arts
  cultural corridor model,
    171–3
  economic significance of,
    169–70
  relationship with economy,
    174–7
  role in regeneration, 169–77
  see also culture

Baltimore, 157, 158

Barcelona, 70, 105, 157
Beirut, 158
Belfast, 43–6, 196–7, 229
  alternative agendas, 123
  Castle Court, 167, 178
  city centre regeneration,
    164–5, 199, 202
  compared with Chicago,
    79–80
  economy in regional context,
    36–43
  education system, 36
  household income, 50, **50**
  Laganside waterfront, 164,
    166, 178, 199
  non-sectarian groups, 178–9
  partnerships in, 199–204
  political recovery, 167–8
  population fall, 44, 66, 75,
    165–6
  proposed strategy for, 74–6
  residential segregation, 44
  role of arts in regeneration,
    169–77
  role of district council, 202–3
  sectarian division in, 165–7
  social programmes for, 87–8
  Vision for the Future, 204
  visioning model for, 158–9
  Waterfront Concert Hall,
    170, 199
  see also Making Belfast Work;
    Northern Ireland

Belfast Areas of Need Programme, 210
Belfast City Council, 198–9
  Laganside partnership, 202
  proportionality in, 199, 204
Belfast City Partnership Board, xiii–xvi, 199, 201, 204
Belfast European Partnership Board, 200, 203
Belfast Harbour Commissioners, 199
Belfast Urban Area, relative deprivation, 51, **51**, **52**
Belgium, regionalism in, 108
Birmingham, 12, 105, 122
Blue Banana (Brunet's), 72
borders, international, 72
Bosnia, 194
brownfield development, 66, 100
Brundtland Report (1987), 205
  on sustainable development, 90
Brussels, 70, 107
Business in the Community (Belfast), 200
business leaders, 160–1
  in City Challenge partnerships, 190–1
  see also industry; small businesses
business model, 157–8
business support, for arts development, 172

Canada, vision planning in, xii
capitalism, 231
  'disorganised', 13–14
  and financial deregulation, 9–10
  and welfare funding crisis, 6–7
capitalist development, phases of, **22–3**, 24–5
carbon tax, as option, 93

Central Business District plans (US), 132
central government
  and democratic deficit, 184
  lack of co-ordination within, 111
  and new planning policies, 110, 142
  and Single Regeneration Budget, 120
  see also city governance; local government
Centre for Local Economic Strategies, policy papers, 124
change agent, role of, 161–2
Chaos Theory, 16
charismatic leader-led model, 157
Chattanooga, 158
Chicago, 79, 81, 88
Chichester family, Belfast, 197
cities
  autonomy for, 107
  changes, 34–6, 208–9, **209**, 211
  collective psychologies, 151–2
  deconcentration of, 66–7, 72
  and deindustrialisation, 17, 19–21, 24–5
  density, 81–2, 100–1, 128
  diversity, 82
  economic advantages of, 80, 81–2
  effect of Urban Programme, 111
  efficient market niches, 130
  hierarchy among, 69–71
  interlocking crises of, 152–4
  inward movement to, 73, 128
  just and efficient, 87–8
  loss of employment, 66–7
  outward movement from, 72–3

population drift from, 20, 66, 106–7
potential for failure, 159
role of neighbourhoods, 84–6, **214**, 216–17
sources of funding, 111, 118
visioning models, 157–9
visioning in successful, 154–5
see also city governance; city regions; edge cities; European Union; free-standing cities; inner cities; rural areas; suburbs; sustainable cities; urban decline
City Challenge initiative, 104, 112–13
funding, 118, 119, 123
Tyneside, 190–1
city governance, 21, 24, 208
building institutional capacity, 192
importance of, 117, 183
multiple initiatives model, 186–7, **186**
North East England examples, 189–92
policy objectives, 183
role for, 35–6
strategic capacity-building model, 187–8
tendencies in, **185**
traditional model, 184–6, **185**
see also cities; local government; urban planning; urban policies
City Grant, 138, 141
City Pride initiative, 122
city regions
concept of, 61–4
flows between, 71–2
integrated planning strategies, 99–100
civic capacity, 159–60
civic pride, 153

civil society, 230
class, and crisis of welfarism, 7
Cleveland, 157
co-learning, 155
coalitions, in local government, 112
collaboration, 208
leadership for, 163
partnerships, 159–60
Cologne, 128
Comedia, 151–2
Commission for Social Justice, report, 124
commodification, 16
communications, 108, 130, 216
communitarianism, 230
Community Investment Act (US), 227
community participation, 122, 123–4, 140, 141
community-led model, 158
competition, 110, 116
between cities, 105, 130, 215
criticisms of, 114–15
and job creation, 211
as management tool, 112–13
competitive bidding, for funding, 118–19
competitive cities, 92
characteristics of, 108–9
connected city, concept of, xiii
conscious city, concept of, 215
conservation, 172, 175–6
consumption
changing patterns of, 9
and economic expansion, 168–9, 211
corruption, 185–6
costs, xi, xv
see also funding
creative cities, 93, 175
creativity, 151
and technology, 175
in urban planning, 155

Cruddas Park Development
    Trust, 189–90
cultural corridor, proposed
    model for Belfast, 171–3
cultural environment, 108, 127
cultural vision, 157
culture, xiv
    commercialisation, 173
    and leisure industry, 174
    social and political role of,
        164, 169–77
    to transcend sectarianism,
        177–9
    see also arts

decentralisation, 205
    in Europe, 108
    resistance to, 72–3
deconcentration, of cities, 66–7,
    72, 153
democracy, 230, 231
    and decentralisation, 205
    in Northern Ireland, 158–9
    and proportionality, 204
democratic deficit, 184, 192
Denver, 158
Department of the Environment
    (DoE), Action for Cities,
    104, 118
Detroit, 157
development, xiv, 90, 216–17,
    229–30
    economic, 116
    funding for, 85–6
    implementation, 221–6
    importance of process, 109,
        221–2
    phasing, 217–19, **218**
    property, 109, 139, 140–1,
        167, 208, 211
    see also brownfield; economic
        development; greenfield
development models
    agency-based, 222
    individualist, 222
    performance, 222–3

diversity, problems of, 194,
    205–6
docklands, regeneration
    projects, 65–6, 73, 116
Dortmund, 107
Dublin, 70, 74, 75, 128
    Temple Bar, 17
Durham, city governance
    example, 191–2

economic convergence,
    European, 227–8
economic development
    diverse aims of, 211–12, **212**,
        215
    diversified, xiv, 108, 127
    as long-term, 215
    role of arts in, 169–70
economic growth
    and consumerism, 168–9
    and instability, 106
    quality of, 91, 128, 140
economy
    1970s crisis, 4–5, 210
    Northern Ireland, 41, 225–6
    relationship with arts, 174–7
    structural weaknesses, 41
edge cities, 93
    in US, 67, 96
education
    informal, 154
    Northern Ireland, xvi, 36, 39
    and skill requirements, 86–7,
        140, 212–13
Educational Priority Areas, 219
efficiency, 87–8, 100–1
electronic cities, 92–3
employment
    creation rate, 38, 211–13, 218
    effect of expansion to
        suburbs, 83–4
    employers' subsidy, 42
    high-wage, 80–1, 82, 128
    moving out of cities, 66–7
    sectoral changes, **45**

skilled and unskilled, 44–5
status, **45**
US schemes, 137–8
see also labour; unemployment
empowerment, in regional
planning, 99, 101
England
Royal Commission on Local
Government (1969), 62
urban renewal projects, 65
English language, dominance of,
71
Enterprise Zones, 65
entrepreneurial city, prospects
for, 107
entrepreneurialism
private, 109
public, 110
urban, 110–13, 161
environment
cultural aspects of, 172
cultural and physical in cities,
108, 127
and sustainable development,
90
see also sustainability
environmental assets, 91–2
environmental costs, 91
in cities, 93, 100
travel patterns, 128–9
environmentalists
differences among, 94
opposition to decentralisation,
72–3
equity, for future generations,
91
ethnic groups, xvi, 205
in Belfast, 179
'Europe 2000 +' report, 74
European Commission
growing role of, 110
Social Policy paper, 224
support for networking, 125
see also European Union

European Monetary Union
(EMU), 69, 228
European Regional
Development Fund
(ERDF), 125
European Single Market, 69,
105, 130
European Social Fund (ESF),
125
European Spatial Development
Perspective, 99
European Union, 104
city trends, 72, 105–7,
127–30, 227
economic convergence, 227–8
financial support from, 99,
126, 130
Great Britain compared with,
227
hierarchy of cities in, 69–70,
71
high-tech industries, 132
investment patterns, 131
periphery, 107, 129, 130, 131
poverty programmes, 125,
228
RECITE initiative, 126, 127
regional autonomy in, 107–8
social cohesion, 228
social programmes to reduce
poverty, 87
unequal development in,
129–30
urban policies in, 125–7,
130–2
URBAN programme, 126
see also European
Commission; France
European Union Special
Support Programme
(Delors package), 200, 202

First World War, 197
fiscal instruments, for urban
planning strategy, 74–5

flagship ideas, 160, 163, 217
  for arts development, 172, 173
flexible accumulation, 9
flexible specialisation, 16, 131
Fordism, collapse of, 7–10
France
  Contrats de Ville, 129
  growth of telecommunications, 69
  regionalism in, 108
  urban planning changes, 65
Frankfurt, 157
free-standing cities
  employment changes, **18**
  unemployment rates, **19**
funding, 85–6, 111, 118, 138–9
  arts subsidies, 172–3, 176–7
  changes in, 123, 141
  competitive bidding, 118–19
  crisis in, 152–3
  for job creation projects, 213, 218–19
  public, 223–4, **225**
  see also private investment; Single Regeneration Budget
futurity (long-term views), 91, 215

Geographical Information Systems, 214
Germany, 75, 107
ghettoization, 75, 153
  in US cities, 75, 96
Glasgow, 105, 157
Glasgow Eastern Area Renewal Project (GEAR), 65
global cities, 69–71, 92
globalisation, 21, 35, 229
  and Americanisation, 15–16
  of capital, 13, 229
  and multiculturalism, 174
  and significance of space, 25–6
  of telecommunications, 68

'glocalisation', 229
Good Friday Agreement (1998), 196
Great Britain
  compared with Europe, 227
  evaluation of policy, 140–2
  expenditure in urban programmes, **138**
  and government of Northern Ireland, 195–6
  integrated approach to sustainability, 94–5
  manufacturing decline, 11–12
  North East development initiatives, 189–92
  sectoral employment changes, **45**
  unemployment rates, **37**
  urban policy compared with US, 136–40
  see also England; Scotland
Great Society programme (US), 133
greenfield development, 66, 100

Hamburg, 70, 107
Headstart programme (US), 219
Helsinki, 157
hierarchy
  of cities, 69–71
  and networks, 69
  in production, 14
  shift from, 154
  in traditional governance model, 184–5
history, specific, 27
homogeneity, in cities, 153
housing
  city rental, 84–5, 88, 128
  Northern Ireland, 199
  prices, 48
  public sector, 87
  socially mixed, 140, 171, 213–14

Housing Action Trusts (HATs),
    118
Housing and Development Act
    (US), 132
human capital
    in cities, 108, 127, 130, 140
    local, 132

immigration, illegal, 106
incentives, role of, 99–100
income, household (Northern
    Ireland), 50, **50**
income flows within
    communities, 220–1, **220**
industry
    high-value niche, 175
    sectoral networks, 217
    small-medium enterprises
        (SMEs), 130, 131, 211–13
    spatial shifts, 17, 19–21
    see also employment; labour;
        manufacturing; service
        economy
informality, shift to, 154
information economy, 154, 216
    and cities, 20–1, 175
information networks, 131–2
information society, 10, 13, 15
infrastructure, 87, 108, 216
    Northern Ireland, xv, 76, 131
    trans-European networks,
        127, 130
inner cities
    advantages of, 220
    Belfast, 164–5, 167–8, 210
    employment changes, **18**
    high-wage jobs in, 80–1, 82
    investment in, 82–3
    share of expenditure, **123**
    unemployment rates, **19**, 141
    urban renewal projects, 65,
        116, 167–8, 210
    US, 97, 132–3
    working class housing, 75

Inner Urban Areas Act (1978),
    65
inner-city partnerships, 109
innovation, in multiple
    initiatives model of
    governance, 186
institutional capacity, in city
    governance, 192
institutions, and networks, 108,
    192
Integrated Regional Offices, 120
integration
    in regional planning, 98–100
    in sustainability policies, 94–6
    in urban regeneration policies,
        113–14
investment
    Belfast, 169
    for cultural corridor model,
        173
    inward, 38, 116, 217
Irish Home Rule, 197
Italy, 108

Japan, 70
Jerusalem, 158
jobs *see* employment; industry
Jobseekers' Allowance, 40, 226

Kahn, Hermann, 156
Keynesian demand
    management, 4–5
knowledge
    separation of, 154
    sources of local, 127, 132, 187
    use of assets, xv, 187
    see also information economy

labour
    and economic restructuring,
        9–10
    employment trends, 11–12
    New Deal initiative, 110
    skill requirements, 86–7, 116,
        117, 212–13

Labour Party (in government), 42
  'City 2020' document (1994), 124
  and community-led regeneration, 124
  decentralisation, 205
Laganside Corporation, partnership with City Council, 202
leadership
  in city partnerships, 204
  and decentralisation, 108
  depersonalising, 159, 160
  institutionalising, 160, 162
  in urban development, 106
  valuing civic, 162–3
  and visioning, 159–60, 162
learning
  life-long, 154, 157
  local capacity for, 187
leisure industry, and culture, 174
Lewin, Kurt, 155–6
libraries, public, 152, 153
Liège, 70
linear megalopolis model, 72
linen industry, 36, 37, 43, 197
links, xiii, xv
  in urban regeneration, 124, 213, 219–20
  see also collaboration; networks; partnerships
Lippitz, Ron, 156
Lisbon, 70
liveable city, concept of, 216
Liverpool, regeneration strategy, 119
local government
  constraints on, 110, 111–12, 114, 118
  and decline of public sector, 110–11
  Northern Ireland, 196, 198–9

Redcliffe-Maud Commission, 61, 62–4
  roles for, 112, 121, 124, 141
  and separation of regions, 63
  and Single Regeneration Budget, 120–2
  single-tier of city regions, 62
  two-tier (for conurbations), 62–3
  see also city governance; partnerships
local knowledge, sources of, 127, 132, 187
London
  elected mayor, 110
  employment fall, 66
  as global city, 69, 71
  regeneration projects, 65–6
London Docklands, 73
Londonderry, 76
loyalist identity, in Belfast, 177, 178
Lyon, 105

Making Belfast Work initiative, 201, 210
  goals and constraints, 221–3
Manchester, 105, 122
manufacturing, decline of, 11, **11, 45**
markets, 8, 216
  and poverty, 87
  and public intervention, 223–4, **225**
  to regulate environmental costs, 94
media, role of, 161
Milan, 70, 107
Ministry of Housing and Local Government, and city regions, 61
Model Cities Program (US), 132
Modernising Planning policy (UK), 98–9, 100

Montpellier, 105, 157
multiculturalism, 174
Munich, 70
mutual city, xiii–xiv

Naples, 128
nation states (Europe), 70
    and borders, 72
National Community
    Regeneration Agency,
    proposed, 124
National Urban Policy Report
    (US), 135
Netherlands, 65
    Social Renewal Programme,
    129
network society, spatial patterns
    of, 68–9
networking, 14, 125
networks
    for community-based regener-
    ation, 123–4
    in European cities, 105, 130
    industrial, 217
    information, 131–2
    institutional, 108, 192
    in regional planning, 99
    and space, 68–9
    see also links
New Federalism policy (US),
    133
new town development corpora-
    tions, 73–4
New York, as global city, 69
Newcastle Initiative, 189
non-profit organisations, 161
Northern Development Agency,
    189
Northern Ireland
    and European policies, 131–2
    government of, 195–6
    household income, 50, **50**
    local government, 196, 198–9
    political crisis, 38

regional economy, 36–43,
    225–6
    as single city region, 76
    unemployment rates, **37**, **40**
    see also Belfast
Northern Ireland Arts Council,
    170
Northern Ireland Council for
    Voluntary Action, 200
Northern Ireland Economic
    Council, 42
Northern Ireland Growth
    Challenge, key goals, 42–3,
    199
Northern Ireland Housing
    Executive, 199

oil crises, and industry, 38

Palermo, 128
Paris, 107
parks, role of, 152
partnership-led model, 158
partnerships, 116, 140
    for arts development, 172
    Belfast approach, 199–201
    in City Challenge programme,
    112
    for collaboration, 159–60
    combined with competition,
    110
    common features in Belfast,
    202–3
    establishing, 190–1
    hierarchy of (Belfast), 201–2
    importance of, 154, 194–5
    inner-city, 109, 141
    interdependent, 163
    multi-agency, 118
    problems in Belfast, 203–4
    role of, 88–9, 112
    in Scotland, 125
    value-added, 14, 221
    see also leadership
peace, prospects for, 53, 221–2

'People in Cities' (1990 DoE), 141
Pittsburgh, 157, 192
place
  importance of, 153
  particularity of, 25–6
place marketing, 116
pluralism, 208
politics
  crisis of, 152
  depoliticising important issues, 161, 194
  impact on city changes, 34
  and urban planning, 73
population, urban decline, 20, 66, 106–7
post-industrialism, 10–13, 14
post-modernism, 14–16, 175, 231
poverty
  compared with social exclusion, 47, **47**
  EU programmes, 125, 228
  and income inequality, 210
  spatial concentration, 166
  see also social exclusion
Priority Estates projects, 118
Private Finance Initiative, 122
private investment
  and economic development, 217–18
  in inner cities, 82–3, 141
  property-based regeneration, 109
private sector
  role in partnerships, 203–4
  US, 132, 134, 218
production
  collapse of Fordism, 7–10
  'just in time', 21
property development, 109, 139, 140–1, 167, 210, 211, 215
proportionality, on Belfast City Council, 199, 204

public art, 176
public sector
  in American cities, 98
  investment in inner cities, 83
  and regional economy, 226
  and urban problems, 110
public/private debate, 230

quality of life, 171, 172, 176
quangos, 198
  role for, 73–4
Quartiers en Crise, 125, 127

Reagan, Ronald, US President, 134–5
RECITE initiative (EU), 126, 127
reconciliation, 158–9
Redcliffe-Maud Commission on Local Government (1966), 61, 62
reflexive accumulation, 14
regional administrations, role for, 73–4
Regional Development Agencies, 99
regional development strategy, 38
regional devolution
  among European cities, 70, 71
  in UK, 110
regional planning
  funding, 123
  Modernising Planning policy, 98–9, 100, 208
  nature of British, 98
Regional Planning Guidelines, vision planning in, xii
regional sectoral specialisation, 36–8
regulation
  role of, 99–100
  in urban planning, 74
religion, 158

Rennes, 107
renovation, 126
republicanism, in Belfast, 177, 178
Richmond, Va., 160
Rochester, 158
Rotterdam, 105, 107
Royal Commission for Scotland (local government), 64
rural areas
  employment changes, **18**
  unemployment rates, **19**

Sarajevo, 158
scenario planning, 156
Schengen Agreement, on European borders, 72
School to Work programmes, 88
schools *see* education
Scotland
  inner city renewal policy, 65
  partnerships culture in, 124–5
  Royal Commission on local government, 64
Second World War, 197
sectarianism, 158, 166, 177, 194
  and employment patterns, 46
  and ghettoization, 75
  measures to overcome, xv–xvi, 221–2
  and role of culture, 177–9
  and transcendent spaces, 178
segregation
  in Belfast, 44, 165–7, 210
  and neighbourhood redevelopment, 85
  and social inequality, 129, 139, 210
Senior, Derek, and city regions, 61, 62–3
service economy, **45**
  effect on cities, 20
  post-industrial, 10–11, **11**, 12–13
services, regenerative role of, 116

Seville, 107, 128
Shell, and scenario planning, 156–7
shipbuilding industry, 36, 43, 197–8
shopping centres, edge-of-town, 67
Single European Market *see* European Single Market
Single Regeneration Budget, 112, 117, 119–22
  resource allocation, 110, 113–14
  revision of, 122
Sinn Fein, 177, 222
small businesses, 130, 131
  support for, 211–13
social capital, 88, 192
social cohesion, 116
  in European city policies, 106, 127, 228
social cost effectiveness, 224, **225**
social costs, of city expansion, 83–4
social economy, critical role for, xiv, 218–19
social exclusion, 208
  compared with poverty, 47, **47**
  definitions, 46–8
  and relative deprivation, 51, **51, 52**, 53
  as spatial, 48–50
  see also poverty
social justice, 91
social reflexivity, 230
social regeneration, 117
space
  and concept of social exclusion, 48–9
  hierarchies of, 14
  and networks, 68–9
  particularity of place, 25–6
  post-modern compression of, 16, 208

public, 216
social production of, 17,
  19–21, 24–5
  see also spatial growth; spatial
  targeting
Spain, regionalism in, 107–8
spatial growth, containment of,
  94–5, 100–1
spatial targeting, in urban regeneration policy, 113, 139,
  214, **214**
specialisation, flexible, 16, 131
speciality, need to establish, 74
Standard Metropolitan
  Statistical Area (SMSA),
  61, 62
strategic capacity-building
  model, for city governance,
  187–8
strategic local authority model,
  157, 187–8
strategic urban planning, 73,
  122, 141–2, 203, 215
  dimensions of, 215
Stroud, 158
subsidiarity, 228
subsidies
  arts, 172–3, 176–7
  for Belfast, 88
suburbs, 80, 81, 96
  development of, 83–4
  employment changes, **18**
  industrial relocation to, 17,
  208
  unemployment rates, **19**
sustainability, 90
  and conservation, 175–6
  integrated approach, 94–6
  see also environment
sustainable cities
  defined, 94–6, 215
  as goal, 92–4
  US experience, 96–8
sustainable development,
  dimensions of, 91–2

targeting
  development, 222
  of social need, 223
  spatial, 113, 139, 214, **214**
Targeting Social Need (TSN)
  programme, 223
taxation
  on emissions, 93–4
  and public funding, 223
  tax credit incentives, 100
telecommunications, 131–2
  effect on cities, 68–9
Thessalonica, 128
time, post-modern compression
  of, 16, 208
Tokyo, as global city, 69, 71
Toulouse, 128
Town and Country Planning
  Association, 66
Training and Employment
  Councils, 119–20, 121
Training and Enterprise
  Councils, 121
transparency, principle of, 228
travel, long-distance
  (commuting), 72, 128
trend planning, xi
'Troubles', the, 198, 210
trust, importance of, 88, 189–90
trusteeship, 160

unemployment, 39, 153, 211
  Belfast, 46, 51, 166, 199, 229
  calculation of, 39–40
  in Europe, 130
  female, 39, 40, 211
  long-term, 40, 50–1
  rates, **19, 37, 40**
  see also employment
United States of America
  current policy, 140
  edge cities, 67, 96
  federal funding, 133, 134, 135
  local development
    inducements, 136

origins of vision planning, xii
post-war urban policies, 132–6
poverty in, 87, 88
private sector role, 132, 134, 218
regional centres, 70
service economy, 12
and sustainable cities, 96–8
urban policy compared with UK, 136–40, 211, 226–7
workforce crisis, 86
urban decline, 35, 109, 210, **209**
in Europe, 106–7
see also cities
urban deprivation, 48, 166, 230
see also social exclusion
Urban Development Action Grants (US), 134, 136–7
job creation under, 137–8
Urban Development Corporations, 65, 73–4, 118
Urban Development Grants (UK), 136–7
urban planning
alternative principles, 215–17
changing purposes of, x–xi, 34–5, 65–6
conceptualisation, 217–21
and deprived areas, 49
implementation mechanisms, 73–4, 221–6
periods of government policy, 109–10, 117–18
post-modern, 175
and regulation, 74
strategic, 73, 122, 141–2, 203, 215
theories of, 3–4, 207–8
see also cities; development; urban policies
urban policies
alternative agendas, 123–4
Europeanisation of, 130–2
funding, 123
guidelines for improvement, 139–40

US and UK compared, 136–40
Urban Priority Authorities, 117, 118, 141
URBAN programme (EU), 126
Urban Programme (UK), 114
resources of, 111
Urban Regeneration Grants, 138–9
Urban Renewal Programs (US), 132

Vienna, 157
vision planning
for Belfast, xiii
concept of, x, xi–xii, 122, 154–5, 188
visioning
five models of, 157–9
and leadership, 159–60, 162
sources of, 155–7
Visual Preference Survey, xii
voluntary sector, 161, 230
role in Single Regeneration Budget, 122

Webber, Melvin M., and 'nonplace urban realm', 68
welfare
social contract for, 139
and spatial targeting, 214
and work-poor households, 47–8
welfare capitalism, crisis of, 3, 4–5
welfarism, failure of, 5, 6–7
Wheatley Commission on Local Government in Scotland, 64
Working Families Tax Credit, 42
World Commission on Environment and Development *see* Brundtland Report

Index compiled by
Auriol Griffith-Jones